NUMBSKULL

A Numbskull's Quest for Spiritual Serenity

BY: THOMAS CODY MULLENAUX

PRESS

A stoic person despises the shedding of tears, but a Christian is not forbidden to weep. Yet the soul may become silent from excessive grief, just as the quivering sheep may remain quite beneath the scissors of the shearer. Or, when the heart is at the verge of breaking beneath the waves of a trial, the sufferer may seek relief by crying out with a loud voice. BUT THERE IS SOMETHING EVEN BETTER. It is said that springs of sweet, fresh water pool up amid the saltiness of the oceans, that the fairest Alpine flowers bloom in the wildest and most rugged mountain passes, and that the most magnificent psalms arose from the most profound agonies of the soul.

May it continue to be!! Therefore, amid a multitude of trials, souls who love God will discover reason for boundless, leaping joy. Even though "deep calls to deep" (Ps.42:7), the clear cadence of the Lord's song will be heard. And during the most difficult hour that could ever enter a human life, IT WILL BE POSSIBLE to bless the God and Father of our Lord Jesus Christ.

Have you learned this lesson yet? Not simply to endure or to choose God's will but to rejoice in it "with inexpressible and glorious joy" (1 Peter 1:8).

"Tried by Fire," from *Streams in the Desert*[1]

Acknowledgements

This book is dedicated to all the people and friends that said I would never amount to anything, as well as to my family and anyone else who was around during all my shenanigans and fell victim to my inconsiderate lifestyle but still stood by me through all my ups and downs.

I especially want to thank Grandma Phyllis. Whether you choose to believe it or not, you are one of God's children, who was always there for me no matter what, even after all the stealing, lying, run-ins with the police, and all the embarrassments and tension I created throughout the neighborhood. I am very thankful to have you as my grandma and a part of my life. I also really appreciate your gesture of support when you got the news about my tumor. Thank you for being willing to go to extreme lengths to see that I got the best care and best surgeons in all of the US, including, if necessary, selling your home, stocks, bonds, and whatever else. I am truly grateful for you, even though I don't always show it. I love you with all my heart and soul. To Grandpa and Grandma Moreno, I don't think I even have to express how grateful I am for everything you guys have given me and shown me along my path. I love you guys very much. You really have shown true love and displayed such forgiveness towards me. I am forever thankful for that support.

I also want to recognize that all my aunts played large roles in the lives of my brothers and me from an early age. I want to give a special thank you to Aunt Vicki, Aunt Suzan, Aunt Erin, and most of all Aunt Cathy for always being present for us, making us dinners, taking us with them on family outings, and just over all showing us unconditional love and support always. There is no way that I could ever repay all of you ladies for the amount of time and energy all of you displayed in helping to raise us and just always being there when we needed a place to go. I thank all of you very much, and I love you.

To my father, Scott Mullenaux, you are a very big part of my life, and I love and respect you in a crazy way. I am very thankful for every day I get to spend with you and be a part of your life. To my older brother Chris, I dedicate Proverbs 19:25, "Strike a scoffer, and the simple will become wary; rebuke one who has understanding, and he will discern knowledge." Even though we have not always seen eye to eye, I love the fact that you are as real as they come. Sometimes being around you is intimidating and even hard to take because you so hard-nosed. Don't ever lose that characteristic. I wish I could say the things you say to people sometimes; I just don't have the guts. I love and care about you dearly. You are my older brother, and I look up to you in so many different ways. I just know you are going to be very successful one day.

Also, I thank all my friends along the way who have stood by my side, especially to all my faithful and loving friends: Mike E., Ali F., Danny A., Samuel I., Mike R., Brittany W., Eliot R., Vinny D., the La Rosa family, Justin and Brandon W., Jonny Boy, Mark and Heidi D, and Kristi S. I also want to remember all of my friends from Calvary Chapel S.B.: Art, Jose, Vince, Luz, Crystal, Frankie, and Louie D., all of you guys. The list goes on and on, and I know I am missing a lot of you. Please forgive me if your name is not there.

Dr. and Mrs. Wachs, thanks for still accepting me to be a part of your lives, even after all the stress and heartache I caused you and your family from a very early age. Thank you for still allowing me to come over to your house and eat dinner with you and your boys and for accepting me for who I am today. You guys are also very much like surrogate mother and fathers to me. I love you guys and respect you guys very much. To Mac M., I love you and respect you so much and am very grateful to call you a friend of mine. You are always in my prayers, and I can't thank you enough for all the great opportunities you have given to Casey and me. You are truly one of my all-time favorite people in the world. To Pete B., I love you Pete.

And I always save the best for last. To my little brother, Casey James Mullenaux, I love you with all my heart and soul, Casey. Don't ever lose faith, and keep your heart focused on what is positive and good for you and your life. You have been through a lot, and you deserve a good life. God bless you. You're my little brother, and I love and care about you more than anything else in the world. I hope that this book is an inspiration to you that ignites a fire in your heart to smarten up and stop being a numbskull!

Please check out the websites of my friends Ante Rotim, along with the website for Alcoholics Anonymous, and Calvery Chaple because all of these people and organizations have been beneficial to me at one point or another in my recovery and my journey to spiritual serenity. Thanks, you guys; I love you all.

www.hello@favoritebodypart.com

www.alcoholicsanonymous.com

www.ccsouthbay.com

Prologue

In life, you can prepare for some things; others take you totally by surprise.

Such is the case on Outrider Road. To the passerby or perhaps other neighbors up and down the street, the Wachs and Mullenaux clans were just two families separated by one other house. Taking off the blinders, however, you would see that our two families, at least the kids, were joined at the hip.

Cody's story has a happy ending because a loop was closed. The long and short of this journey is a successful landing after a rather bumpy take-off.

Every day, something wild and crazy seemed to be happening to Cody. A new drama was in the works on a regular basis. As a father, I remember vividly the intense soccer and baseball games on the hill. Cody and my son Justin were athletes to be sure. And to describe Cody as being competitive would be an understatement. He would more than once break his arm going after a ball or skateboarding down a hill. I would not call him "Mr. Moderation".

As a young boy, Cody was a genuinely affable and sincere person until drugs and alcohol muddied the waters. My wife and I have truly enjoyed Cody's company most of the time. The story Cody wrote speaks for the rest of the time.

We all learned a lifetime of lessons from this young man.

I could not put down this pen without mentioning Papa Joe, Cody's grandpa. He was such a good man. He taught me how to fix a toilet and fix a sprinkler leak. What more can I say? Understanding what specific event changed Cody's life around is difficult. All I really know is that, just in time, under extreme adversity, Cody became a solid young man, not unlike his grandpa.

I always tell my children that their goal in life should be to teach others. Cody's journey is about a lifelong teaching experience.

I celebrate Cody Mullenaux for his commitment and spirit in writing this manuscript. This story truly is from the heart and soul.

Barton H. Wachs, M.D.

It Was Like That
When I Got Here

I was sitting one day trying to figure out my purpose in this crazy life of mine, to come up with a good answer as to what my life is all about. I'm not so sure about the conclusion to my question, but I can assure you that I for sure serve a purpose for some reason or another. Life seems to be arranged almost too perfectly to conclude coincidence. I choose to believe in a much more divine being orchestrating and running the show, if you will. I call Him God.

My name is Thomas Cody Mullenaux, and this book is about my life. I just want to say first that I wrote this book completely and entirely based on my own real-life experiences, and nothing you are about to read is fiction of any kind.

I am a twenty-six-year-old male with a twelfth-grade high school education. I was born in Torrance, California on December 23, 1982, weighing in at 6 lb. 11 oz.

Isn't trying to think back to the day we were born weird? If you ask most people that question, whether they can remember being born, you usually get the same answer: no. I don't remember for sure the exact moment of birth that Wednesday evening at 8:24 PM. But I can honestly say, when I think back to that day, that I remember being in some type of transparent, open-air bedding. I remember that I was struggling. I remember what sounded to me at that point like arguing. I can't be sure what the situation was right then, but I think I was scared. Scared: that's how I came into this world, as a scared little baby boy.

I was somewhat premature; so the nurses were supposedly supervising me regularly. As I got older, I started having problems with my nose. My mom told me that, when I was born, either the doctors had accidentally put me face down on the bed in which they put you when you're being separated from your mom at birth, which for me was an incubator, or I had managed to roll over on my face. Anyway, when I ended up face down, I rubbed a huge sore on my nose. I grew up with nasal problems my whole life. When I think back to that moment in my transparent setting, I associate it with conflict between my parents and the hospital. They were arguing about my situation. Of course they had conflict, but why should a newborn have to undergo such intense physical pain only a few hours after being born because of somebody's inability to supervise? That situation really seemed to set a tone for the type of journey I was about to begin.

My mother's name is Pamela Jean Butler. She grew up in one of the most beautiful places to live in all of Southern California, South Bay-Hermosa Beach. My mom was the third daughter of five girls, smack-dab in the middle. She seemed to live a pretty out-of-control type of lifestyle from a very early age: sex, drugs, and rock 'n roll. Her sisters, Vicky Anne, Suzanne, Erin, and Cathy, all ended up living pretty normal lives. They all got married fairly young, held down jobs, and raised their families like normal people do, all but my mom and Aunt Cathy. Aunt Cathy had a legitimate reason for not leading such a normal life. From early childhood, she struggled with her weight and her health. My mom, on the other hand, attractive, healthy, full of energy, full of life, as Grandma would say, became victim to drugs and alcohol.

I used to ask my dad what my mom used to be like back in the day and what drew him towards her. I remember that my dad told me the story of Pam back when they were in high school at some party. My dad got super wasted one night and passed out on the living room couch at a party. Now back in high school, my dad had a little Porsche four-cylinder, a 914 it was. Now Pam (mind you, this was before she and my dad had ever really met or even hung out) stole the keys from my dad's pocket while he was passed out drunk or whatever, probably super loaded, and decided that she was going to go on a little joyride. My dad said that my mom couldn't have been any older than fourteen back then. She was a freshman in high school, if that. Well, my dad ended up waking up to his missing car. My mom, on the other hand, ended up waking up in the hospital with glass and a huge gash in her head. I guess that she had a few angels watching over her that night, because she survived a near death experience. Either she didn't know how to drive a stick shift, or something happened with the gears and brakes. Anyway, she lodged Scott's Porsche underneath the trailer of a semi truck, completely taking off the top of the Porsche and almost taking my mom's head off with it simultaneously.

Now that I think about this story, my mom and dad actually met through this accident. I am pretty sure that my dad couldn't have been too thrilled to find his car completely totaled by some random girl he didn't even really know. Nonetheless, Scott and Pam went on to become best friends, partners in crime, and eventually lovers. Like I said, my mom was into the whole sex, drugs, and rock 'n roll lifestyle. I used to grow up hearing stories of just how out-of-control Pam was and some of the outrageous things she used to do with a quite normal attitude. Like, how normal is it to take a bowling ball, go to the top of 8th Place Hermosa Beach, and go bowling for cars? If you're not familiar with 8th Place, it is an extremely steep street which intersects the Pacific Coast

Highway. Okay, maybe for a child that type of behavior is somewhat normal or even justifiable. But when you grow up and still make similar choices, you really need to sit down, take an inventory, and try to determine what is causing you to act out in such an absurd way. Maybe her childhood caused her to lash out at times. Or maybe something deeper and much darker haunted her, but who was going to determine that cause and know for sure?

My mom's mom, my grandma Virginia Moreno, was born Virginia Lee Mann and married to become Virginia Lee Butler. Grandma Ginny is one of my favorite women in the world. We called her Grandma Ginny when we were little, because Grandma Virginia was too long and hard to say, and the name stuck. Grandma married at a very young age, eighteen. She had five girls, and by the time she was twenty-six, she was going through a divorce and taking on the responsibility of raising her daughters on her own, because the boy she married, Bob Butler, was involved in all sorts of silly activities, such as drinking, smoking, partying, and being very promiscuous and unfaithful, even though he was married to a wonderful woman and had kids. He was upset that he had five girls because he wanted so badly to have a boy of his own. Bob proved to be a numbskull and was, from then on, not a part of Grandma Ginny's or his own daughters' lives.

I can see that five young girls growing up without a father figure must have been very unusual and even, as the girls got older and understood things more clearly, very uncomfortable. I can just picture what trying to fend for themselves and trying to play an adult role extremely early in life looked like for my mom and her sisters. Such self-sufficiency would definitely take a toll on you as you developed into a mature adult. So although I don't really know what that type of situation really looked like for my mom, I can kind of understand why she rebelled at an early age. I am not going to sit here and justify my mother's choices and drug use, but I just kind of sympathize with her a little bit. Growing up that way must've been very hard. I would've had a lot easier time kind of consigning that type of irrational behavior she chose to her upbringing if all of the sisters turned out like Pam, but none of them did.

Pam was really the only outcast of the girls, and she made a decision early that she was going to lead a life of sex, drugs, and rock 'n roll like her father. I think that my mom always kind of admired her dad or even looked up to him, and just accepting that he was not going to be there anymore was very hard for her. She told me once that, as she got older, she kept in touch with him and kind of actually maintained a relationship with him. She told me one time that he would pick her up early from school sometimes, and he would smoke joints of marijuana with her. Now here's a good role model. For me, when I heard that story, it was kind of a bummer. And she told me as mother to son; in the way she told me, she kind of glorified her dad's behavior like it was cool or it was okay. What did she know, though, as a little girl? She must've felt like her dad having her ditch school to get high was okay. For my mom, ditching school and getting high became the pattern of a downward spiral into life.

Now my dad, on the other hand, Scott Thomas Mullenaux, grew up in a little city called Gardena, a lower middle-class setting. Scott had life a lot easier, with a much more comfortable living situation. His mom and dad were much in love, both young and thriving parents. Grandpa Joe, Scott's dad, was an extremely talented, handsome, hard-working businessman. Joe was one of the hardest working, most honest, most likable men I ever knew. I never once heard anyone say anything bad about Grandpa Joe. Not once. He was extremely lovable. Grandpa Joe's work ethic and dedication to his family proved to be true and strong. Joe was born in one of the smallest and hottest cities in all of the United States, Gila Bend, Arizona, into a large family of nine kids: seven boys and two girls. Joe was the youngest of the boys. From my understanding, most of his six older brothers turned out to be alcoholics.

When he was about eight years old, Joe had an experience happen to him that would change his life forever. Now, what I have heard is that Joe and his brother Claire were messing with a lawnmower or a chainsaw, something like that, a gas-powered machine, anyway. Well, the night was getting late, and Claire and Joe were out in the barn. Claire took off, but Joe was trying to finish some work they had started. Well, Joe, being so young, wanted so badly to impress his older brother Claire that he tried to get the rest of the work finished quickly. He noticed that the machine had no more gas. So he began to put gas into it on his own. The barn was getting dark, and Joe wasn't too sure he was getting the gas in properly. He sparked a lighter to see if he was getting the gas in the hole properly, but he dropped the lighter, which broke out in flames. While adding fuel to the machine, Joe spilled the gas all over his pants. So when the lighter fell, it simultaneously caught Joe's pants on fire. His legs would never be the same.

The fire ended up burning both of his legs severely, with third-degree burns all the way up past his knees and onto his thighs. This accident didn't build character with Joe; no, he already had character. I believe that Joe turned this incident, which could very easily have been a very negative, life-changing event, into a positive experience. He almost lost his legs, but did it stop him? No! I strongly believe that this setback made him more determined to live a much fuller life. Though he was already set to be a hard worker, the accident made him work twice as hard. Grandpa Joe ended up becoming a very successful construction worker, making very good money for himself, and owning his own company in the 50s, 60s, and 70s. He purchased his own estate in Rolling Hills, California, in 1972. That buy proved to be one of the smartest investments he'd ever make. He bought his house on about two acres in 1972 for $91,000. Nowadays, the property is worth a few million.

I really and truly feel and believe that if Joe had not had the accident with his legs, who knows, maybe he would've become an unproductive drunk like his brothers. I strongly believe that our experiences in life happen for a reason. You have to recognize what's going on right in front of you to be something that could change your life for the better or for the worse. Whether or not you want something so tragic to slow you down, whether you want to look at a situation in life that happens and just think, "Poor me," or "I got robbed," or just dwell on it for the rest of your life and not live life to the fullest capacity or potential is up to you. If only we could, for every good or bad situation, take what happens as a blessing, or just be thankful when something happens that could very well be painful either physically, emotionally, or spiritually and just learn from it, dust ourselves off, and grow through it. I've noticed that, when things happen to us that we don't like, usually we become very defensive. Maybe we go into a state of denial and become angry or agitated when another person brings up a certain topic that may be touchy for us. I am really in search of a life of serenity, peace, love, and everything positive.

The reason I mention growing through adversity and remaining positive through trials is that this topic brings me to my dad, Scott. He had a wonderful dad for an example. His mom, Grandma Phyllis, was always around and there for him and his older brother, Joey Mullenaux. The boys had everything; they were just blessed in so many different ways. My dad's brother Joey, who would have been my uncle, was six years older than my dad. Joey kind of took after Papa Joe in the sense that he was handsome, hard-working, and business savvy like his dad. He joined the Marine Corps in his twenties and had intended to serve our country for a few years, make some money perhaps, come home after a couple of tours, and start working for Papa Joe, because if you are a Mullenaux, that's what you do: you work.

Unfortunately, Joey met a woman along the way, and they began dating. They fell in love early and moved in together. At some point, the relationship took a turn for the worse. Some type of altercation occurred between the two of them (I heard that Joey was planning to leave her). Joey, being a Marine I guess, had a handgun nearby, or maybe the psychotic woman had a gun of her own. The argument escalated. This woman, for whatever reasons, grabbed a gun and fired six rounds into Joey's head, killing him instantly. This tragedy is what I'm talking about when I say that certain life-changing experiences can be either motivation or discouragement. You can really let a horrible event have an opposite effect on you, and an experience that was supposed to change your life for the better ultimately becomes an anchor that you can really never detach from you which drags you far down the deep, dark path of life that nobody really wants to live in: a life of resentment, denial, fear, anxiety, isolation, and ultimately heavy drug abuse. As human beings, as people, we have the choice to let something like death really change us in a profound way either for good or for bad, but it's our choice which way. I like the path that Papa Joe took when his legs were pretty much ready to be amputated; he took the bull by the horns and rode that sucker out to his advantage. I loved my Papa Joe.

Scott was sixteen when his older brother and best friend passed away. From that day forward, Scott was never the same. Who knows how you are going to react in a situation like that? Who's to say you will grow for the better through such a cold, hard time? Only those who have been through such heartache really know. I've seen Grandma Ginny overcome adversity when times got rough, and she prospered. I've seen a good friend of mine, Chris Gray, take his own life from a drug overdose. But on the other hand, his little brother Alex, who was fourteen at the time Chris lost his life, took that horrible situation and didn't let it deter him. Alex looked up to Chris so much; Chris was so talented. Alex was always just trying to imitate his older brother. Three to four years after Chris's death, Alex became a professional surfer. Bad things happen to good people, but good people don't turn off the switch, collapse, and quit. They wear the pain, put it on, accept it, and grow through it.

I never really quite knew the whole story about Joey's girlfriend and never really cared to ask. I did hear, though, that Grandma Phyllis used to take in foster children, raise them, and give them a good opportunity to live happy and successful lives, kind work which I think is very commend-able. Then she started taking in foreign exchange students and raising them as well. One of these children or students ended up becoming Joey's girlfriend and later his wife and the woman who took his life. I actually think that the woman may have just been a friend of the family, not an actual exchange student; nonetheless, Grandma Phyllis let Joey's girlfriend live with them before she was introduced to Joey. So I think that the really hard part of the story for Scott to accept was that his mom killed his brother, in a sense. I believe that Grandma Phyllis accepted that blame as truth and just kind of babied Scott from then on. She lived with guilt, shame, and remorse as a result of trying to help someone less fortunate live life fully in a beautiful country. In such a complicated situation, what happens is really nobody's fault; it's life.

Who's to blame when a huge storm comes through, flooding your whole city and destroying thousands of homes and lives? If all the people in New Orleans after Hurricane Katrina hit just said, "Forget it," and just gave up or blamed each other for what nobody can really explain in words, where would the city be now? Nature causes tragedy sometimes; that's life. Don't just give up; quit blaming each other, yeah? Well, if that pessimistic kind of attitude is our prerogative as human beings, I don't want to live. But it's not. We can choose to love and comfort one another. We can encourage and lift up each other in a time of weakness and discouragement. Doing so is our obligation. We're not always going to be feeling happy, caring, tired, stressed, or angry at the same time, no. Our attitudes vary depending on our moods. I strongly believe that family can overcome any type of dreadful situation they may be going through because of the love that they have because of being related. Families are like a strong spiderweb, and when things get tough, that bond is supposed to hold you together.

I can see, though, that for my dad that relationship wasn't the case. Grandma Phyllis felt at fault for what happened to Joey to some degree, and Scott was never going to let her live that down. I can just see Scott growing up after that, going out, getting in trouble here and there. When Grandma Phyllis would get after him about something, such as partying, staying out late, or maybe being disobedient, I choose to believe that Scott used that situation with the exchange student and his brother's death as a scapegoat for his own misbehavior so that he could come and go as he pleased and do whatever he willed. I have my own perspective, and although I am not sure I know exactly how things went down, my intuition tells me that I've made a valid assumption. And if I'm not exactly correct, maybe I should ask, but something similar to what I just explained definitely happened.

My dad, Scott, is a genuine guy. He really has a good heart, means well, and he's a handsome guy. Somewhere along the way, though, Scott lost all interest in being a productive member of society. Maybe the death of his brother was too overwhelming. Maybe never dealing with his anger and resentment towards his mom forced him to become dependent on drugs. Holding resentments or grudges is like you taking the poison in hopes that the other person dies, understand? Or maybe Joey's death was such a traumatic experience that Scott didn't really care either way after Joey passed. I do know one thing for sure, though; Scott didn't try to follow his dad's path and turn something bad around to become an effective member of society. No, I don't know one thing my dad has ever accomplished since I've known him. He has never bought a house or his own car, or even really attempted to set some goals to live life to his fullest potential. I've never known my dad to hold down a job for any lengthy period: maybe a year or so at the most.

As a matter of fact, Scott has never even had to worry about anything, really. By the time Scott was all grown up, Grandpa Joe, Scott's dad, was so successful that all Scott had to do was keep his nose clean, and Joe was pretty much willing to take care of him. I'll say one thing, though; from the time my dad was sixteen to the present day, Grandma and Grandpa's outlook on life dramatically changed, along with Scott's familiar, upbeat energy following Joey's death. I feel that the wall of resentment Scott built towards his mom really started to take a hold of him and grab at his heart in such a negative way at a young age that he began to withdraw from home, stay out late, and party, maybe some nights not even coming home. I'm sure that, once Joe and Phyllis saw this type of behavior, they became concerned. But I also feel that Grandma Phyllis justified Scott's antics because of what had happened and just kind of let him do his thing. Joe was working too hard and was way too busy at the time really to be involved too much, even though he was himself concerned. Joe was more concerned with making that paycheck at the end of the week, which was the only thing Joe was really focused on: providing for his family.

As Scott grew older, his unmotivated, slothful ways continued. Somewhere in his early twenties or so, Scott and my mom Pam started hanging out quite a bit, I guess. Remember, my mom ended up being the chick from the high school party who stole Scott's keys and totaled his Porsche that one night: not really love at first sight, if you ask me. My dad ended up getting Pam pregnant when she was about maybe twenty. When Joe and Phyllis found out that Scott had got this little girl Pam pregnant, they were super mad; they just were not having it. I don't think that Scott was really even working at the time. He and Pam were both just kind of hanging out, partying, and getting high together. They ended up moving to Hawaii before Chris, who ends up being my older brother, was born. His birth date is October 23, 1978. My mom told me that, when they were out living in Hawaii, Scott was actually working and being somewhat productive, at least trying to be a little bit responsible. Grandma Phyllis had always just labeled Scott as a basket case: unwilling and unable. Scott was a completely capable guy, and when the heat is on, he can hold down a job for a while. He can even pay bills and be responsible as a normal person in society. Grandma Ginny even told me that the situation got to the point where oatmeal mornings, noon, and night every day wasn't cutting it anymore. Scott geared up at one point and started fending for himself, and he actually supported Pam, Chris, and himself for a minute or two.

But Pam wanted to come home all of a sudden and live back in California near her family. So Scott and Pam moved back to California and just kind of did the bare minimum required to get by. Some time passed, and Scott and Pam as a couple really started to get into heavier drug use when they made the transition from Hawaii back to California because of their old friends and influences. Pam and Scott were concerned about Chris, but they weren't really as concerned about his well-being as much as about getting their next fix.

Life was getting pretty out of control for both of them. The drugs seemed to become more important to them than their love for each other or even their newborn son.

About that time, my grandparents decided to intervene. Grandpa Joe gave Scott and Pam an ultimatum: either you straighten up your acts, get sober, start taking responsibility for your actions, and raise your kid in a healthy environment, or we are taking him from you two. So Scott and Pam kind of got the message, but they just were too far gone at this point. The drugs had really taken a toll on both my mom and my dad. The lack of motivation, determination, and responsibility to live a happy, normal life had really had its way with them. Scott was unable to keep a job, pay bills, or raise a family. Phyllis decided to convince Joe to get Pam and Scott a place to live. So he did. At the time, Joe was building three houses in the middle of Lomita, three consecutive houses. He and my grandma decided to let Pam, Scott, and Chris live in one under certain conditions. The requirements were that both Scott and Pam get and stay sober, find jobs, and take care of Chris properly; then they could have this beautiful, two-story home with four bedrooms, a three-car garage, and brand-new everything completely furnished. The house was gorgeous. My grandpa even provided cars for Scott and Pam and a live-in maid. The house, the cars, and the maid were free. My experience has been that, when things are given to someone, that gift makes the recipient less motivated to go out and get things of his own. Scott actually was never really a basket case; he just always had everything handed to him on a silver platter. Those gifts made life really easy and comfortable for him so that he could do nothing but get high, party, and really just waste this beautiful thing we call life and family away. I know that, if someone keeps throwing me a rope and bailing me out when I'm drowning, I'll never really learn how to swim on my own, and eventually at some point when I really am drowning and I have no rope to save me, I'm going to drown, because I never learned how to keep myself afloat and I expect the rope to be there. I become dependent. But if you have no rope and you're forced to swim, you'll figure things out one way or another. The worst part about that type of mindset is that relying on other people becomes part of your character, and you never really get to live life like God has intended it for us to be lived: happy, joyous, and free!

Sink or Swim

W hen you love somebody, you want to be there to support him. I'm a firm believer in tough love. I strongly disagree with enabling someone, especially family, into a codependent state of mind or life. Right around the time my mom and dad were moving into their new house, I was already born and a year or two old, I think. I am positive that my parents had not fulfilled Papa Joe and Grandma Phyllis's request to remain sober. Nonetheless, the house was Scott and Pam's. They were both heavier into their drug use now than ever. My dad at the time actually was doing home invasions, robbing houses, and my mom was selling drugs out of the house at the same time she was pregnant with Casey, my youngest brother. For me, hearing this stuff from my relatives as I grew older was so disheartening. Scott and Pam were basically handed a great opportunity to raise us in a regular household; they received everything they needed to take care of Chris and me in a positive and healthy manner. Their waste of this gift is such a shame to me.

Seeing that my parents' lifestyle and choices didn't change much from adolescence to early adulthood, I don't wonder that raising children was so hard for them. Raising kids is hard enough when you're established career-wise and emotionally. Through all this confusion, my parents decided that maybe bringing another kid into their lives would be smart. They ended up having Casey about a year or so after they moved into their free Lomita house. God really gives you a good gift when you're really young of being so innocent and so unconnected to the chaos and true recklessness of the people living around you. Sometimes, though those people are your parents, your family, and the ones you're supposed to have as role models, you end up having faith in and believing in people who are just as confused and scared as you are.

I know for a fact that the day I was born I was loaded, high. I was born on heroin, and who knows what other substances were my mom's system at the time she gave birth to me. And thinking back, as I started growing older and started really remembering things, when I was probably around three or four my mom and dad never seemed to be around. I have more memories in that house with our house maid then I do with my own parents, because as I found out when I got older, they were always locked up. And other times, they would just take off for days on end.

I remember one Christmas when my mom and dad were gone late and just Chris and I were home unsupervised. Chris lit the Christmas tree in the backyard on fire. No one was even home. All I remember was water coming over from the wall next door from our neighbor, who saw the flames and blasted the tree with his hose from across the wall, putting the fire out. When you're little, your imagination is so creative that you can turn something so basic, so simple, into something so complex. I could never figure out what the water was, or how or where it was coming from. That image never really made any sense. As I became older, the situation was clearer, but boy, did I have a crazy imagination!

I remember this one morning when I was still in diapers; I tried to follow Chris to school. His school was only a few blocks away from our house. He used to try to leave quickly in the mornings, specifically so that I wouldn't follow him. I looked up to him greatly. So one morning, although he didn't know I was there, I watched him go out the front door, and I tried to follow him. I lost him. The crowd was all kind of a blur. But as I was walking the streets aimlessly, now lost, the sheriffs picked me up. All they saw was this little boy cruising up the street in diapers. They had no idea I was just looking for my older brother. I had no way to identify myself; so they had no choice but to take me to the substation. Eventually, someone came and got me. Although that first encounter wasn't really an arrest, my relationship with the Lomita sheriff's station started early. And this trip to the substation wouldn't be my last.

I really have no other memories of my family in that house. Actually, after that incident, my memory gets kind of blurry. The next vivid memory I have occurred after we moved into a smaller place in the city of Torrance, a much smaller place. So now, three of us boys were in the family. My parents were still out of work, and their drug use was just getting worse and worse day by day.

Chris used to love to torment me. Casey was still too young to be interesting, but Chris loved messing with me. I specifically remember one night when mom and dad had gone out and appointed Chris the duty of babysitting me. He would watch that show *Unsolved Mysteries* with the really creepy guy that hosted, Walsh. The worst part was the super-intense theme song on that show in the beginning, which frightened me. It used to scare me so badly that I would cry. Chris knew how scared I was, too; so he would turn off all the lights and crank the TV all the way up just to watch me tremble. I don't know why I was so frightened by that show, but my fear probably had to do with the creepy people on the show and the unsolved murders. The host coming on with his wrinkly face scared me enough, but then he would say, "If you know anything about the whereabouts of these men," at which point a picture of the murderers would show on the TV, "please contact us at," and then a number would appear at the bottom of the screen. I always thought for sure that the guy in the picture about whose whereabouts the police had no clue was sure to be standing right outside our window, waiting for me at the front door. He never was, but Chris loved messing with me. He really knew how to push my buttons.

Now trusting Chris was really hard when I was growing up. I came to the conclusion early on that either Chris really didn't like me or he really loved to see me scared or in pain. I remember one time in the backyard when I was helping Chris break up some bricks for whatever reason. He was having me hold the bricks while he took a hammer and just smashed them for whatever reason, breaking them all up. But Chris was a smart kid. He knew I looked up to him; he also knew he could manipulate me into doing things I really didn't want to do. That hammer came down so hard on my thumb that evening that I just about popped out of my shoes. I took off running down the street so fast to my aunt's house that I must have left a trail of fire with smoke coming off my shoes. My thumb swelled up like a pumpkin. My aunt Vicki wrapped it up with ice, and I ended up crying myself to sleep on her front porch. After that night, I really lost a lot of trust in my brother.

My brothers and I never really had much supervision. We felt like my parents were never home. Grandma Ginny would come down every so often to check on us. So would Phyllis and Joe. I remember that Grandma Ginny would pull up in her little blue Volvo in the alley right next to our house. I would hold onto her window, begging her to take me home with her. Sometimes she would, and other times I would end up staying home with Chris, wondering what he planned to do to me next. Somewhere along the line, life started getting so bad with Scott and Pam using drugs and all that my mom and dad left our grandparents no other option but to take my brothers and me and raise us themselves. They did give

Scott and Pam an option, though: get clean and sober, and the kids are yours. All my parents really needed to do was to show some signs of growth and healing, like some consistency in a job and some sobriety, and we were theirs again. Put it this way. After Grandma and Grandpa intervened, we never, ever again lived in the same house with my mom and dad as a family, a situation which was probably better for us. Needless to say, sobriety was not an option for Scott and Pam, no matter the circumstance. Their lives went on this way for years and years to come.

But we boys finally got a break. Grandma Ginny took Casey and me, and Grandma Phyllis and Papa Joe took Chris. Why they separated us, I'm not sure. But as I got older, their reasoning was clearer to me. After raising their own kids, watching them go through their ups and downs, for my grandparents to make the decision to take on the responsibility of raising their grandkids, a second generation, was a hard choice. So the best solution financially for them was to separate us and plan accordingly. They made an extremely hard choice and took on a very large commitment: doing all the paperwork to get us enrolled in school, clothing us, and taking care of all our medical expenses. For Casey and me, our medical bills turned out to be a never-ending story. I can't express the gratitude I have today for the courage and love my grandparents displayed in such a time of need for us.

Chris was living in Rolling Hills with my dad's parents, and Casey and I were in San Pedro with our mom's mom and Papa Herman. Herman had gone through this set of responsibilities once already, and I'm not too sure he was very thrilled about a second time around. Papa Herman never actually had any kids of his own, but he did end up raising seven kids. Here he took on the obligation of raising all of Virginia's girls, and now he had to make time to raise two more crazy little kids? I don't think he was too thrilled. Why didn't he have to raise any of a Vicki's kids, Suzanne's kids, or even Erin's kids? Why just us? We would always hang out with the cousins, but they lived at home with their moms and dads. Why were Scott and Pam's kids different? When I was younger, I never really thought about our family in that way. But as I grew older, the thought haunted me until my late teenage years.

Because Grandma Ginny and Herman were still working full-time when they took us in, getting us to school on time or fulfilling scheduled appointments was difficult. Pam was never around much after the grandparents took us in. Most of the time, she was either in prison or not allowed to come around because she was too intoxicated. But Scott was around a little bit. Scott was living with Chris up at his parents' place in the pool house, once again free of charge. He really never had much responsibility. So from time to time, Virginia would ask Scott to come through and help out with his kids. For example, if my dad would get us to school in the morning, then Virginia would pick us up from school when she got off work if she didn't have to stay late for teachers' meeting or whatever, as she was required to do quite often.

Now because Scott had not a care in the world, you would think that he wouldn't mind helping Grandma, seeing that we were his kids. But having to be of the least bit of service to someone always seemed to make him mad, even if he were helping someone who had taken on the responsibility of his own kids. I could understand not wanting to help out with the neighbor's kids or something, but come on, your own flesh and blood is different. I can remember so many times being late for school or waiting on the curb after school for hours on end, thinking that Scott would be there any minute. I would seriously just stare at the corner, hoping that the next car was my dad. Sometimes, he wouldn't even show up, and I would have to use the phone in the school office to figure out a ride situation. As I grew older, that neglect made me very punctual. As weird as my reaction may seem, I always loved my dad so much, and even when he would show up late, as soon as I got in the car I would almost instantly forget that he left me stranded for as long as he did.

I remember one incident that occurred one night with Casey and me at Grandma's place. We used to love putting a plastic bag on the corner of the door and getting some type of little ball. One of us would guard the plastic goal, while the other one would take off down the hall to throw the ball. Whoever was defending the goal would try to block whoever was making a shot from scoring. Well one night, we were playing for a long time. We were having so much fun. I came down the hall full blast, jumping with the intention to slam the ball. But when I landed, I got caught up with Casey and landed awkwardly, splitting my head open and gushing blood everywhere on the edge of Grandma's oak dresser. I was probably in third grade at this time. Before Grandma could really evaluate the situation, she was instantly upset. She told me just to go lay on the bed until she could figure out what to do. I remember vividly that the sleeping bag on which I was lying had a huge puddle of blood. I ended up needing seven stitches in my head to fix the wound.

Hospitals weren't really Grandma's forte, and so she called Scott. I guess my dad had a date that night; so when he got the call, he was very bitter. Unfortunately for Scott, his plans for the evening changed. When he got to my grand-mother's house, he was heated. He continued to be upset at the hospital, like he was the one with a huge gash in the back of his head. Scott just seemed to be very agitated anytime you needed him for anything that wasn't really concerning him. I remember sitting next to him in the car when he was mad. You could always feel the negative energy coming off him. I always knew when to be quiet. Most of the time, he would be smoking also. He would always bum me out. Unfortunately, trips to the hospital became quite a normal part of my life as I got older. Every year or two after that head-gash incident, I was back in the emergency room.

One time before soccer practice at Ladera Linda, where our AYSO team used to hold practices, my dad taught me how to do a cherry drop off the top of the pull-up bars. What you do is climb up on the top of the bar, putting your legs where your knees are in between the bars while you're holding on with one arm to either side of the poles. You tighten your legs and drop straight back, rotating like an arm on a clock. When you drop back and start to come up and around, you release your legs and let your body fall, landing on your feet. The trick is really a lot easier than the description sounds.

After my dad taught me how to do this trick, I thought it was the coolest thing. As soon as I got to school the next day, before class in the morning, I decided that I was going to show everyone on the playground what I had learned the day before. First, I did a successful one on the lower pull-up bar, but that success wasn't enough for me. I had to take the trick one step further to the higher bars. Not being satisfied with something good I had accomplished, I always wanted to do more or something better. As I got older, this trait would become problematic with me. I got up to the high bars, sat on them normally, and dropped back. I didn't calculate the difference in the drop time and released too early. Well, my momentum had not gone to the top yet, from where you were to release. I released too early, causing me to do an extra half rotation. So instead of landing on my feet, I landed with my arm out in an awkward position, breaking my ulna and radius in my right arm.

I remember that my body went into shock. I don't even remember really crying or anything like that. I just remember looking at my arm and thinking how mad my dad was going to be when he found out about this one. I was thinking, "Hopefully, he's not getting ready to go on a date right now." To be honest with you, I was pretty scared at the time. I was in third grade when I broke my arm. I missed over a week of school due to my injury. Right then, I can remember just starting to fall behind on assignments. My grades were never really great from the start, not that I wasn't smart or anything like that, but I think that all the stress of moving around at an early age was hard and very confusing for me.

For a brief moment, after I had moved in with Grandma Ginny, Pam came back around trying to get Casey and me back. Papa Herman owned a little house in San Pedro. So Virginia and he came up with the idea that they would let Pam stay in it with Casey and me, seeing that she seemed to be doing a little better at this point. Or did she just manipulate them into thinking so? Well, whatever the situation was, Grandma and Grandpa's marriage seemed to me to be on shaky grounds because of Casey and me. We definitely were not the easiest kids to manage. Herman was actually considering a divorce because of us, or so I thought. I would not have blamed him. We were getting to be too much. Later on, I found out that my mom just really wanted us back in her life and that really Grandma and Grandpa were just as happy as ever, only very frustrated with my mom and her decisions.

So they gave us back to Pam, and Casey and I stayed with her for a short while. When you're young, remembering for sure how long things like that lasted is really hard. I think that we lived with her for a few months at most. Some of the worst memories of my life were living in the house with my mom for the short period that I did. My mom had never exactly cleaned up her act at all. She was still using. The worst part about the situation was that I was grown up a little more now; so I got to witness some pretty bad stuff that ended up sticking with me for the rest of my life. Pam would have the dope man come over, introduce me to him, and have me hang out in the living room while they would run a lighter under a regular spoon with heroin in it. As I remember the images as a little boy, Pam and the dealer would take this little tiny sac that almost looked like a raisin or something, put it in the center of a spoon, and draw a lighter underneath it. I'll never forget the smell that little sac would produce when they would do that in front of me.

All through my life from that point on, whenever I would smell something remotely close to that smell, the odor would instantly take me back to that particular day and the insanity in which I grew up. It's strange how certain smells or songs can really take you back in your mind to a place in life that happened maybe years prior, but instantly you're right back in that moment as if it occurred a few minutes earlier. Whether or not you were having a good day, a memory can really change your attitude and mood. Whether that memory was something necessarily good or bad doesn't matter; an appeal to the senses just triggers something in our brains. Just a smell I remember from when I was younger can really put me in that uncomfortable state of mind for a few seconds.

I never actually watched Pam shoot up in front of me. But many times, I would find her nodding out on the bed. Sometimes she would have a cigarette in her hand when she was slipping in and out of consciousness on her bed. Holes were burned into almost every blanket we had in the house. Sometimes she would just nod off and not regain consciousness for what seemed to be days on end. Sometimes I would shake her, even smack her if I had to, in order to get her attention. Sometimes she wouldn't even respond. This stupor used to scare me so much. She wouldn't wake up, and she never kept food in the fridge, either. She used to buy just a few burgers or Fillet-O-Fish sandwiches from McDonald's, I remember, and she would keep them in the fridge for days. They always seem to go bad after a day or two. Casey and I never really had any decent food around to eat. I try to think back to where Casey was and what he was doing in those days, and I don't even really remember him being around much. Maybe because of all the stress I was under, I failed to acknowledge my little brother at times. As I grew up, I never failed to acknowledge that Casey was right there with me, going through the same hell I was enduring.

Pam had this boyfriend that I just hated. Even as a young boy, my intuition gave me good reason to believe that he was a bad guy. I actually walked into the bathroom a few times to find him tying himself off and shooting up dope in my grandma's house where we, my mom, Casey, and I, were staying for free, thanks to Grandma and Grandpa Moreno. Really, the house was my Papa Herman's property. The nerve of Pam to manipulate her own mother into thinking she was even the least bit sane enough to raise us was insanity.

My mom's boyfriend, whose name I don't remember (we'll call him John), used to take me into the backyard and really put on this strange attitude that he was my buddy or something, trying to convince me that going up to Grandma Phyllis's and getting her jewelry, clothes, radio, and other stuff and bringing it back to him and my mom was okay. He tried to sound like doing what he asked was really okay for me and that, if I carried out this favor for him, he would take me fishing and to Disneyland and all sorts of other fun activities. Yeah, the dude was crazy, and I knew he was full of it. The crazy thing about the situation was that my mom actually was in agreement with John and assured me that taking from Grandma was okay.

I'll never forget that day driving up to my grandma's house with my mom and John. Because Grandma Phyllis lived in a gated community and my mom knew she wasn't allowed back there, she dropped me off at the library, which is part of a high school bordering my grandma's backyard property. Behind the library was an undetectable back way into this gated community. Pam knew that I knew how to take this trail up to Grandma's house. At the time, I had a feeling that what I was doing wasn't right. At the time, though, I didn't want to let my mom down.

I can remember the feeling that came over me as I entered Grandma's house surreptitiously. Grandma and Grandpa were home at the time. I already knew what I was going to get before I set foot in the house. John and Mom made what I was to get very clear. As I went straight to the hallway closet, my heart started thumping; I was extremely nervous and scared. I thought I heard someone coming, and I closed the closet door. False alarm: nobody was there. I opened the door again quickly before someone found me. As the nervousness began to flow uncontrollably through my body, I grabbed a portable mini-TV. I was so nervous that I left after I grabbed the portable TV; I made a quick and clean getaway. I was so nervous that I didn't feel I was able to get to Grandma's bathroom for the jewelry; so I split. I ran back down that trail so fast into my mom's car. I was determined not to have anyone see me.

There John and Pam were, waiting for me. An emotion came over my whole body that was indescribable. Part of me liked the whole sneaky behavior for which my mom and John had enlisted me. And another part of me was very confused. But John and Pam seemed happy, and that's really all I cared about. I would search for that feeling of getting away with something dishonest continually as I grew older. The feeling was, I can say for sure, a high of some sort, but on a different level of perception distortion.

Not long after the theft, I was living back with Grandma Ginny. I didn't see Pam very often growing up, because of her chronic drug addiction. She has only experienced brief periods of sobriety, none of which have lasted long enough to make her a permanent part of my life. Apart from the occasional phone call, we have no contact, a situation which, although tragic, is healthy and sane for me.

Back at Grandma Ginny's, sports started becoming my number one priority. I remember that, the last year I played AYSO soccer, I got home from practice one night, and the

All-Star team coach had called me. He asked me how I would like to join the All-Star team. Getting that call was such a good feeling that I said yes right away. He told me the time and place for the next practice, which was pretty much the gist of the conversation. I hung up the phone, and I kid you not, ten minutes later I got a call from a traveling soccer club team who wanted me on their team also. What? I'd just told the All-Star team that I would play for them, but All-Stars was still AYSO, while club was the next step up. I was caught in between two great honors, but at the end of the day, any AYSO kid would way rather play for a club team than an All-Star team. I told the club coach that I would call him back.

I hung the phone up and told Grandma and Grandpa that both the All-Star team and the club team wanted me at the same time. "What should I do?" I asked. I remember that my grandpa said, "Do what you want; just follow your heart." I ended up calling the All-Star team back and telling them that I wouldn't be able to play for their team this season. Then I called the club team and started playing for the Palos Verdes Raiders club team. That choice was difficult to make, because all my friends were All-Stars, but it turned out to be the right choice. Once we had a scrimmage game against the All-Stars. During the whole game, my buddies were jokingly calling me a traitor. But my team ended up winning; so I don't feel too guilty on the choice I made to play for the Raiders. We had a stacked team; they had a slacked team: ha ha.

After soccer season was baseball. I loved baseball, too. I made All-Stars for baseball that year, and I remember hitting a home run in one of our All-Star games. I'll never forget that game. A good friend of mine, Eric, hit two grand slams and a home run in that same game where I went yard (hit a homer); that game was crazy, very memorable.

I got a call that year from one of the coaches telling me that something was going on with our little league field, and Kellogg's was to be filming a commercial there. It was a

Kellogg's Apple Jacks cereal commercial. The theme was baseball, and the company chose me and a couple of my teammates to be in the commercial. I was so honored. Shooting the commercial was a half-day job, but we got paid for a full day because the company filmed on the weekend. I seriously didn't do anything for eight hours but throw a ball around in the background, and when my check came, it was almost a thousand dollars. I was so incredibly shocked at the amount of money that Kellogg's paid for the amount of work I did, which really was nothing.

I took the check to school and showed all my friends that I had a thousand dollars even though I was only eleven years old. I bought some type of new top-of-the-line roller-blades with a lot of that money; at that time, rollerblading was quite popular. But buying those rollerblades was one of the worst ideas ever. I should have just gotten some new baseball equipment or some soccer cleats.

One day, Chris and I were up at Grandma Phyllis's house. Her house was so nice and so big, with a tennis court on the property. I had my rollerblades on, and I was skating around the tennis court. All of a sudden, Chris came down to the tennis court with our dog Pinky. He had her on a leash, and he started to chase me around the tennis court. At one point, the leash got tangled around my legs as Chris was trying to keep up with me, and I fell flat on my face, breaking out my two front teeth. When I think back to that day, Chris seemed to have purposely jumped in front of me with the dog and tried to trip me. I see and remember the incident exactly that way.

I was so mad at Chris for just breaking out my front teeth that I started crying. My dad was in the pool house where he was staying at the time. I was so reluctant to tell my dad because I knew how he reacted in situations like these. Every time I hurt myself, my dad was so mad. Chris and I came up from the court. I had my teeth in my hand, and I very shyly told my dad what had happened. He blew up right away, just as expected. I was actually in counter mode; so I was ready for his response. The injury wasn't really a big deal. My teeth got fixed, and they look pretty good now. Every now and then, they'll bite into something hard or accidentally bite down on my fork, and they'll break off. That only happens once every five years or so. I knew that Chris hated me growing up and wanted to kill me if he could. He would always tease and torture me from a very young age. I never had a very brotherly relationship with him growing up.

I had a situation happen to me in the pool house when I was growing up that stuck with me my whole life. This random guy Craig used to hang around when we were younger. I think he was a neighborhood friend or a friend of my mom's; his tie to the family was never very clear. One day, we were swimming all day with some of our cousins and friends. When everyone had gone, Craig ended up staying for some reason or another; so we started watching TV together.

My dad used to have all sorts of pornography videos lying around the house. These videos were the first encounter with any type of sexual intercourse between a male and a female that I'd ever seen. Craig was snooping around when he found one of my dad's pornos, popped it in, and started to watch it with me. This situation, which was very awkward, happened several times afterwards also, once when Casey was there. Then one time, Craig, Casey, and I were in the pool house. Craig was acting strange. He was in and out of the bathroom, and then he went in there for a while and then came out again. His behavior was very awkward. Keep in mind that this guy Craig was an older man. He started grabbing and touching me in a very aggressive manner. I think that Casey had gone upstairs by this time. He then began to pull his shorts down and forced me to perform oral sex on him. I was forced. I was totally against complying, and I did not feel comfortable with the act at all. But in the end, he forced me. What he did was torture; it was an experience I'll never forget. The memory was very demoralizing for me growing up. I'll never forget that.

The abuse was a deep, dark secret that I dared not tell anyone lest they judge me. I held on to these feelings of hatred and bottled up unhealthy emotions from a very early age. Even though Craig only actually abused me once, that one experience was all that was necessary to shut me down emotionally. Craig came around several times after that afternoon, and then he kind of faded away. I never really remember seeing him again after. I was ashamed for many, many years afterwards. I closed down a certain part of me that was fun and exciting, and I started becoming angry, withdrawn, hostile, and easily agitated. Ultimately, I started getting into a lot of trouble from that point on. Thinking back, I don't think I can say that the abuse was the worst thing that ever happened to me, but it was right up there for sure.

Chris actually one time tried to kill me. Once, when Grandma Ginny was out of town or out to dinner, one of the two, my dad was babysitting Chris and me at Virginia's house. Ginny lived on 18th Street in San Pedro. Her house was on the top of a huge hill that overlooked the Long Beach / San Pedro port. Her street has got to be one of the steepest streets in San Pedro for sure. Chris and I were outside messing around with this little bike we had, and we were taking turns going down the hill into some ivy plants. Chris went down and into the plants, and then he came back up. Then I took my turn, and I went down and into the plants successfully. Back up the hill I came. I noticed that the chain had come off the bike. I don't remember how old I was, but I remember I was too young even to consider being able to put the chain back on properly. So for some reason, I felt that maybe I could trust Chris to put the chain back on correctly. I should have known better.

Chris attempted to put the chain back on, but I feel somehow that he rigged it or something, because he wanted me to go back down right after that without taking another turn himself. So I did. I jumped on the bike, but I failed to look at the chain. I just trusted that Chris had fixed it properly. Remember, I looked up to Chris. But Chris didn't even fix the chain. He just thought that seeing me go down the hill with no brakes would be funny. I didn't have shoes on at the time. I was barefooted, and I was wearing shorts and a T-shirt. As I started going down the hill, I realized that the chain was not on the bike. As I became aware of that fact, I had already picked up so much speed that I had no way to stop without brakes. I had no choice but to put my feet down. I was probably doing a good forty to forty-five miles an hour with no brakes and no shoes. But your natural instinct in that scenario is to put your foot down. A split second of my foot touching the ground is all it took to create a blister on the whole bottom of my foot.

I went flying down the street through the stop sign where, at any given moment, oncoming traffic could approach and send me to an early grave. I was fortunate enough to survive this situation with only minor injuries, no collision with any cars. Luckily, I ended up coming to a rolling stop, eventually. I had the biggest and worst blisters on the bottom of my feet that you ever saw. I escaped death. If for some reason I was not supposed to live past a certain point, that day would've been the day. God must have something great planned for me, I imagine. I survived another horrifying life experience brought to you by my oh-so-loving older brother, Chris.

You're in the Army Now

From an early age, I personally struggled with watching my buddies getting picked up by their parents after school. Usually, Grandma picked me up. I never understood why, but not having my parents there after school bugged me a lot of the time. Really deep down, I felt different from all of my friends, and I thought about that difference a lot. One thing that really helped me take my mind off my family situation was sports. I love playing sports; I can get out there and just run all day. One thing I learned about myself early on was that I'm always very competitive. I would get out there, put my heart into the game, and give my best, whether I was playing soccer, baseball, tennis, skateboarding, or whatever else. The feeling of satisfaction I got when I scored a goal or hit a line drive into the center field or struck a backhand winner down the line was exhilarating.

I did really well early on in sports, but I was having my struggles inside the classrooms. Besides my grades not being good, I was getting sent to the principal's office more than your average elementary school student. I was always a kind of real spunky, happy-go-lucky kid with a lot of energy, despite the problems at home. I excelled on the field but not in the classrooms. My energy got me into a lot of trouble during my last year of elementary school. I remember having to be segregated from my peers because of my inability to stay in my seat and not disrupt the classroom. I was put in the back of the classroom with a huge, sectional divider which acted as a wall so that I would not disrupt other students while they were studying. I just hated that segregation. I just wanted to go; I wanted to experience life. I didn't want to sit in some classroom listening to some guy talk about some numbers, some fractions, or whatever it was. My mind was moving at a million miles an hour.

I'm not quite sure, but I think that, at the beginning of fifth grade, I moved from Grandma Ginny's house to Grandma Phyllis's house in Rolling Hills. Grandma Phyllis sent Chris to military school in Carlsbad, CA near San Diego; so my moving made keeping Casey easier on Grandma Ginny. I also really had a crazy connection with my dad, and I insisted on going and living at Grandma Phyllis's house with him. I remember Chris going to military school. When you're young, military school sounds like a huge, kind of intimidating deal. I can remember getting in trouble in fifth grade and justifying my misbehavior with, "It's okay; I'm going to go to military school next year, anyway." I knew I was going to be shipped off at one point or another.

Well, I didn't end up going to military school that following year; no, instead I started my first year of junior high at Miraleste Middle School. I remember being really nervous starting sixth grade. You know, starting middle school is like starting at the bottom of the food chain again. You don't know all the big eighth-graders. Just when I'd finished five years of elementary school to get to be a fifth grader and feel comfortable, now I had once again been taken out of my realm and thrown into a completely new environment, not to mention moving in with Grandma Phyllis, where I was still trying to adapt.

Middle school is where I really started to act out in all sorts of absurd ways. I used to have a Casio calculator watch which also had the option to be a remote control for your

TV/VCR. I remember that in my fifth grade English class, I would turn the TV on and off just to distract the class and put some attention on myself. My teacher at the time, Mrs. Davidson, had no clue what was going on with the TV; mostly only kids around me knew. But everyone started laughing. Mrs. Davidson would have to stop class and call maintenance to look at the TV, because she couldn't teach when the TV was shutting on and off; it was too much of a distraction. When she started to catch on, eventually one of the kids in the class told on me, and she took my watch away. I'd actually bought that watch with the money I had made from my cereal commercial. I think I got detention or something for that little prank. I'm pretty sure I failed English that year.

I remember getting in a fight with this big Asian kid named Michael Cho. Over what, I don't remember. But I do remember that this kid was big, and I wanted nothing do with him. Our trouble had to do with an argument with a friend of mine. I just stepped in the back of my buddy like a normal friend would do, and before any actual fist fighting broke out, Michael and I were being reprimanded and taken into the principal's office. That fight was the first time I got suspended from school and actually sent home. I don't think anything happened to Mike.

Because the school officials already had their eyes on me, they had already labeled me as a troublemaker. Placing the punishment on me for whatever the absurd acts would be was easy for them; the fingers would point my way automatically. My situation is pretty understandable when you grow up and find out that, once you start acting a certain way, the authorities put you in a certain category.

The punishment for the fight was a three-day suspension. Then, a couple of the kids I knew were throwing rocks over a fence down on the field at lunchtime one afternoon. Being competitive and all, I cruised over to where they were and right away picked up a rock, threw it over the fence, and directly hit a car, smashing the front windshield. All of the kids scattered and thought nothing of the incident, as the car was on the other side of the fence in traffic. I guess we just thought that no one would find out who had thrown rocks. I was sitting in class during the next period, when my name was announced over the loudspeaker and I was prompted to go to the principal's office. Now the kid with whom I was throwing the rocks was in the office as well. The principal called my aunt Cathy to come pick me up; a five-day suspension was in order. The other kid, well, he went back to class. I'm pretty sure he actually told on me.

Then, my next suspension was for throwing Wite-Out all over the boys' bathroom stalls. I remember leaving math class to use the restroom. And this bathroom trip was so quiet, with nobody in the hallways and no one in the restroom when I got there. I started to use the center stall when I noticed a bottle of Wite-Out sitting on top of the urinal. I didn't even think about what I was doing. As I finished, I grabbed the bottle, unscrewed the top, and just started throwing Wite-Out all over the bathroom. How could anybody have found out what I did? Detection seemed impossible. Why did I throw Wite-Out? I don't know. I think that something about doing something I knew was bad but trying to be sneaky about it was exciting to me. Before I ever did any drugs, I sought after the high that you get from adrenaline on a regular basis. But after I sat back down in class, the bell rang for lunch, and over the loudspeaker again I heard, "Cody Mullenaux, report to the principal's office." Once again, I was sent home suspended, missing more school work and getting more behind and more stressed and confused.

By the time the first year of junior high was coming to an end, teachers and staff agreed that I was too much of a distraction to return the following year as a seventh-grader. As a matter of fact, I agreed with them, too; they pretty much had expelled me at that point. So I got what I wanted, I guess. I got to go to the same military school where my older brother went. Now getting shipped off to military school so young was supposed to be a punishment, right?

At first I didn't really know what to expect. I really didn't know how to act. Besides, I was this kid who couldn't stay out of trouble for the life of me, and the same was true with all the other kids that went to the boarding school, too. We were shipped away because we all had one thing in common: trouble. I didn't know anyone who got sent to reform school for being an overachiever. Well, guess what happens when you put a whole bunch of kids together who single-handedly create more drama than the 1990s Los Angeles riots? You know as well as I do that I've just described a recipe for disaster.

At first, getting situated and once again adapting to a new living situation was challenging. The school had a very straightforward day-to-day program. What was strange about this school was that I was about eleven or twelve years old going to the same school and programming with kids that were already in high school, as the school was a seventh to twelfth grade school. So in a sense, I started high school two years before all my buddies back home did.

My first year there, I didn't have much trouble. I went to school, got decent grades, and met some real cool cats. I actually started to feel really good, and structure seemed to work in my favor. The program was pretty intense. Every morning at 6 AM sharp over the loudspeaker the school played reveille, which was a very annoying trumpet song; we'd wake up to it every single morning, military status. So right at 6 AM, you jump out of bed; from then, you have almost fifteen minutes to get dressed, clean your room, make your bed, and head out to formation.

Now we would wear full military attire, which actually consisted of about four to five different uniforms. We had regular PT attire, which was physical training. There was white wool, which was a standard white button-down collared shirt with wool dress pants. On Wednesdays we would wear our BDUs, or battle dress uniforms, which were straight-up, full-on camouflage uniforms with boots. Then there was the garrison attire, which looked basically like white wool but was all gray. We also had coatee attire for formal dress events. Your uniform had to be perfect, with your shoes shined daily and your gig line straight. Your gig line meant making sure that the buttons of your shirt lined up directly with the center of your belt and the zipper on your pants.

So in the morning before we left our rooms to line up for formation, we would make sure that our beds were six inches and eight inches, which meant that our beds had to be made perfectly. The folder, the sheet which came over the blanket, had to be six inches, and the top part of the bed where just the bottom sheet was exposed had to be eight inches.

Now if you failed to make your bed properly, see to it that your uniform was properly worn, or get to formation on time, well, that failure meant getting demerits, and demerits meant marching on a white line during your free time. Demerits also meant that you had no free time. The demerits were basically a write-up for failure to fulfill basic instructions. We would perform our marching hours on this white painted line outside of our dorm rooms. The amount of demerits you accumulated would equate to the amount of hours you would march back and forth on that line.

You could also get demerits for things such as not looking completely to the front in formation or scratching without permission in formation. Seriously, if you had a scratch, you would stand with your right arm straight out in front of you, and when approached by an officer of rank, you would ask, "Sir, personal permission to scratch, Sir." Then you had three to five seconds to adjust yourself, if you were granted permission. Some kids would get caught looking around or scratching without permission, and sometimes instead of giving them the demerits, the officer would pull the offender out of formation and put his nose against the wall with his arms out at his sides at what was called double arm interval. I hated that one. That position was, pretty much, one of the worst punishments that you could get.

Basically morning formation existed to account for everybody. The officers lined us up according to what company we were in. The junior schoolers, like me for example, were Echo Company, followed by Charlie Company, Bravo, Alpha, and Headquarters. And each company had a company commander, a senior or somebody who had been there awhile and acquired a certain stature of rank. And a commanding officer called the battalion commander was over everyone else.

The battalion commander was the highest-ranking officer in the whole school. He was the type of guy that comes to military school really young, with intentions of going to West Point or going into the service from the beginning. The battalion commander was a kid, only sixteen or seventeen years old, and he had about five to seven hundred kids under him. But he was our leader. At first he was intimidating. To me, he was like the president of the United States or something. He even had his cabinet, guys under him, his chain of command, his captains, lieutenants, sergeants: a really genuine military format. And whenever you would approach someone with a rank of lieutenant or higher, you had to salute him. Most of the kids in the upper-classes, ninth through twelfth grade, had this type of rank. So you found yourself saluting quite often. I guess that habit taught you respect.

So after morning formation, we would go straight to the mess hall, where we ate. From there, we came back to our dorms for about an hour and then went off to school. This schedule was our regular Monday through Friday routine. After school was our free time; from about 3 PM to 5 PM we had recreation. Because the school was on a waterfront property in Carlsbad near San Diego, CA, we had access to the beach every day after school. I would get out of class, grab my board and wetsuit, and head straight to the beach with my buddies. I remember that the surf was usually good down there. Even at three in the afternoon, surf was usually really nice. The school also had a recreation hall which had TV, movies, video games, pool tables, a snack bar, and also a beautiful view of the Pacific Ocean.

The school was pretty nice. I got spoiled. I actually started really liking that school. My grades came up, and I made the Dean's list, which required a GPA of 3.3 or higher. If you made the Dean's list, you were able to study in your room with your roommate, if he was on the Dean's list too. If not, and if your grades were below a 3.3 average, you had to study in the study hall with everybody else, where you had to be watched over and extremely quiet every night. Being on the Dean's list was chill. You could hang out with your roommate, listen to music, study, or just do your thing. You had your freedom. The first semester, I didn't have that privilege. Being on Dean's list taught me the basic fundamentals of achieving and showed me the benefits of hard work. One lesson that I could for sure see that paid off for me later on as I grew up was how neat and clean I would keep my stuff, my clothes, my room, even the house. I kept everything very organized, and still to this day, I'm very tidy. Military school paid off also by giving me a different type of understanding and respect for people.

For me, making friends was never very hard. I started hanging out with some pretty cool kids. I remember I got my first pair of Sal Barbieri's, a certain type of skateboard shoe that was in high demand at this time. I didn't really even skateboard very much back then; I just remember that the shoes had the number twenty-three on the side of them. That number was my favorite one ever since I was little, because my birthday fell on December 23. The shoes were white with black soles and black laces, and the number twenty-three on the side was black as well. They just looked really clean. Even now, I wouldn't mind a pair of Sal's.

Anyway, this kid Judd who went to school with me was a real skater kid from San Diego. His older brother went to the school with us also and was supposedly a really good skater. Judd knew all about skateboarding. He knew all the names of skaters; he knew the names of all the maneuvers performed on a skateboard. The kid sure tripped me out when I met him. He approached me because of my shoes. He said, "What's up? You got the new Sal's: nice." He introduced himself, "What's up? I'm Judd. You skate?"

"Yeah, I skate a little," I said. I didn't really though. I knew the basics; that was pretty much it. Judd and I became pretty good friends. He would sit behind me in class. We used to wear these hats that pretty much looked like an envelope put on your head with the ends of the envelope towards the front and rear of your head. They were really silly looking. As we weren't allowed to wear our hats under covers, which meant inside, Judd used to pretend that his hat was a skateboard. So in class all day, he would sit in a totally different world. He would flip his hat around and land on it with his fingers, doing all sorts of weird skateboard maneuvers, like sliding it on the side of the desk. He was definitely obsessed with skateboarding, and he really got me interested in it. He would flip the hat around in a certain manner and ask me, "Cody, what trick was that?" I would have to guess. I would say, "Kick flip?" He would say, "No, that was a heel flip." Then he would do another trick, flipping the hat around, and say, "What was that trick?" Then I would guess again. Judd's game is how I started to figure out different types of tricks and maneuvers on a skateboard.

I became really interested in skating from that point on. Being competitive, it was no wonder I'd become pretty good. We students weren't allowed to have wheels or trucks, which are the metal brackets attached to the skateboard in order to mount wheels. So kids would just have regular skateboard decks with no grip tape or wheels, etc. Skateboarding actually got really interesting to me when we would play S-K-8. If you ever played basketball, our game was the same thing as horse but on your skateboard. You alternated back and forth, trick for trick, trying to match the trick of the person who went before you.

I've always been kind of a natural athlete; I just picked up sports like I was born for them or something. Sports came easy and felt right to me. I got pretty good on my board. I ended up skating a lot as I got older. I also played baseball and basketball at military school. I was granted a God-given ability to play baseball, which was like part of my soul growing up. I had this killer arm, was fast, and could hit the ball very well from an early age, thanks to Papa Joe, who almost every day would take me to the batting cages and bribe me with a dollar a ball to hit every ball that came out of the machine over the pitching fence. I loved that man. I played center field and usually would bat first or second in the lineup because of my ability to beat out ground balls hit to the infield. I remember being captain of my junior school team.

But I liked skateboard a lot also. If you skateboard, though, a certain lifestyle seems to go with the sport, and most people frown upon you, especially Grandma Phyllis. She hated that I skateboarded. She was, I think, more concerned about me hurting myself than anything else. My first year at military school was going pretty well, actually. The school kept us busy with all sorts of weekend activities. We used to go paintballing, miniature golfing, or to laser tag sometimes. Sometimes the school would just take us to the movies and to the beach down in San Diego and let us skate the strand. Whenever we left campus, though, we usually had a good time and good memories. I remember one time even one of the counselors took a liking to me and another one of the kids at this school; the counselor took us on a private trip kind of under the radar. We were out in Lake Paris, where he took us gliding. Gliding, which was pretty crazy, is where you are in this really small, aerodynamic airplane that has no engine. A regular plane pulls you up into the air behind it with some type of rope, and you elevate into the air higher and higher. Then, when you get to a certain elevation, you are released from the plane that pulled you into the air. The glider is stable, but it has no engine. It's just a little two-seater. That trip is something I'll always remember; that was definitely a fun time.

The school wasn't really all that bad in the beginning. On certain weekends, if you didn't have to stay at school for drill practice or practice for marching in a parade or something like that, you were allowed to go home on a visitation leave. I used to take the Amtrak train from Oceanside to Union Station in downtown Los Angeles and have my grandpa, dad, or grandma pick me up. I rode the train home pretty often. Coming home was kind of a trip, too.

I got home for a week during Thanksgiving break in 1995. I called up one of my good buddies at the time, Brent Launer, with whom I grew up playing sports. That day was just a normal day, nothing out of the ordinary; we were playing some tennis and did a little rollerblading. Every time that I got on my rollerblades there seemed to be a disaster waiting. Brent had a little ramp, homemade and small but fun. We were cruising down his driveway and doing tricks off it into the street. Things were going fine until I tried to do some stupid, out-of-control trick off the end. I thought that I was pretty cool; so I decided that I was going to do a flip or something off the ramp and into the street. I landed wrong. As I rotated, the momentum I had going forward did not compensate for a stable landing. My feet came out from underneath me, and I landed with extreme force on my right arm, the same arm I had broken in the third grade, but this time only worse. My arm looked like the same as it did in third grade, only this time my bone was exposed through my skin in a compound fracture.

I went from a normal afternoon to a long evening in the emergency room. Brent's mom was in more of a panic than I was. I remember going into the house with my arm in hand, sitting across the living room from Brent's brother and Brent while Brent's mom tried to contact my family. Unfortunately, my family was unavailable at the time. As my hospital had been Kaiser ever since I was little, we hopped in the car, and off we went. I was pretty calm. I was in shock, but I wasn't crying or panicking. We got to the hospital, where the doctors and nurses took me into emergency, immediately x-rayed my arm, and determined that I would have to go in for immediate surgery.

I remember sitting in the waiting room of the emergency room in the hallway. Brent's mom had gone to the car to get some information from her purse, while Brent stood next to me. Out of nowhere, Brent turned white as a ghost and passed out in the middle of the hospital. The funny thing is that, when the doctors went outside to try and get Brent's mom to let her know that her son had just passed out, Brent's mom, thinking that the doctors were talking about me, said, "No, that's not my son; that's my son's friend." They said, "No, your son passed out; the kid with a broken arm is sitting there calmly." It was definitely a funny situation. I immediately went into surgery. The doctors put eight screws and two metal plates in my arm: one on the radius and the other on my ulna. Three years later, I'd have to go back to have the plates removed. Well, three years went by rather quick, it seemed, and pain pills sounded pretty good to me around that time.

I went back to military school after the break was over. I was so bummed to tell my friends that I broke my arm roller-blading. I always had a million different stories to tell people how I broke it. Well, I ended up doing well the rest of the year, and then I came home to relax for the summer of 1996.

And I Huff, and I Puff,
and I Blow My House Down

As soon as September came around, I went back down to Carlsbad for my second year of military school, which turned out to be only about three more months of military school for me, actually. I started my eighth grade year pretty smoothly: no broken bones, my front teeth intact, and my arm healed pretty well. I have this nasty scar now on my arm, though. But chicks like scars, and that's true because I know from experience.

Back at military school, I was actually promoted in rank and ended up moving up to the junior school drill team stoles guard, which was quite an honor. Stoles guard was a huge privilege if you were in junior school. It was the highest achievement you could attain as an underclassman. We got to spin rifles and wear dark blue berets with a dark blue cord as part of our uniforms to signify we were on drill team. Everybody in junior school either tried to be or wanted to be on stoles guard. But you couldn't just volunteer for stoles guard; you were handpicked by your peers to join the squad. Like I said, stoles guard was a privilege.

So I was in eighth grade. My grades were good, and I was feeling pretty good. I started getting very comfortable about how things started going and feeling a little cocky. This one kid I never forgot, Stiff Stickler, used to mess with me. I think he was kind of jealous of me or something. Stiff was a heavyset kid that no one really liked. I was this little tiny guy, barely breaking one hundred pounds, who was probably an easy target for kids that thought they were bullies. Stiff used to pick on me every chance he could get. He wouldn't really do anything too serious, nothing physical; he more or less made verbal threats. He just talked a lot.

One of my best friends at school was the biggest guy at our school, Phillip Lancashire. I seriously used to love this guy. He was a senior when I was still in junior school. But for one reason or another, he liked me a lot. He was a lieutenant; so he had some so-called juice. He kind of took me under his wing. He used to tell me, "When I get older and have kids, Cody, I want a son like you." He'd always tell me to let him know if I ever had problems with anyone. Phil, honestly I can say, was the biggest kid at our school, a good 6 feet 5 and probably two-hundred-forty-pound high schooler: come on.

I told Phil about Stickler. I told him the threats he made to me and how he would just always annoy me. Well, after I told Phil, I don't know what Phil said to Stiff, but every time after that, when I would see Stickler, he would come up to me and ask me how my day was, if he could get anything for me, or if I needed help with anything. I'm dead serious. The kid changed his whole tune with me. The type of turnaround I got from this clown was so sick. I felt like no one could mess with me anymore, and I started using this to my advantage.

At the time, as part of stoles guard, I was required to do special events, such as marching parades and preparing for certain rifle-spinning ceremonies. One of the coolest experiences I had at military school on stoles guard was performing in front of thirty thousand fans before a Padres game in San Diego. We had a whole routine down, and we stood in front of a huge crowd before the game and performed flawlessly.

Afterwards, we got to watch the game, too. Oakland Athletics were in town, and Padres ended up winning that day.

As my classmates and I were eighth graders now, we had a little more flexibility with our free time. Weekends, instead of going home, we were allowed to stay at school or go into town if we so chose. Carlsbad was beautiful, with a lot of nice shops and restaurants. We would go eat or try to pick up on chicks or do anything creative. Sometimes we would skateboard.

One of the boys I used to kick it with smoked cigarettes. As much as I hated cigarettes, I was in town one night with three other kids, and we all decided that we were going to have a smoke. The smell reminded me of when I was young and of my mom and dad always smoking. I had always promised myself that I wouldn't smoke just because my mom and dad did, and I wanted to be nothing like them. I remember hanging around outside of the restaurant in town that night, smoking one cigarette after the other. At one point, I seriously felt like I was turning green. Smoking made me super sick. That night was definitely amateur night for me. At military school, smoking was kind of the thing to do, I guess. Most of the kids smoked, but not too many of us junior schoolers did. I actually never saw anyone doing drugs while I was there: no weed or anything like that. After that night, whenever kids would offer me a smoke, I would usually say, "No, I'm good."

Some kids, though, used to take aerosol cans, put a sock over the top of the bottle, and inhale the compressed air inside of the cans. I remember the first time I saw some of the kids inhaling aerosol; I'd just walked in on them. What they were doing seemed pretty odd to me. As a kid, your intuition tells you right from wrong. I knew right away that what they were doing was not a good thing. And it actually kind of made me nervous; I was very reluctant even to try what they were doing. I was scared. I really didn't even want any. At that moment, I left that room.

Some point later on down the line, I came across these huffers again, reluctantly tried their aerosol, and ended up liking it. I knew that huffing was bad and that I could probably get into trouble for doing it. Deep down inside, I knew I had an addictive personality because of my parents. I think that was what scared me the most about smoking or doing any type of drugs, the fact that I could possibly become addicted very easily. Those kids and I ended up turning into a bunch of aerosol-huffing idiots. We would huff at every chance we got, before and after formation. We would huff a lot. When we ran out, we would go into town and stock up on more cans. We would even huff in town on the way back to campus.

The habit really ended up getting out of hand pretty quickly. I started being late for formations all the time. I found myself having to march off the demerits quite often. My friends and I all ended up becoming pretty much prisoners of these bottles of compressed air that smelled like flowers. We heard stories of how kids actually died from huffing aerosol at this school in the showers, of how their lungs froze. You think those stupid stories of what actually happened at that school at some point deterred us? The stories didn't really scare any of us, to tell you the truth.

One night, we had just gotten back from town, where we had stocked up on about twenty bottles of aerosol between maybe six of us, if I remember correctly. Because of the weekend, most of the kids were home on family leave, and so the school was very quiet and still. Most of the sergeants and lieutenants were not around, and their absence meant that we didn't have very much supervision around. So we thought we could get away with sitting up in one of our rooms and just going at it, huffing our little junior school heads off. Well, we did. We ended up huffing so much aerosol that we would pass out or just get into this stupid state of mind where everything was really kind of slow, but nonetheless, we would continue to huff and huff.

All of a sudden, unexpectedly, one of the junior school sergeants walks in on all of us and finds us passed out in a room with empty aerosol bottles everywhere and a strong stench of potpourri in the air. Nothing we could do would save us; we were caught red-handed. We were all sentenced to a suspension: five days home suspension with means of termination from the military academy. We all had to face a military hearing in front of the board of administration after the five-day suspension was served. Although we were all granted one last chance to stay at the school, we were stripped of our rank. Being demoted back to the rank of cadet was basically the worst possible scenario, besides being expelled. Also, the kids who were on stoles guard were removed and placed in a regular platoon. We all knew that we had really screwed up. We had taken things way too far. We got caught up in a destructive habit that evening and were not paying attention to what was beneficial at that point and time in our lives.

Going back to being a normal cadet at school with these kids, when at one point you had some seniority, some rank, some pull, was really hard. We had to go back to study hall and do all the normal things that we began to do when we first arrived at the school. All the trust we had gained was taken away. When the administration said that we had one more chance, they really meant that we had one more chance. The whole situation scared me so much that I straightened up and decided that I wasn't going to screw up again. I think that mindset lasted about a week.

For whatever reason, I was up on the second story of the upperclassmen's dorms, on a huge ledge that went across from the sidewalk up and over a fifteen-foot gap. The ledge was up about twenty feet across the way where the sidewalk was; like I said, about fifteen feet or so. A whole bunch of kids were gathered around one kid, who was up there pretending that he was going to jump off the ledge and onto the sidewalk, clearing the gap, but he hesitated. So I went up there. I knew that I could clear the gap without any hesitation; I was going to get up there and jump it. I could most definitely clear the gap and land on the cement where all the kids were crowded around. I went to the very far end of the ledge, ran as fast as I could, and cleared the gap by at least a good five feet if not more, I'd say. As soon as I landed, I remember looking up and seeing Captain Donovan coming straight at me. He looked so upset.

That jump proved to be my last chance to be a student at Army and Navy Academy. I got kicked out of reform school in less than a year and a half. I mean, come on, I was doing well for a little bit, and I actually liked it down there. But I had screwed up something good again. I was sent back home. My grandparents were so upset with me, too. Military school wasn't cheap; plus now I was back under Grandma's supervision. The last thing Grandma Phyllis wanted was to supervise me. I enrolled back at my old junior high school, Miraleste, for the remainder of my eighth grade year. I was back to the same school where I was going to be expelled when I was in sixth grade.

Military school ended up paying off for me a little, I suppose. I remember coming back to school as the kid that went to military school. The kids were all scared of me or something, as if I had gone to war and were carrying guns around and killing people. You know, when you're a kid, you visualize something you don't really have any clue about, or you just have this picture in your head about something without even a basis. Well, I think that all the kids visualized military school as me going away for a year to some one-on-one, hand-to-hand combat training. Now that I was back, everyone seemed to think I was the worst kid ever. Everyone really thought that, since I went to military school, I could kill you with my bare hands. Well, I probably could if I really wanted (just kidding). Military school was cool, but not even close to what their little minds had them visualizing.

I remember walking into class that first day back and seeing chicks there in the class....What? I thought: *I am going to like this for sure.* For whatever reason, I got to class that day thirty minutes before lunch, and when I entered that classroom, the room got awkwardly quiet. I was gone about a year or so with no chicks around, and I came back to junior high school just starting to hit puberty: good luck. Everybody thought I was some stone-cold killer or something, when all I wanted to do was hang out with some chicks and finish my eighth grade year with no problems. I did really well at Miraleste, actually, at the end of my eighth grade year. I finished the year well. I graduated junior high at the beginning of that summer and started getting prepared to become a freshman at Peninsula High School in Palos Verdes.

I started Peninsula High in September 1997. My high school was a huge, very fast-paced, dog-eat-dog type of environment. I think for me from the start the atmosphere was very intimidating and overwhelming. I struggled with my studies straight out of the gate. The only class I finished my first semester was biology, which I completed with a B. I remember hating English class, and so I would always ditch. The health class was okay only because some cute girls were in the class. If nothing else worked to get me to class, somehow good-looking females would usually get the job done.

I was living up in Rolling Hills when I started high school. The first weekend of high school, I remembered, was party time as soon as the bell rang after last period. Everybody seemed to be making plans before school was even out. Grandma Ginny was out of town that weekend, and Chris was put in charge to watch the house for the weekend. Before school was out that day, I was telling everyone that I was having a party that night and that my house would be open and to tell everybody to come by and party. I knew that people were going to show up, but I didn't expect half the school to show.

The first rager of the year was at my place. Everyone was drinking, smoking weed, getting loud, and being obnoxious, being teenagers, really. At that party was the first time I ever drank beer, and I didn't even like it. That night was also my first time ever smoking weed. The party was fun; everyone was having a good time. People were pouring hard alcohol into my dog's water bowl and getting my dog pinky drunk. Then they were trying to get her to fetch the ball, but she was having trouble standing up straight. We were kids having innocent fun.

That night after the party had died down and everybody started to take off, a couple of my good buddies, James Narino and Magnum Regay, stayed the night. None of us had ever smoked weed before, and we knew that my brother Chris, being the stoner that he was, would have some weed for sure. He was in the living room with his girlfriend at the time when I approached him to ask if he had any weed we could have. That moment was really awkward for me, as he didn't know I smoked weed. Actually, I didn't know I smoked either, and I wasn't sure how he was going to respond. He looked at his girlfriend, started laughing, and calmly pulled out his sack of weed. He pinched me off what was probably about twenty bucks' worth.

I went out back and showed my boys that I got some weed; now all we needed was some type of pipe to smoke it. James and Magnum thought that I had smoked weed before that night. I never had smoked weed, ever. I told them both, though, that I used to smoke weed at military school and not to worry, that everything was cool, that I knew how to smoke. I ended up having to go back and get a pipe from Chris so that we could smoke the weed he had given us. I packed Chris's pipe with the weed and headed back out to Magnum and James. Now all we needed was a lighter; we were such amateurs. I was embarrassed to go back in the third time to ask Chris for a lighter; so I went upstairs and found some matches.

Well, right away my boys knew that I'd never gotten high before from the way I was holding the pipe. I wasn't covering the carb, and I was inhaling improperly. I played it off as if I'd only smoked joints before. I didn't even remember a significant head change. Maybe I didn't hit it right, or maybe Chris was smoking the swag weed. But that night was a bonding experience for James, Magnum, and me. So now I smoked and drank, and high school had just begun.

I remember hearing on the announcements one morning about baseball tryouts being held that week and what I needed to bring and where I could go to get more information. Playing sports was really all I ever wanted to do. I knew I would make the team. For some reason, I totally missed tryouts and wasn't able to play baseball that year. Did weed and skateboarding have anything to do with my blowing off tryouts? Probably. I remember being so depressed about not being on the team. I really wanted to play baseball more than anything. I ended up hanging out with all the skater kids, ditching class, and smoking pot all day. Now, instead of sports, all of a sudden my mind was fixed on skating, pot, and chicks. I started on a downward spiral really quickly.

Grandma Phyllis used to love taking and hiding my skateboards. She always used to make me come home right after school; I used to hate that rule. All my friends would go skate after school, go hang out with their buddies at the mall. I had to go straight home, and I wasn't allowed to skateboard. I started building resentment towards her very early. And the animosity in the house made wanting to go home on time really hard. So I would sometimes just stay late after school anyway, knowing and not caring that I was going to get in trouble. I wanted to skate with all my friends and be a regular kid. So I would. I would go skate, stay out late, get high, and be a kid. Sometimes my grandma and grandpa would come rolling up in the car, embarrassing me in front of all my friends and taking me home. As a kid, for your parents (even more embarrassing for me because it was my grandparents) to come looking for you, telling you to get in the car, not allowing you to be a kid and have fun with your friends was so embarrassing. Well, that resentment towards my folks kept getting bigger and bigger as the months passed.

Now, I came to a point where I said, "You know what? If I can't skate after school, well, then I'm going to skate during class." So I stopped showing up to all my classes. I didn't like school anyway, and all I really wanted to do was skate. So that's exactly what I started doing. I started getting more into skating than ever. I told myself early on, "Don't do drugs; don't be like Mom and Dad." I knew deep down that I was more prone to drug addiction because of my parents, and I was always scared of turning out like them. Well, when you're not working and getting high all the time is your main prerogative when you wake up but you don't have any money to get some herb, believe me, you're going to figure out a way to get some weed, no matter the circumstances. I started to go about things that way. If I wanted something, I was going to get it. Or if I wanted to do something, I was going to do it. I didn't care how I got or did what I wanted, even at someone else's expense. I was determined, for good or bad, with no differentiating.

I started stealing first from Grandma's purse and eventually from Papa's wallet. Besides, I never really had respect for Grandma Phyllis growing up; she always seemed to be so close-minded about things. I would show up to school with sometimes fifty bucks, sometimes a hundred bucks, or sometimes a couple of hundred bucks near the beginning of the month. Right away, I'd get some buddies together, usually before first period, and we would find someone at school that had a hook-up on some weed. We skated all day, smoked, and wasted my early years of education away. I had no direction. I really didn't feel that anyone at home had my back or really even loved me. My parents were losers, and I felt so inadequate in so many ways. I stopped caring about life. Things just kept getting worse and worse. And I just kept withdrawing more and more.

High school got so bad for me so quickly that Grandma Phyllis and Papa Joe felt that they had no choice but to send me away again to another boarding school. This time they weren't messing around. They had been doing their research for quite a while, I guess, trying to come up with a good solution and a good, stable school for me to attend. They ended up finding a school in the middle of Utah called Sorenson's Ranch School in the middle of Koosharem, Utah, on an old Indian reservation. I remember that, when I found out I was going away again, I told my friends, and I just started getting as high as I could for the last few days I would be at home.

When the day came to go, I had all my stuff packed, and off to Utah Grandma, Papa, and I headed. We flew to Las Vegas, rented a car, and drove the rest of the long and drawn-out way to Utah. We seemed to be about eight hours outside of Vegas when we arrived at the school. Talk about a desolate environment! I could see nothing for miles. The school was a ranch, a straight farm. I think that my grandparents drove me out to Sorenson's from Vegas so that I wouldn't know exactly where I was. Well, I am extremely observant, and I notice everything. I remembered what freeway we took from Vegas; I remembered every different freeway we took as we entered Utah. I was paying very close attention to the directions the whole ride from Vegas to Sorenson's Ranch School.

When we arrived, we went straight to the office, and the town sheriff, J., who was also one of the main guys in charge of the school, showed me around. Koosharem was a ghost town. This school was the biggest thing there. The town didn't even have a supermarket, just one little gas station and a convenience store. If you needed anything serious or needed medical attention for anything life threatening, the closest city nearby was this little town called Richfield, Utah about thirty miles away. Pretty much, I wasn't going anywhere. J. showed me to my room, and my grandparents headed back to Vegas to drop off the rent-a-car and fly back into LA.

I ended up hating that school with a passion. It was completely different than military school. All the kids were very out-of-control, and I became very homesick within the first week. The school was on a farm setting, hence the name Sorensen's Ranch School. When we students weren't going to school, the administration had us doing slave labor on their farms. I'm not kidding. I thought that these guys were very clever to have this farm in the middle of Utah run by a sheriff, working us day and night while our parents were paying them thousands of dollars monthly to supervise us and reform us, if that's what you want to call the program. I mean, we would maintain the farm, feed the pigs, chickens, and horses, and clean up after them. The administration would have us in residential Koosharem sometimes, fixing the irrigation systems on the desolate properties of the residents. We would even load huge trailers full of hay bales. Here I was, about a hundred pounds or so, loading seventy- to eighty-pound hay bales all day, while these guys running the school were making money off us kids. We were working our butts off for these people.

What didn't make sense to me was that most of the kids there were court-ordered. Because they failed to comply with the terms of their probation, a judge sent them to camp. And that's what they called it: camp. I had camped before. Camping was fun. This ranch seemed to be the next step towards hell. Also, the administration had these recovered drug addicts, an ex-Navy SEAL, and just some really hard-core guys in charge of us and running the school. I had a problem getting along with most of the other kids, because

I was just a little fifteen-year-old kid who didn't like to go to school and liked to smoke pot. Those characteristics were pretty much the whole reason I was sent away. I didn't beat my mom or dad like some of these kids did. I wasn't an arsonist. I didn't do robberies. Besides my non-violent record, I was one of the youngest boys at the school. I couldn't relate to most of these kids, but Grandma Phyllis felt that slaving myself on her expense was for my benefit. Or was her benefit that I wasn't home creating mischief?

We students used to have physical training on the weekends. The Navy SEAL guy ran the physical training program, a three-hour, vigorous, intense workout that we had to do on the weekends if we either got points off on our room inspections or just got into some type of mischief throughout the week. The workout was so intense that most of the kids couldn't even finish it. Then after the workout every Saturday and Sunday, Sorenson's made us hike what they called the Hog's Back, which was a mountain range behind the school about ten miles away. Every weekend we hiked. This kind of exertion made military school seem like Disneyland, no joke.

I remember getting in a fight with some gangster Mexican kid from Colorado and having my nose broken for the first time. I was lying on my back on the bed, talking with my buddy G'Money, when this kid came in and decided that he was going to try to punk me. He sucker punched me right in the face. I thought that my buddy G'Money would back me up because I was the little guy and he was my buddy, but I guess that he just wanted to see if I could hold my own against this bigger Mexican kid, who was some type of out-of-control bully. I gave the kid a real run for his money. I stood up off the bed as soon as he punched me in the face, and we began wrestling. We went like cats and dogs through the cabin for good five minutes. Though the kid was bigger than me, I held my own; I got him a couple of good times in the face. We must've been really loud, because one of the counselors came in, saw us fighting, and punished both of us. The kid used the race card, saying that I was saying derogatory racial slurs towards him, which was a completely false statement.

This school was like a bad dream turned reality. I just did what the men in charge told me to do. I went to school, obeyed instructions, and tried to stay out of trouble and mind my own business. Most the kids didn't like the fact that I was going with the program, sticking to the script, if you will. I think that they saw me as a threat or something. I didn't even really like most the kids; so I wasn't going to hang out with them. Keep in mind that I was seriously at most a hundred pounds soaking wet with boots on. So I was just this little guy who, for guys who think they're bullies, was a prime target.

One day, the other kids were acting all cool to me for some odd reason, and I mean their behavior was strange. I was ignorant. The other kids wanted me to hang out with them in their room and play cards, they said. I thought the invitation was strange at first, but I didn't think much of it at the time, really. I was actually kind of surprised, and so I cruised. I got up to their room, and they started convincing me that they wanted me in on the poker game they were about to start. I had food, chips, candy, and soda, which were considered cash at this school. Being fifteen years old and all naïve, I just went along with them. Something inside of me told me that something was wrong. I can't really remember what was going on for sure; I just remember feeling uncomfortable and very uneasy.

I could sense the energy in the room becoming really dark and low. The other kids pulled one of the beds out into the middle of the room. About eight of them all of a sudden rushed me, grabbed me by each of my hands with belts, put a pillowcase over my head, and poured water all over my body. As they watched me struggle, they tied the belts around each of my arms and legs and attached them to each corner of two different bedposts. They started kicking me and beating me profusely. Then they started pulling the bed away, slowly separating me from the midsection. Simultaneously, punches and kicks were raining down on me at such a rapid pace that I can remember gasping for air a few times when I had the wind knocked out of me. That violent beating was such a traumatic experience. Finally, one of the kids told the others, "Stop, stop, that's enough." Yeah, it was enough; yeah, it was plenty. I'd stopped squirming twenty minutes before. None of these kids got into any trouble for this episode. Either the counselors didn't believe what I told them had happened to me, or they didn't really care.

Either way, I was deeply angry at this point. From that day on, I was plotting my escape and my vengeance against these punks. Things started going a little smoother after that incident for some reason or another. Maybe the kids got something out of their system, because the harassment pretty much ceased from that point on. Maybe I took the beat down a lot better than they had anticipated, and they now had gained some respect for me. Or maybe the counselors did talk to these punks and let them know that they would now be watching them a little more closely from that point on.

The only fun experience I can remember at this school was the actual real camping trips we used to take. Sometimes we would go out into the Zion National Forest in the middle of Utah in dead winter for a weekend to do some camping. Those trips were good times. Camping trips were one of the very few times we got off school grounds. Usually, leaving school grounds meant possible cigarettes or the hope of coming across some type of mind-altering substances. And for us out in the middle of nowhere, drugs weren't exactly accessible. We managed to come across some propane and some 87 octane, which were both huffable. Inhalants seemed to be the easiest type of high that you could get while you were in boarding school. You couldn't get any real drugs, cigarettes, or any alcohol; obtaining them was literally impossible. We sometimes would try to fortify our own fruits to make what kids called pruno, which was similar to alcohol but tasted like sour, muddy, swamp water. So if we wanted to get high or have a head change of any kind, we would have to improvise, which usually meant huffing.

On one camping trip, some other kids and I stole some gas from one of the chainsaws. Even though the guys in charge would make us think that we were only going camping for the weekend, we would pull a trailer with us and spend half the weekend cutting down trees and loading trucks. Remember, I was about fourteen years old, maybe fifteen at the most, performing strenuous manual labor and doing backbreaking work at the cost of my grandparents. The wood that we would cut and load on the weekend would be used at the school or sold for firewood at the local town store to residents in the Koosharem vicinity.

The propane we stole from the miniature barbecues the administration brought for us on the camping trips. So my friends and I would set up our tents as far away from the counselors as they would allow us. The first night we got there, it was on. Three or four of us were crammed into a little tent, taking turns huffing the gas and the propane. The little propane bottle we were using was basically sucked dry in a matter of minutes. Huffing gasoline was different; the fumes from the gasoline would never seem to go bad or even evaporate for at least several days. So we all took turns passing this huge plastic trash bag with a minimal amount of gasoline in it. We would put our heads inside and just start hyperventilating as if we were gasping for air at a fast pace, but couldn't catch our breaths. I guess you could say that the head change gasoline would produce was similar to huffing nitrous oxide. As gas was so strong and potent, getting high off it was easy.

The gas we had was divided amongst a few of us in the tent. We got to a point where we were getting agitated waiting for one another after passing the bag. We decided that we would pour some of the gas from the bag and make our own contraptions. We all had our own twelve-ounce Coke bottles that were filled a quarter of the way up with gas. We poked a little hole in the upper side of the bottle, which acted like a carb on a bong, and then we simply put our mouths over the top of the bottles and began breathing heavily as we did with the plastic bag. And just like the aerosol at military school, the gasoline produced quite a good head change, very similar to the aerosol, just more amplified. I can remember just sitting there for what seemed to be hours on end, getting high with these guys. We looked at each other and laughed. Some of the guys would just kind of slowly start to pass out, all of a sudden decide to take a break for a second, and then continue huffing.

I actually passed out a few times in that tent that night. Passing out on gas fumes was not like being fully unconscious. You could still feel your body, but you just couldn't move. Once I actually passed out with the bottle to my lips as I started falling backwards. I felt a really slow consciousness, but I was unconscious like timber, if you can grasp that sensation. I was actually sitting down. I lay fully out on my back, but the whole time, I kept the bottle on my lips. So when I actually went down, so did the gasoline, right down my throat. I remember feeling the gas slowly entering my throat and coating my stomach like Nyquil or some type of thick, liquid substance. I pretty much had taken a shot of 87 octane gas, maybe a little more than a shot. I remember being unconscious from reality but in a conscious panic in my blackout. I seriously thought I was dying. I remember coming out of the fog like: *Wow, I literally just drank some gas.* I was feeling it all in my throat and tasting it in my mouth; it was all over my shirt, too. Instead of being kind of scared that I seriously did probably almost just take my own life, I was actually more concerned with the amount of gas I had just wasted, opposed to losing my life, potentially. My casket was near. I had already developed the drug mentality in my early teenage years that victimized my parents their whole lives.

The next morning, I woke up reeking of gasoline and feeling extremely sick to my stomach. I walked outside to use the bathroom in the woods. My liver and main intestines were very unhappy with me, as they kept letting me know. Moving my bowels hurt so badly that morning that I literally was in tears; I am not exaggerating. Afterwards, I turned to look, and my stool was full of blood. It seriously looked like I'd lost part of my intestines, as I probably had.

As bad as I hurt and as sick as I felt, I still had that urge to have more gas and seek that significant head change from the neck up. I wasn't so much into huffing the gas as I was the head change that the gas produced. I didn't care what I did, as long as it would give me a certain feeling from my neck up, which was all I needed to feel on a normal, day-to-day basis. I eagerly sought a distorted perception of life at a very young age, whether it was going to kill me or not.

My friends and I all headed over to breakfast that morning with a pungent gasoline smell, which we obviously didn't notice. When we got over to the breakfast area, the counselor from El Salvador who was in charge of us looked at us and said with his deep accent, "Who has the tinner?" We said, "What?" "The tinner," he repeated. We couldn't understand what he was trying to say because of his thick accent; he sounded like he was saying "dinner." Dinner? We all thought: *What are you saying?* "DINNER! Who has the DINNER!" he shouted. "We don't have it," we replied. "I can smell it on jew guys," he insisted. "What?" we repeated, confused. "The faint tinner!" he exclaimed. Oh. He was trying to say "paint thinner." When we figured out what he was actually trying to say, we said, "We don't have any paint thinner."

Well we didn't; the guys in charge knew that something was up, though. They could smell us; we just couldn't smell ourselves. They searched our tents and found the bottles of gasoline. We all got busted. When we got back to school, they put all of us in orange jumpsuits and gave us each a sleeping bag separated by about fifteen feet from each other in a huge field, five hundred acres of just plain rocky field behind the school called isolation. They put us there for seven days straight. We slept and ate there, and if we used the restroom without permission, we were creating more isolation time for ourselves. So if we really had to go to the bathroom and couldn't get permission at that time, we pretty much just had to go right next to where we slept. We were like animals. The staff would actually have students bring us our meals morning, afternoon, and night. They would let us shower once every three days, and they didn't even allow us to go to school during the week as part of our punishment. That week seemed like the longest week of my early teenage life. As soon as my long, long week of isolation was finished, I went straight back to work.

One afternoon, the administration had us loading hay bales at a nearby resident's house approximately eight miles from campus. The resident turned out to be a relative of Mr. Sorensen, who owned the school. All of the people out there seemed to be related in some way or another. So, the house where we were loading hay bales turned out to be Mr. Sorensen's cousin's house. Crazy Alkey, who was an older man who was always drinking his whiskey on the low, was supervising us that day. Everybody knew that Alkey was an alcoholic; excuse me, a drunk, which is why we called him Alkey. He was missing most of his main teeth, and he spoke with a really raspy tone in his voice. He was very unstable most the time. Fortunately for him, he was a Sorensen. He was one of the main guys who would take us to load hay or perform any physical tasks the staff would ask us to do throughout the week.

About six of us boys were packed into a four-door Ford pickup truck pulling a forty-five-foot flatbed trailer for the hay. We pulled up; everything looked pretty normal. Every time I got off campus, supervised or not, my mentality was to look for some type of escape from that hellhole of a school where my grandparents had sent me, obviously with no good, solid research. We started loading the trailer from a huge stack of hay at this house. As soon as we pulled up to the place, I saw on the end of this man's property towards the back what looked to be like a work truck in operable condition. Alkey had gone inside the house to talk with one of his relatives, whoever it was; they were both Sorensens. We had quite a bit of work to do; so he probably figured he'd sit down for a few and have a cold one or something. That's what I thought anyway.

Whatever the case was, as soon as he was out of sight for a few minutes, all I could think about was whether or not that work truck at the end of the property had the keys inside. I couldn't focus. I kept looking at the door to the house and then glancing over at the truck, from the door of the house to the door of the truck. I was becoming anxious and nervous while working. My heart started palpitating. The feeling was similar to what I felt entering my grandma's house years before to steal for my mom and her boyfriend.

None of the kids knew what I was thinking. Five minutes passed. Without hesitation, I jumped off the bales of hay, broke into a fifty-yard dash in probably under four seconds (all jokes aside). I got to the truck, and the driver's side was locked. But as I glanced over at the passenger side door, I could see from the little orange indicator that the passenger door was unlocked. I ran around the front of the truck, opened the door, and found the keys in the ignition. I opened the door, grabbed the keys, and jumped out of the truck, closing the passenger side door as quickly as I could. As I looked up, I saw crazy Alkey coming out of the house. Out of fear that he saw me, I threw the keys underhanded fifteen feet into the embankment on my left. Fortunately, he didn't notice me, and as quickly as he'd started to come out of the house, he went right back in. Wow! I was seriously startled. My heart was racing. I ran over to the keys, put them in my sock, and sprinted back to the trailer with the boys as fast as I could.

Now all the kids knew that I had just taken the keys out of the truck. I kept pretending that nothing happened, but they all were asking me if I got the keys or not. They knew. I didn't say anything; I just kept working. I didn't really trust all the guys I was working with that day. We stacked the truck to the top with hay and headed back to the school to unload. Once we finished unloading, we headed back to our rooms.

As soon as we got dismissed from work, I headed straight to my room. I got with a couple of my boys that I liked at that school, because I felt I could trust them. I showed them the key to the truck I had and explained to them, "I'm straight out of this school, and if you want to roll, what's up, let's roll." I told them, "Don't even trip. I was driven here by my grandparents, and if I can somehow get back to that truck, I know for sure I can make it all the way to Vegas at the least."

The time came for bed, and I went to bed with all sorts of bad thoughts in my mind. My boys were down, and they got some of their friends in on things, too. I gave my friend T. the key that night because I trusted him, and because he was down and older than me, I knew that I could trust him to come through for me. My friends woke me up that night very abruptly and told me, "Let's go; we're making a break for it." This kid T. from Utah, who was seventeen at the time, was court-ordered to Sorensen's for all sorts of crazy probation violations and violent crimes. I guess you could say he was our ringleader, as he was the oldest of the group. This kid Dwad from Nevada, a guy I just couldn't stand because he thought he was something else, was coming with us, along with this kid we called Wind from Chicago, who I actually thought was pretty cool. Then a guy named Sloth from Riverside, my buddy G'Money from Indiana, and me, the youngest from California, were all going.

Now I could never figure out this part. How did six kids at a school where parents had paid to send us to be under supervision twenty-four/seven manage to wake up in the middle of the night, steal a truck, a truck from a relative of the school's owner at that, and escape from a school that was virtually inescapable? But the getaway seemed too easy. I was so exhilarated that my heart was going a thousand beats per second. I was scared but excited. Really, I didn't think what we were attempting was possible, but we did something that night that had never been accomplished in the history of Sorensen's Ranch School. We made a successful getaway.

I jumped out my back window to the guys, who actually seemed to be more pumped than I was. We went by one of the cottages and out into the isolation field. The night was pitch-dark, completely black in the middle of that field; in no way was anyone going to see us. We walked at a fast pace and ended up getting into town. We were just walking, stoked and full of adrenaline, through this town with the streetlights shining brightly on us on our way to the truck. The truck was about eight miles down the road from the school. Only one road ran through this town, a two-lane road going either into or out of Koosharem. We finally got to the open road. A car started to approach us from a distance on the pitch-black highway. When we saw a car coming, we all jumped down the ravine on the side of the road and hid until it had passed us.

Afterwards, I told the other guys that the truck was pretty far, and maybe we should go up into the field on the right and walk through the shrubs so that we weren't seen. So that's exactly what we did. The shrubs were about chest high for miles, but we didn't really have any other options. We felt like we were trudging through a rugged terrain in the middle of the Congo jungle. The difficulty didn't matter, either; we were all very determined to leave this school. We were getting all dirty and cut up, but we didn't even care. We had one thing on our minds, and that was escaping Koosharem successfully. We were all on our way to the truck that was our potential ride to freedom; so we were happy to take any type of crazy escape routes if necessary. Besides, all the training we had done throughout the weeks and weekends at the school, the Navy SEAL training, hiking, and PT had paid off. We were all in such good physical shape that our escape seemed normal, almost easy. We did take a few hours, but we got to the truck.

We had to cut down through the field to the road as we started to approach our destination, because larger shrubs and bigger trees blocked our path as we drew closer to the house. The irrigation systems were on that night, which was freezing, and we all were so tired and dirty. We hopped this little white fence and ran over to the truck. It had not moved an inch, thank God! It was still in the same spot from the day before, with the passenger side door unlocked, a situation which meant that no one realized the keys were missing, we figured. T. hopped into the driver's seat, and I was glad he did, because the truck was a stick shift five-speed 1994 Chevy Silverado extended cab long bed. None of us besides T. knew how to drive a stick shift.

The truck started right up. It had a half a tank of gas, which would just be enough to get us pretty far away from the school before we had to come up with another solution on how we would get some more fuel when the time came. We cranked up the heater and cruised at a slow speed with the lights off into this field on the opposite end of the guy's property. We thought that turning around would have been easy, except that we had the lights off on the truck and didn't anticipate the field having a trench. We were so relieved to get to the truck and have it start right up with half a tank that we felt that our first step was completed. We were all full of energy and excited. We didn't want to turn the lights on as we entered the field to turn around because we were scared that somebody might see us. But a huge hole in the ground right in front of us almost cut our escape short. We were seriously stuck in this hole and making a lot of noise trying to get out of it. Fortunately for us, the truck was four-wheel drive. T. cranked it in high gear and miraculously got us out of that situation. We turned around and headed slowly through the middle of this guy's property, passing his house, and turned onto the road on our way to Las Vegas. We had beaten the odds and successfully gotten safely to our destined truck, and we were thankful that things went as smoothly as they did. Honestly, I felt like God had His hand on our backs, pushing us forward, getting us the easiest way out as He possibly could from that hellhole of a school.

Just Call Me Houdini;
I Can Get Out of Anything

As soon as we were on that road, we got so loud, and we started jumping all over each other as we were doing about a hundred miles an hour. The escape was like a movie. T. put the pedal to the metal, and as we cruised down the road that night, I think that we all felt a sense of relief come over us. T. put the radio on, and we all just kind of started laughing. We took that road at full speed out of Koosharem that night, hitting rabbit after rabbit. The road was pretty straight, and we sure didn't feel like slowing.

We got to this point where you could go either left or right. I told T. that I for sure knew to turn right, because when my grandparents drove me to the school, I memorized the way back to Vegas. From that turn, I knew the rest of the roads to get to our next destination as well. We ended up stopping in the next town we entered, feeling that we may run out of gas. We pulled up to some sort of truck, and Dwad jumped out and somehow really quickly got a hose and siphoned some gas from the truck. That infusion gave us another quarter tank, but we knew it wasn't going to be enough to get to Vegas from where we were.

That quarter tank ended up being enough to get us into a little town somewhere along the way outside of Koosharem.

A gas station there was open, but because we didn't have any money, we had to come up with a solution fast. T. had a really nice watch that he ended up trading for some cigarettes to the gas station clerk; the clerk also gave us five dollars in gas, which wasn't much. So all the guys were happy that we had some smokes, but back then I didn't care for cigarettes much, because I just liked to smoke weed. We cruised through that little town in search of gas. We were also paranoid about the littlest things; we seriously thought that every car that kept approaching us was going to be a cop car or something. And that suspicion really kept us on our toes.

We pulled off to the side of a little run-down city, where Dwad once again jumped out of the car and began going through little sheds in search of gasoline. He ended up scoring a few different five-gallon tanks that gave us just enough to get from Highway 9 in Utah to Highway 15 through Arizona and into Nevada. The sun was just starting to come up as we were leaving Arizona and entering Nevada, when a state trooper began to follow us. We hadn't slept all night, and we were all a complete mess. Being in a stolen vehicle with the patrol car behind us after we had just crossed three different state lines was a bit sketchy. Each time across a new state border in a stolen vehicle became a new felony theft charge, as I discovered later. We were all tripping. We thought for sure that this was it. The trooper followed us for quite a while, running our plates or something, I think, and the plates must have come back clean, because he ended up passing us. All of us exhaled in a big sigh of relief as he passed; that near-miss meant that nobody knew we were gone or that they just hadn't filed the report yet. Either way, Vegas was just over the horizon. We had successfully made a clean escape. We beat the odds and seemed to be free.

Before entering Las Vegas, we had to make another stop, because our fuel was running low once again. We pulled down the off-ramp, which looked like it had the most traffic. As none of us had any money, we had to split up and panhandle individually to try to get as much money as we could for gas. Dwad and Sloth went across from a little casino, and T., Wind, G'Money, and I were at a gas station trying to approach anyone who pulled up for some gas money. We just looked fishy. Six kids all under the age of eighteen in the middle of Nevada trying to panhandle for gas at 6 AM looked a little skeptical to people we approached, I'm sure, but the truth was that we needed gas money, not money for drugs or alcohol, nothing like that. We really just needed some fuel. Our efforts took a while, but we finally convinced someone to get us enough gas to get us into Vegas and drive around for a solid half day. We hopped back on the road, and off to Vegas we went.

As we were just arriving into Vegas, we saw all the casinos, all the tall buildings, and the skyline was beautiful. I think we were all pretty amazed at how far we came with nothing, no money, just the clothes our on our backs, and we had gotten all the way to Vegas. That achievement was pretty astonishing. I don't think that any of us expected to escape as smoothly as we did. Getting away was almost too easy.

By the time we got to Vegas, we were starving. We had no cash; so we decided to sneak into an all-you-can-eat buffet. We stopped at the Circus Circus, walked right in the exit of the buffet, and stacked our plates with enough food to hold us for a few days. Things were going so easily for us and working out for us so well at that time that God almost seemed to have arranged everything to work out in our favor. We were cruising around, just laughing and eating ice cream.

But now that our second step was completed, making it to Vegas successfully, we had to figure out what our third step was to be. Wind lived in Chicago. G'Money was from Indiana. Utah was behind us, where T. lived, although he didn't even want to go home. Dwad was from Nevada, but he didn't want to go home, either. Sloth and I were both from

California, and as I was the one who actually got the keys from the truck, we decided that the third step was to take Sloth and me back to California, dropping me off first in Palos Verdes.

So after we left the buffet, somehow we panhandled some more cash, got some more gas, and took off to the streets to look for some drugs to score. We scored some hash, and we made sure we stayed in underground parking structures, because we wanted to make sure that the truck went unnoticed. We parked at the New York New York and smoked some hash out of a Pepsi can. I don't even remember feeling a significant head change from the hash, which wasn't very potent. Besides, we all hit it maybe once before it ran out. It was more of a tease.

After a little more panhandling at the nearest terrible gas station, we left Vegas and headed straight for Los Angeles. We reached Barstow, California before we had to stop again in search of more gas money. Towards the end of the trip, Dwad was getting pretty good at approaching people and manipulating them or convincing them, however you want to put it, to help us out with our situation. Some chick actually ended up filling our gas tank for us, a gift which ended up getting us all the way to Palos Verdes from Barstow, which was the last place we stopped for gas that I can remember on this trip.

We arrived in LA. Everyone was passed out by this time except T. and me. T. had to drive, and I wanted to make sure that we ended up in LA, not San Diego or somewhere way off target. I had only been away about two months at this point when I finally got back to LA and back into my hometown of Palos Verdes. We went straight to my buddy Arby's house, and because we came in the middle of the night, I knew he'd be awake. He was what you call a tweaker. We pulled up, and his light was on, just as I expected. I yelled to him through his window, because we had come too early in the morning to knock on the door or ring the bell. Because we were all underage, going to Arby's house was brilliant, because he had a fake ID. So when he came down, I told him that we had just stolen this truck and escaped from boarding school and that basically we were all fugitives. He wasn't tripping. He jumped in the truck with us, and off to the liquor store we went. Arby must've been real high on something that morning, because he didn't even really act too surprised. We were so thankful for Arby that morning for getting us a handle of tequila, Jose Cuervo. After we thanked Arby for the bottle, we took him back to his house and dropped him off at home.

From there, we headed straight down to RAT beach, a local name which stood for Right After Torrance. We parked at the Rolling Hills Preparatory School parking lot and headed down to the beach. Dwad asked me if the place where I'd parked us was going to be okay for sure. I assured him that the parking space was perfectly okay, but for some reason, he was tripping about it. He was always tripping about stuff. I don't think he really ever liked me for some reason. He was just one of those high-strung, ADD, bipolar kids, you know.

Getting from the middle of Utah to the beach in Southern California in less than twenty-four hours with no money was not only crazy, it was unbelievable. We all got up on the lifeguard tower and started taking pulls off the tequila bottle. Within a matter of moments, we were all pretty well drunk. I just remember being so exhausted, so tired from the whole experience, and being passed out pretty drunk in the freezing cold on top of the lifeguard tower.

I woke up abruptly, because Dwad was kicking and hitting me and calling me all sorts of crazy names. I guess that he went back to the truck to go to sleep in it and found a ticket on the windshield. He was really mad at me. He woke up everyone and told me and everyone else that we had to leave. I wasn't really worried. I was already home.

They could go wherever they wanted; I'd stay at the beach. The ticket on the truck meant nothing, I told him; rip it up and throw it away. The truck wasn't even ours, but Dwad acted like because we got a parking ticket now everyone knew where we were. This kid was a real hassle. He just wanted to leave me at the beach, even though my house was pretty far over on the other side of the hill, but I didn't mind. I figured I'd come up with a solution. Besides, I had pretty much gotten us out of Utah alive. But Dwad was so sure that the cops were on their way because of the ticket that he wanted to leave as quickly as possible.

I convinced the others to give Sloth and me a ride up to a park a little closer to my house, Hesse Park. It was about 3:30 AM, and I hadn't really slept now for about a day and a half. I thought that, if I got at least to Hesse Park, I could get some rest, wake up, and figure out what our plan was to be in the morning. The other guys dropped us off, and they took off on an adventure in their own direction. We left on really weird terms; they seemed upset. Anyway, no sweat off my back: I was home. I was home.

Morning came quickly; we probably only slept two or three hours before the sun came out. I didn't even know where the rest of the guys were headed, and frankly, I didn't care. All I cared about was being back in my hometown, not in the middle of Utah. I was determined to get back home somehow, and I did. That morning, when Sloth and I woke up, we walked all the way to my house. I don't really remember why home was my destination, but I didn't really have anywhere else to go. Plus, it seemed to be the closest thing to me at that point. From Hesse Park that morning to my grandma's house in Rolling Hills was about a ten-mile walk. I felt like a champion that morning. Something about accomplishing what I really thought deep down would be impossible was very satisfying. I think I must've felt what

Thomas Edison felt after inventing the light bulb: pure satisfaction at a successful mission.

Sloth and I got all the way up and over the hill to my
street. This one tree on my street looked like a really big,
brushy shrub of some sort; you could actually go inside it.
My neighbors and I had used that tree as one of our forts
growing up. I told Sloth to hold tight and chill out in the tree
fort while I went home and tried to talk my grandparents into
letting me stay home.

At about 8 AM, I walked straight into the house and
into the kitchen, where both my grandma and grandpa were
sitting. I tried to explain to them how cruelly and poorly I
was being treated at that place where they had sent me and
that, if they were to let me stay home, I would do my best to
attend school and at least try to be a better kid. They were
really upset with me. My grandpa said that I was definitely
insane for what I'd done. The school had notified my grandparents about what had happened before I even got to the
house. Although they didn't really get as mad as I thought
they would and didn't seem too upset, I guess my grandma
had ulterior motives. Her plan was to stay calm and notify
the school ASAP.

I went down to the pool house where my dad was staying
at the time and told him what had happened, but in a silly
elaborate lie of a story, thinking that I was protecting myself.
He was surprised to see me, but he was also happy to see
me. I guess that when I went downstairs to visit my dad,
Grandma called the school and told them I was home. At
that very moment, the town sheriff in Utah hopped in his
unmarked vehicle and drove directly to my house in Rolling
Hills straight from Utah. The whole thing about coming
home and the reaction of my family was so overwhelming
that I completely forgot about Sloth in the tree, and by the
time I went back to get him, he had already vanished. I went
back down to the pool house with Dad, where I felt safe.

That night, I fell asleep with my dad in his bed, and being home felt so good.

Those good feelings of being safe and home were only temporary. In the middle of the night, J. from school arrived at my house with his wife, having travelled all the way from Utah to Rolling Hills in a record-breaking time. J. pulled me out of my bed, waking me up aggressively, put my pants on me, and belt-looped me, as it's called. Being belt-looped is when you put your pants on and someone grabs you by your belt to make sure you don't go anywhere, basically like handcuffs or something. People do it to ensure that you can't run anywhere. The school got me. J. threw me in the car, and off to Sorensen's Ranch School we went.

I remember thinking how mad I was that I went home after everything. Besides, everyone else was still on the loose. I lay down in the back of the car and slept the whole way to Utah. When we finally arrived back at the school, the counselors and the sheriffs sat me down in a room and immediately began to interrogate me. I just told what had happened and how we got the truck and everything. They wanted to know everything. They wanted to know how we planned so intricately to stop at a sheriff's house in another city during our first stop where we siphoned gas. They were amazed that we planned to make that house one of our targets. The truth was that the stop at the sheriff's house was a complete accident. That truck from which we'd siphoned gas when we first stopped just happened to just be a sheriff's house; we didn't even plan that stunt.

The truth was that we had no actual plan upon arriving at the truck; we just wanted to get out of Koosharem as safely and as quietly as possible. The authorities thought we were so good that somehow we knew where the sheriffs stayed about thirty miles from the school and had actually planned to steal gas from his truck during our escape. They didn't believe me that they were convincing themselves of bogus fairytales.

Then they started questioning me about the whereabouts of the rest of the group. I told them that I honestly didn't know, which was the honest truth. I told them what happened at the beach and that, after T., Dwad, G'Money, and Wind dropped Sloth and me off, we'd walked to my house. I explained to them that the other guys didn't tell us where they were going; they didn't really have a plan. I told them that, when Sloth and I got to my house, I hid him in the tree down the street, and by the time I was done dealing with my family and eventually got back to see what he was doing, he had vanished. They didn't believe half of what I was telling them to be factual. I had no reason to lie, really. I was already busted and back up the school anyway.

When they were done interrogating me, they put me back in the orange jumpsuit and once again in isolation all by myself for two weeks. Meanwhile, the other kids were still fugitives on the run. The school took about a week and a half or so after they captured me to locate the other kids. The boys had driven all the way to El Paso, Texas, where they were trying to cross the border into Mexico so that they could sell the truck and live down there for a while until they figured out what they were going to do. I thought that their plan was brilliant, and I wished I would've stayed with them. I would've made my little escapade a little longer, and if I didn't get caught or take myself right back home, the others would've probably been gone longer. I think that the authorities knowing the whereabouts of my location made locating the rest of the bunch easier for them. My being home made the police realize that the other escapees were at least on the West Coast portion of the US.

Unfortunately for those guys, the police saw them coming and closed down the border. The kids told me that the sun was so hot that day while they were going through Texas that they were all pretty much stripped down to their boxer shorts. So when they got arrested, they were pretty much naked. Helicopters circled, and police from every angle were pulling the kids out of the truck with guns drawn in a huge scene that made the Texas prime-time news that day. Well, the school finally got all of us, all but one: Sloth. Where was that guy? Sloth ended up being gone the longest, and we actually never heard from him after that day I left him in that tree fort. No one knew where he was; he took off on foot and was nowhere close to his house when I left him. I would never actually see Sloth again.

The boys got shipped back to the school the next day and put in isolation with me upon arrival. Dwad had this assumption that I told the school of their plan. I think this idea was his way of messing with me some more when he got back. He loved to pick on me. T. was the oldest out of all of us, and as he was already court-ordered to the school, he was sentenced to do jail time upon conviction. He was seventeen, but the state tried him as an adult. He never came back to Sorensen's. The rest of us got a grand theft auto charge, fines, and three hundred community service hours, which were to be worked off at the school in a timely manner.

I remember just coming to the school as an immature kid who like to get high, skate, and not go to school. Now I was a convicted felon with a record at the age of fifteen. My family should have sued the school for not supervising me properly and allowing me to obtain a criminal record at my grandparents' expense. Were our parents or grandparents paying almost four grand a month per kid for us to be supervised improperly? You would expect a little more supervision.

I worked off a few of those hours and convinced my grandparents to bring me back home. They made a deal with the school, paid off my community service in cash, and brought me back home within a couple of weeks. I really wasn't even ready to come home yet. Actually, the school didn't even change my mind about getting high or wanting to party and chill with my friends at all. It actually just made me more resentful towards my grandparents and forced me to lash out in a manner that would ultimately create confusion and chaos in the years to come. It also made me realize how cruel and unruly this life really was, as well as very evil and unjust! I still wanted to smoke weed and hang out with my friends. Sorensen's Ranch School actually made me worse, I believe. When I came home, everyone knew what had happened with the whole truck situation. I told the story over and over again until it was getting to a point where glamorizing my criminal behavior was actually becoming bitterness in me. I did not realize the effect that bitterness was having on my heart. I took the name Felon, labeling myself as a criminal from that point on. I started doing anything and everything I was not supposed to be doing. My heavy pot smoking would eventually lead me into other bigger and better drugs.

I have to say that I was one of the most out-of-control and uncontainable kids in my neighborhood. Whatever had to do with other people didn't matter to me; life was all about me. "All eyes on me" was my mentality. I began hanging out with older and cooler kids and experimenting with other drugs, such as ecstasy, speed, mushrooms, etc. I started going out partying and running extremely wild. My one-time dream of becoming a sports icon had slowly been stripped away from me by this false dream of wanting to be accepted by my peers.

One of my best friends growing up was my neighbor, Justin Wachs, who lived two houses down from me. We grew up playing sports together: soccer, baseball, basketball, and skateboarding. He actually even played on my club soccer team, the Raiders, when I was younger. I remember always being jealous of him when I was growing up with him. He lived with his mom and dad, first of all, and he always had the top-of-the-line stuff: video games, clothes, bikes, sports equipment, everything. His mom and dad would hook him up. I used to go over and hang out with him every day after school for a few hours a day. His parents would make him do his homework; so either before or afterwards we would hang out, ride bikes, go swimming, play catch, skate, whatever. Sometimes he would come over to my house and play tennis with me.

This friendship was all when I was younger. When high school came around, it was a different story. Justin didn't smoke pot. He went to a private school, worked hard on his studies, played sports, and really kept his nose clean early on in high school. I started rebelling, and Justin and I kind of grew apart. We were still buddies, but on a different level. He was on a path I wanted to be on, but I was heading down a path of distraction nobody wanted to be on. The sex, drugs, and rock 'n roll lifestyle started becoming a way of life for me.

From a young age, I would always take stuff from Justin without permission, like I thought that taking his stuff was okay or something. I would take his bikes and ride them without permission. I would take his video games and use them without asking. I would go into his room in his house when nobody was home and take things that didn't belong to me. I'd get that really sneaky feeling in my gut that I used to get when I was younger doing favors for my mom, and I liked it. I started getting into trouble with Justin and his parents pretty early on about taking and borrowing stuff without their permission. This stealing started off with borrowing little things, like I said, and it escalated a lot more into problematic situations as I got older.

The Wachs would go on vacations quite a bit, snow-boarding, Mexico, Canada, family vacations. Sometimes they would have me feed the cats. I would go over, feed the cats, and maybe play some video games. Sometimes I'd even take the keys to the housekeeper's car, which the Wachs had specifically bought for their maid to take Justin and his brother to and from school and to run errands with them on a weekly basis. The car always sat right in their driveway. Sometimes the keys were just in the ignition. Leaving them there was never too much of a worry, because we lived in a gated community where the only way to enter our estates was through authorization. I would hop into this little Honda Civic they had, just cruise around my neighborhood for a little bit, take it back, and park it. Then I went home and hung out with my grandparents, eating dinner with them and acting like nothing happened. Keep in mind that this joyriding happened when I was about fifteen; my grandparents had no clue. The type of feeling I would get when doing something so sneaky and getting away with it really had no comparison to any type of drug or high I had experience at that point. Well, sneakiness was a different high, anyway, and I really enjoyed it.

The Wachs had taken a vacation one winter and had locked every window and door in that house. The situation was getting to a point where coming home and finding stuff either missing or out of place was normal for the Wachs. They stopped trusting me and allowing me to feed the animals or even care for their house when they would leave town. Justin's and my friendship had become a bit untrustworthy on my part. I was so out of control at this point in my addiction that I was staying out late partying, not coming home sometimes, and obtaining the life that my mom and dad had lived their whole lives. Usually, when the Wachs would go out of town, they would have me watch their animals and kind of keep an eye on the house. But things got so bad between us that they weren't even letting me hang out with Justin, and I wasn't even really allowed to go to their house anymore.

I remember that the Wachs had had this trip to go up North planned for quite a while. Because Justin and I attended different schools, our Christmas vacations fell on different weeks. Friday, before getting to school, I had already in my mind visualized throwing a party at their house. I told everybody that I was throwing a phat party that night at my buddy's house because they were out of town and had asked me to watch the house for them, which was a complete lie. After school got out, I got a ride home and went over to the Wachs, thinking that one of the doors would be open. I showed up, and not really surprisingly, all the doors were locked, along with the windows. The Wachs had finally caught on to my schemes. I wanted to get into the house that day so badly because I had already told my friends I was throwing a party and I didn't want to look like an idiot. I was already committed. I had to find a way to get into the house.

Along the side of the house was a little bathroom with a really small, miniature window. Somehow, I managed to open the window, climb up on a limb, and squeeze through it. Once I got in, I unlocked the front door and began calling all of my friends, letting them know that the party was on that night for sure. Everybody showed up that night, including people I didn't even recognize. Actually at one point, friends of Justin's came to the party. I had random people I didn't know asking me, "Isn't this Justin's house?" I just let them know I was watching the house for the weekend. Now seriously, what would possess anyone to have this type of disrespect towards anyone, especially close friends and neighbors? Was I raised completely wrong? Or was there just something wrong with my head?

A day or so before the Wachs had gone out of town, my grandma had sold a piece of antique furniture she'd had in the dining room for years. The man who came over and bought the piece of furniture wrote a check for $1050, made out to Mr. Mullenaux. The check sat in our kitchen for several days. That Friday morning before school, I told myself that, if that check was still there before I left, I was taking it. That morning, the check was right in the same spot where it had been for several days. I took the check and my ID to Bank of

America, and without any problems from the teller, I cashed that check. Besides, I was Mr. Mullenaux.

So after school was out that Friday, I got a whole bunch of weed and two hundred dollars' worth of ecstasy, which was equivalent to about ten pills. One pill alone is enough to make you feel like you're in a false heaven for almost four to five hours. I took two of them at the beginning of the party. By the time everyone had arrived, I was feeling like Rico Sauvé.

When older chicks approached, whom I would normally be shy around, I was being really physical and confident. That crazy feeling made all my usual anxieties go completely away. I was able to talk with words that I didn't even know were in my vocabulary. Ecstasy gave me confidence I never knew existed. I felt so comfortable around everybody that I was able to approach people I didn't even know and tell them I loved them with open arms, and I really felt in my heart that I loved them sincerely. The feeling was crazy. I started to give away ecstasy to everybody around me, because I wanted them to experience what I was feeling. I was giving pills to people I didn't even know.

As the party went on and got bigger and bigger, people were in the pool and Jacuzzi, and people were all over the kitchen and in all the rooms of the house. The party was getting to a point where it was out of control. But the craziness really didn't matter to me; I just wanted everybody to have fun. I really was just looking for everybody to have a great time. I was getting concerned at one point because of the number of people that actually showed up. Being so high, though, those concerns were only temporary. I started really expressing my feelings towards everybody, telling them how much I loved them. I started to tell everyone, "Take whatever you want; you can have whatever you want in the house. Don't even trip; it's totally cool." That generosity was what I felt in my heart at that time to be true. I don't even know what came over me; I just felt so good that I wanted to give to people. I wanted everyone to feel good. I crossed a line I should've never approached, not realizing my words at the time.

These guys at the party did exactly what I gave them permission to do, which was taking whatever they wanted. The party was still going on, and strong at that. I wasn't paying too much attention to everything going on in the house; I was outside on drugs, trying to take my mind off life. All my worries, all my stress, and all my anxieties were gone. I had not a care in the world.

The party ended super late that night, with a lot of the people passed out in various places around the house. When morning came, my ecstasy had worn off, and reality began to set in. That temporary feeling of anxiety and fear being gone only made their return worse and more agonizing. The house had pretty much been robbed. TVs were missing; videogame consoles, clothes, jewelry, and anything else that looked to be of any value were gone. The house was a complete disaster, with beer cans everywhere and trash and bottles in the pool. People passed out in the bathroom by the towels with barf all over them. I couldn't believe what I did to my best friend's house. It looked like a pigsty. An enormous feeling of guilt and shame plagued me. I knew that I was in for some trouble when the Wachs got home. I cleaned up everything the best I could, but there was no getting around all the stolen merchandise and household items.

The Wachs got home later that next week, and although I tried to hide from them throughout the week, hiding from the feelings of shame that I was holding on to from my actions a few nights before was impossible. Guilt ate at me and bothered me, but I kept smoking, drinking, and getting high. I pretty much stuffed my real emotions with drugs, masking any type of guilt or remorse I actually had.

When the Wachs got home, they immediately contacted my grandparents. The Wachs knew that the destruction had to have been Cody. Justin had gotten the whole story from a buddy of his who was actually there that night partying anyway; so they knew the solid truth. So I had no way around this one. I'd only been back from Sorensen's Ranch School a few months, and already my behavior had become so out-of-control that my grandparents did not want me staying in the house with them anymore. Besides the fact that I was more than a handful, I was burning bridges with good friends and creating tension amongst good neighbors. The only solution my grandma could find was having me go back to Grandma Ginny back in San Pedro. Phyllis and Joe didn't know what else to do with me. They had already tried sending me away, but as I would either get kicked out of those places or escape, the options were limited.

Grandma Ginny kind of balked at the idea of me coming and staying with her, but being the loving and caring grandma she is, she agreed to have me stay with her and make the arrangement work. At the time, she had her hands full with raising Casey, who was attending school in the Torrance district because our aunts worked there. Casey was starting to have trouble of his own with school. Having Casey at a school where my aunts were able to keep an eye on him made life a lot easier for my grandma. Also, as Grandma Ginny was still working at the time when school got out, Casey could go home with our aunts and stay with them until Grandma or someone could pick him up. Meanwhile, Chris was living up in Santa Cruz, where he was attending the University of California at Santa Cruz, taking care of himself, and doing his own thing. He's on an upward track now, but we don't see each other often.

Our whole family pretty much came together in raising all of us boys. One thing I really appreciated as I grew older was having such a good and close relationship with our family. Grandma Ginny let me move into the place she and Herman had built above the garage at her house. The room was actually detached from the main house and was kind of like my own apartment. From my room, I had a gorgeous view of the city and the Port of LA. Papa Herman was a longshoreman in that port for over forty years. I saw how he lived and always told myself that one day I wanted to be a longshoreman like Papa Herman. Besides, all I needed was a high school diploma to be a dock worker, a job with good union wages and great benefits. I didn't plan on going to college. I hated school so much that I figured working hard was the only way I would be able to make any good money.

The summer after my freshman year went by fast. I was living with Grandma Ginny now and really wasn't getting into much trouble throughout the summer. Even though I was living in San Pedro now, when sophomore year started, we still used Grandma Phyllis's address so that I could attend the Palos Verdes school district. Peninsula would not allow me to continue as a sophomore because of my grades and the amount of absences I'd had as a freshman. I was a candidate for continuation school; so Rancho Del Mar Continuation School is where the school district sent me. I fit in with all the troublemakers and all the lazy ADD kids who seemed to stir up large quantities of trouble on a daily basis. This school had a total of only eighty kids at the most.

The schedule was very lax. You started at 8 AM and got off school at 12 PM; four hours of school a day was all. Why would I want to go to Peninsula full time when I could be at Rancho four hours a day? I actually liked the school a lot; the classes were smaller in size, student wise. I got individual help when I needed it, and at the same time I was able to work at my own pace. At the beginning of the semester, the teachers would give you a syllabus on all the work to be completed throughout the semester, almost like a college does. So when you finished the syllabus, you finished your class and got your credits. Completing your credits could take you a whole semester or only a month depending on how quickly you wanted to work. This schedule was either a good thing for you or a bad thing. A lot of the kids were able to catch up on some classes and go back to regular high school. Some of the kids actually stayed there at Rancho and graduated early. The rest of us slacked off around campus, smoking cigarettes and doing the bare minimum, and when the end of the semester was near, we crammed all of our semester's work into a few weeks, a task which was definitely possible. The balance worked out. So in between, we students could kind of come and go to school as we pleased. Most of the time, we were off campus smoking weed. I remember that, every day before school, I was always meeting up usually thirty minutes before class to get high behind the classrooms where everyone would show up early to smoke weed. I was keeping my nose clean, though. I was doing okay besides the fact that I liked to smoke marijuana.

I remember at one point not too long into my sophomore year, I decided that, as things were going so smoothly, maybe I could sell weed. I smoked plenty of it; so I figured why not smoke some and make a little money on the side, right? I really didn't have money, but I did have a good friendship with the weed man, because I saw him pretty much every day. I asked him one day to front me an ounce, which is equivalent to about three hundred dollars' worth of herb. To front someone means giving a person the weed with no money up front. I was just allowed a certain amount of time before I was to pay back the lender, usually a week or so.

So here I was going to school with all of this weed in my backpack. I had separated the whole ounce into grams and was selling individual grams for twenty bucks. About twenty-six grams made up one ounce. I figured that, if I sold all twenty-six grams for twenty bucks each, I could basically smoke for free and have a little extra cash on the side after I paid back my dealer at the end of the week. That was the plan. I was always this really well-known guy through high school because I was selling weed, and I figured that I'd better keep some type of protection on me. I didn't want to get jacked and have problems with my dealer about paying him his money back. So I got a switchblade knife that actually I stole from Justin at one point or another, and I kept it in my backpack next to the weed.

One day in art class, I was just hanging out with some kid from class. I was showing him the chronic I had for sale. He saw my knife I had in my backpack, grabbed it, and began to open it up in the middle of class. Well, the teacher saw me getting aggressive with the kid, trying to get my knife back. The last thing I wanted to do was draw attention to myself in the middle of class, but unfortunately, I did exactly that on that day. As the teacher approached us, the kid ran out of the classroom and threw the knife into a trashcan inside the men's bathroom. He then tried to play like he didn't have anything. Well, he ended up telling the teacher that he'd thrown away a knife and that the knife was mine.

I got called into the principal's office with the kid. He showed the principal where he had stashed the knife. Now having a switchblade knife alone is a felony, but having it on school grounds was even worse. This incident occurred after the whole Columbine shooting, and the schools were not going easy on anyone with intentions of bringing knives or guns on school grounds, whether your intentions were to do bodily injury or to protect yourself. I was so stressed out over the whole situation that I had totally forgotten about the weed I had in my backpack. I didn't really forget; I just wasn't really paying attention. I was probably high at the time, no doubt.

Because the principal was furious with me, even though we had a good relationship, he made a decision to call the police. I ended up causing a huge scene at school that day.

The cops came into the office, searching me first and then searching my property. They found the stock of weed and the pipe I also had in my backpack. They just looked at me with this very sarcastic look on their faces and laughed at me. Now because the weed was in individual baggies, the officers charged me with minor in possession of a controlled substance with intent to sell. The intent to sell part makes the crime worse. If the weed had not been bagged individually, then I could've said that it was for personal use, and I may have only gotten a misdemeanor. But the police ended up charging me with a felony. And for the knife, they charged me with possession of a deadly weapon with intent to do bodily harm. I guess they put two and two together and figured that the knife was for my protection because I was selling weed. Well, that weapons charge was a felony, too.

Here I was on my way to sixteen years old, and I had just been making really bad choices. Any good opportunity for me to have a successful life and future seemed completely out of reach. I was basically a clone of both my mom and dad. Did my childhood cause me to act out in such a wild and out-of-control manner, making poor choices daily? Or was a life of crime just my destiny from being born a drug-addicted baby? Or should I blame both? Whatever the case, I was doomed! Although I was only fifteen, I had three felony convictions, and these felonies weren't some Mickey Mouse charges. I was recognized as a criminal. The only charges worse than grand theft auto, minor in possession of a controlled substance with intent to sell, and minor in possession of a deadly weapon with intent to do bodily harm, charges that I already had at fifteen, were armed robbery or murder. I was now definitely labeled a felon.

The police took me to the Lomita Sherriff's station and booked me; because I was a juvenile, they ended up sentencing me to four months in juvenile hall, with three years of formal probation upon release and a three-thousand-dollar fine, along with the felonies to go on my record. Also, I had to submit to monthly urine tests as a requirement of my probation. At the time, I was still getting high, smoking weed, and taking pills. The corrections department gave me a code name. I would call a recording on a daily basis, and when my code name came up on the recording, I was to appear at the probation department the following morning for drug testing. My code name was orbiters. I was heavy into my pot smoking at this point in my life, and I had just begun to experiment with other heavier substances, such as crack cocaine and methamphetamines. I liked pills a lot, though, too. Missing a drug test would go down as a violation, and a violation meant that my case could go back to court. Doing so also meant breaking the terms and conditions of my probation, in which I agreed to take random drug tests. Failure to do so or producing dirty drug tests actually meant going back to juvenile hall for me.

Even after all this crazy stuff I kept getting myself into, I really didn't think that I had a problem with drugs as much as I did. I always blamed the kid who took the knife out of my backpack or the cop who pulled me over. I was always looking for a scapegoat, never willing to take the blame for my very own actions. Putting the blame elsewhere was so much easier. I wasn't ready to put the pipe down yet; even the time hanging over my head wasn't much of a concern.

When I got out of juvenile hall, I managed to stay sober for about maybe two weeks, tops. Because I was an addict, I tried to come up with every solution possible to avoid getting dirty tests, except not using. I still really wanted to smoke; so I managed to find a solution. The solution was chlorine pills. Basically, you drink a lot of water before your tests, like a gallon or so, and take these pills, in which the main ingredient was niacin. The niacin made you sweat a whole lot, releasing all of the toxins through your pores. Basically, the pills were a detoxifier. Well, the chlorine pills worked.

On my first two drug tests, I was smoking weed still, but I managed to pass my drug test.

Around the time I had my second drug test and passed it, knowing that I was under the influence, I got a real sense of how clever I really was. I started using a lot of meth. I then also started smoking crack cocaine. And for those who have never smoked crack: don't. It is by far the worst drug known to man. I was all high on crack one night, actually, the first night I ever smoked crack, for sure the worst drug that I have ever done. The high was very intense but very short with a horrible come down. Your first high on crack, meaning your first hit, was the ultimate high. That high you experienced from the first hit would be something never to be experienced again, only to be sought after and never attained. Guys become crack-heads because it really is the best feeling, only so very temporary. After your first hit of crack, during the next and the next and the next you are trying to feel that high you felt the first time, but it never happens. Your head keeps telling you it will, and you seek it. Coming off it was horrible: WOW! I actually hated that last part.

I was coming down one morning off a sleepless night full of crack when I remembered that I'd failed to call my probation tape line the previous night. So in the morning I called, and sure enough, my code name was up, meaning that I was to appear at my probation department that afternoon ready to be tested. I didn't actually have enough time to clean my system out; so I tried to drink as much water as possible to flush my system. Unfortunately, after smoking crack all night, no amount of water in the world could somehow magically clean my system in less than ten hours.

I got down to the department, and I was so nervous because I knew that I was dirty. My probation officer stood behind me in the men's restroom, waiting for my urine sample. I was so nervous and scared that I couldn't produce a sample. The probation officer left and told me that he'd give me ten minutes to drink some water so that I could produce a sufficient amount of urine to be tested. Well, I came back a second time, and the same thing happened. The officer gave me one last chance. The third time, I could only produce a very minimal amount of urine, which ended up being insufficient for testing. My probation officer told me to go home, that the insufficient amount would be turned in as a non-test. A non-test was not a dirty test, but it was definitely better than being positive for crack cocaine. And the fact that I showed up for my testing looked good; so somehow I dodged a huge bullet. I don't remember that test really ever going against me or affecting my probation negatively. I was such a crazy, lost soul with no direction and nowhere to go.

Even though I wasn't living at Grandma Phyllis's anymore, I was still hanging out there quite a bit. My dad had moved out and rented an apartment in San Pedro near Grandma Ginny's. Sometimes he would be over at Phyllis's after I got off school; so I might get dropped off there to say hi and get a ride from him down the hill back home to Grandma Ginny's. At the end of Grandma Phyllis's street lived this girl named Chow Chow, who also attended Rancho with me. She had just moved into the corner house on my grandma's block. She was pretty cute, and we became pretty good friends. Her mom had just recently married this guy whose family owned Sav-on drugs; they had quite a bit of money. So four girls lived just a few houses down from my grandma's house now: Chow Chow, her sister, and Mr. Sav-on's daughters. Actually, all four of the girls were pretty cute. We were all pretty close in age.

Though I was staying in San Pedro, I was hanging out with Chow Chow a lot. She was pretty out-of-control, too, just like me. We used to smoke weed all the time together; we eventually started doing a lot of ecstasy and taking a lot of speed together, also. She always had money; so she always had drugs.

Somewhere along the line there, things were getting really bad again. Grandma Ginny decided that I'd better check into a drug rehab program before I landed back in jail. I got shipped out to the city of Orange in Orange County, to Chapman Medical Facility, which was actually a hospital with a drug treatment center on the lower level. I didn't mind rehab; actually, I seemed to do well in structured settings. Patients got to play video games and do sports activities weekly. In the playroom, we had a fridge, which the staff kept stocked full of drinks and frozen foods. Our program consisted of meetings in the morning before breakfast, in the afternoon before lunch, and in the evening before dinner. The meetings were more or less AA formatted. In the evenings, the staff would take us to AA meetings all around the greater Orange County area.

Rehab was pretty cool. I enjoyed it, and I was getting sober. At that point, I actually had really kind of surrendered to admitting that I had a drug problem, a confession which for me was progress from months before. I was at Chapman for three weeks, and I was then released. For whatever reasons, I moved back to Rolling Hills with Grandma Phyllis and Papa Joe. I was told to get a sponsor and go to as many meetings I could upon leaving rehab.

But I really didn't want to go to meetings. I didn't want to identify as an addict or an alcoholic. If I could be strong enough just to stay away and resist temptation, I figured I'd be cool. Obviously, I didn't have enough of the program, and I was still running on self-will. I did well for about a month without meetings before smoking weed again. Every day afterwards, I was down the street at Chow's, getting high again and staying out late. Sometimes I wouldn't even come home. The whole point of me going and checking into rehab, actually, now that I come to think of it, wasn't really Grandma Ginny's idea. Actually, somewhere along the lines I violated my probation and was supposed to go back to

My little brother Casey and me.

Pamela, far left, and her sisters.

Grandma and Grandpa Mullenaux.

Top view of 18th Street
(where I rode on the bike with no brakes).

Bottom view of 18th Street with no stop signs for
oncoming traffic.

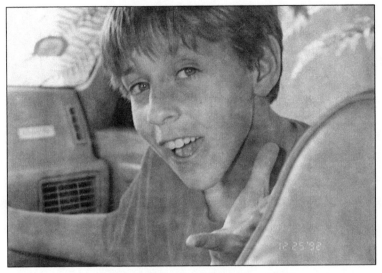

Me just being me: Christmas 1993.

Grandma Ginny is so lovable.

AYSO All-Star game.

The Wachs.

Military school dorm where I got caught huffing aerosol,
for which I was expelled later.

Military school again. There is the actual dorm where
I lived for a year and a half.

Brandon Wachs and me, buds for life.

Sorenson's Ranch school (Utah): I'm throwing a FAT grab
off the ramp I built there.

The G20 Infinity, my first car.

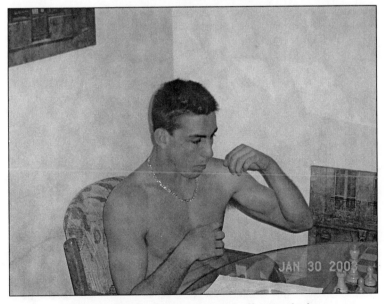

Me, probably high, at my dad's condo in
Rancho Palos Verdes.

My G20 Infinity a month after I bought it;
I flipped it and totaled it.

Lake Mead with a couple of my good friends.

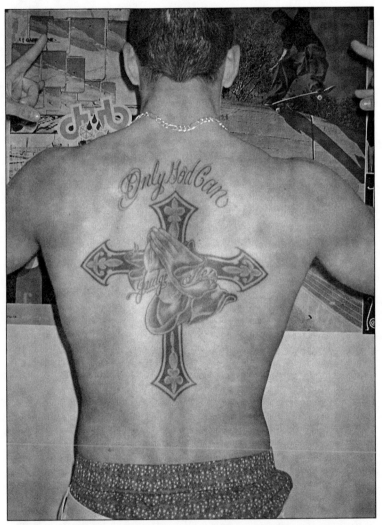

I got my first tattoo at age nineteen: Go BIG or go home.
My dad said that I should have gone home.

My dad, Scott, and my brothers.

Scott again with Grandma Phyllis.

This is the lifeguard tower where I broke my ankle when I was on drugs. Such a NUMBSKULL!

Papa Joe's eightieth birthday in San Pedro.

Candy and me during my sophomore year at
Rancho Del Mar High School.

My cousin Hollie and Tyler and me in Catalina: June 2003.

This is the canyon down which I went charging on acid
with my buddy in 2000.

All of my female cousins from my mom's side.
They're all so beautiful.

The Hermosa beach house.

Some good old times with some good old friends.

Halloween 2006, Manhattan Beach, CA.
I'm having a good time sober.

Staying sober at my friend's wedding.

Long Beach: the El Camino bus stop where the one-legged
veteran picked me up and took me to work.

The stop at which I prayed for God to reveal Himself to me
and He did. I will never again be the same.

Traded the truck Papa Joe bought me for this Jaguar;
I'm loving sobriety.

A little brotherly love. Casey and I at my dads in
Racho Palos Verdes

My best friend ever, Bino, and me on his
twenty-sixth birthday.

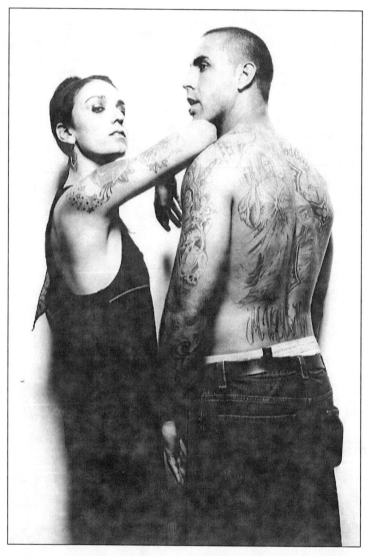

Random night in Los Angeles at a club: good times.

God grant me the serenity to accept the things
I cannot change.

Two days out of brain surgery and four hours away
from a focus seizure.

Kristi and me at the Bahia in San Diego,
our first getaway: great times.

Grandma and Grandpa Mullenaux's home in Rolling Hills.

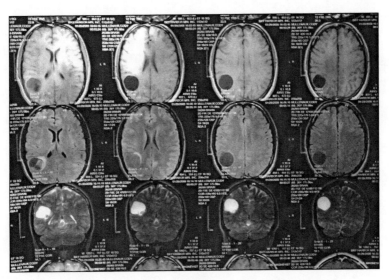

MRI of my Ganglio Cytoma! WOWZERS!

From Respectable Citizen to Gangsta-Lite in Less than No Time

I was lying on my bed one day when I got a call from one of my aunt's good friends, Elizabeth. She was the manager for a catering service called Patina at the Hollywood Bowl. She hooked me up with a great position as a runner, and I eventually became an expediter, making solid cash throughout the summers. The Hollywood Bowl is this huge, outdoor theater where all sorts of musical groups perform. I had the privilege to see The Who, Santana, Radiohead, Tony Bennett, Diana Krall, and all sorts of awesome live shows that people would die to see for free. I worked for Patina for a few seasons.

The Hollywood Bowl offered what is called the box service, a place where all the high-end customers would sit before an event to eat dinner with their families and friends. All the food was pre-ordered, usually weeks in advance of the actual concert or event. At concert time, caterers would get a printout of all the hot and cold entrées going out for that night, who ordered them, and which box seat they had. My job was to account for all the cold entrées before the evening began. As the expediter, I would get tickets with orders of cold entrées on them, go into the walk-in refrigerator, find

133

which entrées matched the ticket, and bring them out, setting them on a shelf for the waiters to take out to the customers.

I would usually carpool to work with my cousin Hayley. She had been a waiter there for a while, and when she heard from Liz that Patina needed some extra help, she threw my name out there (God bless her little heart). The job couldn't have come at a better time. Hayley and I would usually show up pretty early for work, just to make sure that all the food was present for the night on my end in the cold fridge. Hayley would have to locate and set up all her tables for the night. Our other cousin Hollie also worked with us.

After we had all of our entrées tallied in the fridge and the girls had their tables ready for the evening, we usually had about an hour of downtime before we were to begin serving our customers. We would all usually go over to these sticky tables, as I remember them, where the Bowl had designated for the employees to eat and socialize before our night was to begin. I would usually smoke some weed before work most of the time. At the time my cousin Hollie smoked too, but not like I did.

I had some really good weed one day. Hollie ended up smoking with me before work and getting really high, I guess. When we got back to our workstations, she either asked one of the other waitresses if she looked high or said that she was high, something along those lines. Our boss was the older sister of the girl Hollie asked. Hollie kind of shot herself in the foot that evening and ended up getting fired from work for being under the influence of a controlled substance while at work that night. I think she always held this resentment against me from that day.

Because I was working, I was pretty busy. The job was seasonal, which meant that I only worked June through September and a little bit of October. The shifts were only about three hours long. I was making really good money in tips, plus my weekly wages. My grandparents were happy that I was working, an activity which seemed to keep me out of trouble throughout the summer. I saved enough money that summer so that, when my grandpa matched what I saved, I was able to buy my very first little car. I saved about thirty-five hundred dollars one summer, and I was able to pay some of my probation down. The sister of a friend of mine at the time (we called him Goliath) was married to a Los Angeles police officer. I was able to hook up with him and get a real good deal on a 1994 G20 Infiniti from the police auction in Santa Monica. I bought the car for little under five grand. Believe it or not, when I bought the car, it had a bullet hole going through the passenger door and blood on the passenger side floorboard. From the start, I should've known that the car was bad luck.

I was pretty happy that I was able to save the amount of money I did in such a short amount of time. I was also very grateful that Grandpa Joe was willing to match what I'd made, even after all the trouble I'd caused with him. I couldn't have had the car for any more than one month. I was driving around with no license or insurance on the car, but my attitude was basically that I didn't care what anyone said about me driving, because I had bought that car on my own. That mentality made justifying my actions easy. My grandparents, even my dad, were mad that I wasn't driving around legally.

In the summertime, I picked up my buddy S'Dub one morning, got some weed, stopped by a few friends' houses, smoked, and when I was all high, I decided to hop in my car and drive like a maniac around Palos Verdes. I didn't know what "take it easy" meant. Everything I did growing up from twelve to about twenty-one I did with no regard for anyone else and as recklessly as possible. This kid S'Dub was pretty annoying. I didn't really like him, actually; we just so happened to have one thing in common: smoking weed. If he had weed, we were cool. I had at least one thing in common with anyone who smoked pot. I had these kinds of friendships with kids growing up: "You get high? Cool, so do I; let's hang out."

Here I was driving like an idiot through my neighborhood behind the gates, eyes bloodshot red from the bong hits all morning. I knew the streets well, really well. They had sharp, tight turns that were really dangerous to drive if you had just turned sixteen, didn't have a license or insurance, and had no regards for the law or anybody, including yourself.

I came into this really tight right-hand turn with a stop sign before entering the turn. I had S'Dub riding shotgun, and his pipe was in the center console near my emergency brake. I came into the turn with way too much momentum. The car was a front wheel drive car; so it didn't handle very well anyway. The tread on the tires was pretty worn out, and the tires were balding, too. The rear end of my car lost control, and we did a thirty-foot sideways skid. I lost complete control of my vehicle doing a good sixty miles an hour, and to our right was an embankment, like a forty-five-degree slope. So as the car was sliding sideways out of control, it made contact with the embankment. I managed to flip my car completely, starting with my side rolling over the top onto the passenger side and back onto the wheels. I had just totally managed to kick flip my car.

Can you believe that the car was still running? It never even shut down. But every panel on my car was destroyed, with both mirrors gone, and the front windshield was shattered and pushed in. S'Dub and I both somehow were completely fine, not a scratch on either of our bodies. After coming to a complete stop, I looked at S'Dub; both of us, in complete shock, stared silently into each other's eyes. I couldn't believe that I'd just totaled my car that I had just worked all summer to buy. I had no insurance or even a license, no registration, nothing. Luckily for me, though, no one witnessed the accident.

As the car was still running, I drove away from the scene of the accident. Even though the car was literally completely wrecked, it still drove fine. It was amazing. As I started driving off, shards of glass began flying up in my eyes and S'Dub's. All of a sudden, S'Dub realized that his pipe was missing. He said, "Dude, my pipe is gone; you got to turn around." When we flipped, the sunroof was open, and his pipe must've flown out when we were rolling. I'd just totaled my car; the last thing I wanted to hear was, "Dude, my pipe is missing."

I was upset, and at the same time, I was scared, too. I didn't know what I was going to do about my car. The wreck happened only one block away from Grandma's Phyllis's place. I knew that I couldn't go home with my car looking like it did; so I dropped S'Dub off and headed down to play football with a bunch of my friends from high school at a nearby park. I was seriously driving my car around like nothing had happened. When I pulled up to the park, my friends couldn't believe that I was actually still driving the car because of the condition it was in. They couldn't believe I was still alive. They also couldn't believe that, under the circumstances, I wanted to still play football. I played anyway; I got out on the field, made a couple of touchdowns, hopped into my car, and went to my dad's place in San Pedro like nothing was even wrong.

Scott could always keep a secret, especially because he didn't want to hear from my grandma and grandpa. I had to hide the car at his place. As I got older, I came to realize that, when I would hurt myself, my dad wasn't actually mad at me; he was mad at the fact that he was going to have to deal with Grandma Phyllis and her reaction to the situation. And as I got older, I began to realize how he felt.

I couldn't do anything with the Infinity; it was a complete loss. Within a week, I sold the car for three hundred bucks. A salvage yard came out with a flatbed and paid me cash as I signed the title over to them, and off to the weed man's house I went. I took the cash for my car, got some really good Mexican food, bought some really good weed, stayed in that night, and drowned my sorrows. When in doubt, some good Mexican food and some weed smoke would take my losses and fears away, and that remedy was the solution to all my problems. It was a temporary solution, but it was still a problem-solver for me. I had to keep smoking and drinking and partying to forget about my worries and my thoughts. My car was gone, just like that. My sophomore summer came to an abrupt end. Now the time had come to start my junior year back at Rancho Del Mar Continuation High School for Numbskulls.

I never liked or wanted to go to school; I was too active and too high strung. Rancho made coming and going as you pleased very easy. As long as your credits were where they were supposed to be at the end of the semester, everything was fine. Everyone at Rancho seemed to get high or to be an outcast in his own way. My friends and I used to get high in the bathrooms or behind the classrooms or in our cars in the parking lot. Or sometimes we would even climb trees to smoke pot in them and to have a better view of the security guards.

For me, junior year was a more or less experimental year, drug wise. If anything was giving me a substantial head change, I was definitely doing or using it. Early in high school, I was experimenting more or less with other substances but never really as much as I smoked pot. I like pot the most; it calmed me down, relaxed me, and put me at an even keel. Weed really ended up becoming my best friend all through high school. And if weed was your friend, then you were my friend, and that's how things went.

Then, as I started hanging out with Chow Chow, speed started becoming a very good friend of mine also. Chow and I would stay up for days on end, getting high on speed and sometimes taking ecstasy along with it. Weed relaxes you, while speed does the exact opposite: the harder the drug, the stronger the high; the stronger the high, the harder the come down.

I remember when I first started messing around with speed; it would make me so obsessed that I would want to clean everything in sight. I wanted to organize and arrange my room in one hour five different ways, or I would get so zoned out on drawing a picture that I would work on it for hours and hours, not realizing that I was going over and over the same spot, trying to make it perfect, when really the quality didn't matter one way or the other. I was going to continue to go over that one spot and over it again. I would actually draw through the paper at the end, and what started to become something so beautiful on paper ended by becoming a huge blob of ink. The drawings would actually start off pretty decent at the beginning, but at the end they usually looked like a huge mess on the paper.

I associate speed with the devil absolutely: the more you take it, the more you withdraw; the more you withdraw, the more depressed you get. When you start getting really depressed on speed is about the time you become dependent on it. If you can't get or afford it when you want it or need it, you're going to find a way to get some money together to get more, even if you have to go into Grandma or Grandpa's purse or wallet again, even if you have to go into the Wachs' house when they aren't home and take money from their kids' safes, even if you have to go into Chow Chow's purse as soon as she leaves the room for a minute to use the restroom. I did all of those things.

I have to say that, along with speed for me came robbery, lying, fear, and most definitely insanity. Along with all those would eventually come more court cases. I got to a point where I would look in the mirror at myself and just wish that I was seriously comatose. I hated myself. I hated my actions. I was living a lie, and I wanted to die.

One night, I was coming down off speed really, really hard. I think that I had been awake for a few days. In the middle of the night, I began to write an eight-page letter to my grandparents, apologizing and asking for forgiveness for my behavior. I knew that I had been selfish. I knew that I'd been trouble. I knew that I'd caused a lot of grief and stress in my family's life and in my grandparents' relationships with friends and neighbors. At that point when I was writing the letter, I really meant my apology; the type of guilt I had and the type of shame I was feeling really resonated in my heart. The next day came around, though, and I was right back to square one with my addiction.

Though I hated what I was doing and how I felt and though I wanted to die, I couldn't escape speed addiction. It was like a really bad dream, a horrifying nightmare, but I was living in it. That's why speed is the devil's drug. All he wants is for us to feel no good, useless, worthless, scared, depressed, and suicidal. He was having his way with me, and I was losing the fight along with my mind. I had ruined everything good in my life. My best friends didn't even want to hang out with me anymore; my family, though they loved me, didn't trust me or want me around. I just kept digging myself into a hole so deep that I was hoping someone would just come by and bury me alive. At that point, ceasing to exist would have been a great solution, and I would have agreed with it. It would've saved me and a lot of other people a lot of pain and agony. But it would've been very selfish and cowardly, also. I had to ride it out.

I became good friends with these older Asian guys in my neighborhood who sold all sorts of dope, mostly ecstasy, though. Basically ecstasy is all sorts of different drugs put into one little pill. People used old, abandoned warehouses to throw parties which they called raves, or "E" parties. Everybody would be on either ecstasy or some other type of hard-core drug, such as speed or cocaine or maybe even ketamine. The people throwing the party would play really loud, fast percussion music with loud bass, because dancing to this music while taking X really amplifies your high.

Back in high school, I can remember raves being a lot of fun. My friends and I used to drive all over Los Angeles and Orange County and even into San Diego to stay up all night, drop X, and dance the night away. I didn't care if it was a school night or not, I was going to find a way out of the house to go raving with the homies. Most nights, though, were local nights, when I'd take some E and lay low with a few friends at either Chow's or one of the homies' houses.

Thinking back on those times, when you're caught up in the moment, what you're doing seems like fun, but you don't really realize the effect these poor choices are going to have on you in your future. You've compromised your health and wasted your youth. You don't see consequences that way when you're young, though; you just want to have a good time.

A good friend of mine, Seth Howard, was a few years older than I was. He took a liking to me because I was pretty out-of-control, wild, and down to party. Plus, we both always seemed to be able to manipulate the cute chicks into liking us, getting high with us, and hanging out with us, because we were said to be very charming. Seth really used to like to do acid. If you have never experienced acid for yourself, then explaining the effects of acid is really hard to do. It's nothing like people portray it. You really have to have experienced it to understand what kind of psychic change you get from that drug. It really changes your whole perception about reality and makes you really think in depth about life and the possibilities of this world we live in. I call acid the thinker's drug. I had some very interesting nights on acid, very fun when in the right setting. But if you're in a room with negative energy, very easily your sanity can become very unstable. I could definitely see people losing their minds from that drug.

One night, Seth came over in his 1974 El Camino to pick me up. He had a bunch of acid on him, and he wanted to get high. So did I. I did a lot of speed and smoked a lot of weed with Seth throughout our friendship. He picked me up, and we cruised down towards the beach. Along the way, we picked up little B'zer Wachs, Justin's younger brother. He was a good friend of my little brother Casey. I was always that kid who was either a good influence because of my athleticism or a bad influence because of my thrill-seeking, adventurous mentality and lifestyle. Both ways for me, positive and negative, I had a way of influencing my younger peers, who respected and looked up to me, as did Seth, and I looked up to him.

Now B'zer, Seth, and I were on our way down to the beach as we each put acid on our tongues. For acid to kick in and really affect you fully takes about thirty to sixty minutes. The acid we had taken that night was mild compared to some of the stuff I had taken in the past, but nonetheless effective. We were tripping out in Hermosa Beach near the water, and we decided to go on top of the life guard stands and smoke some weed. We were out at about 8:30 PM, and a cold breeze was coming from our backs. The lights from the strand seemed amplified a million times. Everything seems amplified when you're on acid; your senses are a million times stronger. I think that an acid trip is how cats feel at all times of the day, seriously.

The wind felt good, and the high was very memorable. As we smoked, Seth provoked me to jump off the lifeguard tower into the sand. Being the competitive and impulsive one, I looked at the twenty-foot drop and thought: *For sure I can handle that drop into the sand. No sweat, right?* I got to the edge of the lifeguard tower and sat over the edge with my legs dangling down and my hands to both sides of me, tripping on acid and feeling very confident. The more I looked, the higher the tower seemed; I hesitated. Seth challenged me that, if I jumped, he would jump the next time, fair enough.

I took a deep breath, kicked my feet out in front of me, and pushed off the lifeguard tower with both my hands. Upon landing, my body being in such a relaxed state of mind from the acid, my knees came to my chest, and my chest and chin hit the sand simultaneously. The feeling on the way down, with the wind coming through my hair and all over my whole body while I was high, was very exhilarating. I didn't feel any pain hitting the ground, which was kind of cushioned. So I went running back up the ramp, hopped on the lifeguard tower, and climbed back up to the top, where Seth and B'zer couldn't believe what I'd just done.

Well, Seth did not stick by his word. Being all energized from the whole situation, I tried to motivate Seth to jump. He told me that if I jumped one more time, then he would jump for sure. Without hesitating this time, from a standing position I ran and just jumped off of the very top of the lifeguard stand, making the drop now a good, solid twenty-five feet, almost landing in the same position as I did the time before, but this time with more weight on my right side. My right ankle broke in half upon landing. I tried to walk the injury off, as I was in shock, not realizing at the moment that my ankle was sideways. I fell to the ground and began to yell at the top of my lungs to passersby on the strand to call for help. My cry for help scared Seth and B'zer to a point where they ran off the lifeguard tower, gave me a cell phone, and basically abandoned me by myself, high on acid with a broken ankle in the middle of Hermosa Beach.

I hobbled off the beach the best I could and called my dad several times before actually getting an answer. He rushed down to where I was, picked me up, and took me to the hospital. I remember that my ankle was the size of a softball. It had swelled badly, and its awkward position really made me forget about my high and the good time I'd been having. Every time I think back to that night in the hospital with my dad by my side, I don't know if I was paranoid or not. But I really and truly felt that my dad knew I was on acid or something all right, and was really doing his best to trip me out. He seemed to be walking like a robot and making all sorts of weird body movements with a smirk on his face. He wasn't mad; I remember him actually being somewhat comforting. Maybe it was the acid or maybe it was just me, but I'll never forget that night. What was weird was that Scott had a totally different attitude that night than all the other times I had injured myself, and he made me feel good in a sense. I guess that, as Grandma Phyllis wasn't there to nag, Scott was just being Scott.

Another time, Seth and I took some very potent purple gel acid tablets and decided to go up to a very beautiful view-point in Palos Verdes to sit, reminisce, and trip out, if you will. The top of Crest Road in Palos Verdes overlooks all the greater Los Angeles area, from the South Bay beaches to the shores of Orange County, in one panoramic view, definitely one of the best views in all of the Los Angeles area. The girls with us didn't want to stay anymore because we were getting out of hand. We smoked weed with them to chill us out, and then they dropped us off at our destination point, the top of Crest Road, so that we could begin our journey that after-noon after school on Friday.

From our feet looking down was about a thousand-foot sloping canyon that went into a deep and dark ravine. Across the way was actually the very end of Grandma Phyllis's street in Rolling Hills. Now I knew this geography from growing up in Rolling Hills and from the fact that I used to smoke weed at that viewpoint quite often. I would always look across the way and point out to friends, "See that house? That end house right there? That's the very end of my street, Outrider Road."

So as Seth and I were tripping out, enjoying the view, enjoying our high, a crazy thought came into my head. Because we were dropped off, we didn't have a ride either way. I told Seth (and this is how I said it) that all of a sudden I had this ingenious plan that I mapped out so well in my mind. He thought I had a brilliant idea: that just maybe we could make it down the slope, up along the bordering fence of the last house on my street, across it down their driveway, and onto my street. The plan was a long shot, but we were tripped out anyway. From our vantage point, visually the trek looked possible, but physically, anybody in his right mind would never have even thought that running down this thousand-foot canyon sloping at a forty-five-degree angle would even be an option.

Well, Seth seemed to be as hyped about the whole idea as I was. We cruised down the road a little to a decent spot where we could begin to charge. As soon as we found a somewhat comfortable spot, I just started charging full-speed down this embankment. I felt like I was a gazelle in the jungle, leaping over twenty-foot gaps of shrubs and bushes. Seth was following right behind me at a steady speed. We were getting cut, and we were sweaty. Our clothes were dirty, but we didn't even care. We reached the bottom in a very timely fashion. Once at the bottom of this canyon, we had to climb down a sheer cliff into what seemed to be a dry riverbed with trees and bushes overshadowing us. Getting up on the other side of the canyon was almost impossible. Seth was struggling, climbing up trees, and trying to get to the top of the embankment. He became so frustrated at one point that he started yelling at me and saying, "Look what you got us into! We're going to be stuck down here!"

I wasn't too concerned. I knew that, as soon as we got out of the riverbed embankment or whatever it was, we were semi-stuck. My street was right there. Plus, my high was so intensified from running down the side of the canyon that I was in good spirits. Seth and I helped each other get to the top of the canyon wall, and we proceeded to walk along the fence just like I'd visualized it in my head perfectly, over the top part of the fence and right down into the driveway. What we had just done was so crazy that I really could not believe it.

Seth was mad because he was all dirty and sweaty on a Friday night. I just figured we'd go home to my place, shower up, and go over to Chow Chow's. Our climb was a mission well accomplished and another very unforgettable moment in my life that I was actually pretty proud of, to tell you the truth. If you were to go up to that viewpoint and see the actual canyon and I were to tell you that I actually ran down the canyon and over onto my street one day, you would perceive me to be a liar, because the journey seems impossible. I do still today go up there and tell people about the climb, and that's the exact response I get from them. But they aren't like me and I'm not like them. I'm crazy. It was a true story, and I lived it out, as Seth did as well.

We actually ended up cruising over to Chow's after breaking into my neighbor's pool house so that we could try to chill out a little because we were so amped up. I remember that once we got into that pool house, we couldn't sit still. I felt like an untamed wild animal or something. I attacked Seth, and we began to go about the room in a wild, uncontrolled manner. We wrestled for thirty minutes before tiring each other out. We headed down to Chow's after that.

We were so tripped out on acid that Chow didn't want us around; she actually told us to go home. At this point, Chow's and my relationship started to become kind of sour, because I was hanging out with Seth so much, and he didn't have a very reputable track record. Seth had a reputation for being a kleptomaniac, and I had a reputation for being a little drug addict/kleptomaniac myself. We weren't a very good match to say the least. But we had very similar characteristics and qualities and liked each other's company, and so we didn't care what everyone else thought. We terrorized all of Palos Verdes for several years.

Chow's house was furnished very nicely; it had a very nice playroom with a big-screen TV, soft leather couches, and a ridiculous sound system. Off to the right in the corner was one of the most high-tech digital color printers available at the time; its retail value was maybe a thousand dollars, if not more. You could take a picture, place it on the printer, close the top, press copy, and the machine would print you a near-perfect image of what you were expecting, in crystal-clear photo quality. We got the idea to copy dollar bills. So we started Xeroxing dollar bills, and then we escalated to five-dollar bills and twenty-dollar bills. Pretty soon, we were printing our own fake money. The quality was that of a professional workshop, but in an upscale household environment, accessible to anybody basically, and free. The quality of the fake money we began to produce was almost a joke.

Now being young and immature and addicted to drugs, for us to be introduced to a money-making machine was a problem waiting to happen. We started turning out fake bills and spending them at local convenience stores. The scam worked the first couple of times; we couldn't believe our luck. I showed some of the money to my best friend at the time, James Narino. He was so impressed with the fake twenty-dollar bill that he wanted to see if it really worked or if he could spend it. We hopped in my dad's 1978 Ford pickup truck and drove up to the local 7-Eleven convenience store up on the hill. I told James not to spend that particular one because you could see that the back side wasn't exactly lined up perfectly, but he insisted. My warning didn't stop him.

He cruised right in, grabbed something for about a dollar, and proceeded to make an exchange with the fake currency. I was right outside the window in the truck; so I saw the reaction of the 7-Eleven employee. Simultaneously, James turned around and ran out of the store like he'd robbed it or something. I had the truck started already, as I was anticipating James getting caught. The bill he tried to spend was a practice one which didn't give justice to how well I could actually print quality fakes. James hopped in the truck as we raced back to my house and parked the truck in the driveway.

About an hour or so later, the Lomita sheriff's department was at my door. The employee at 7-Eleven got the license plate number on our truck as we fled the scene. The police knew that James was the one trying to pass the fake bill as cash since they had him on surveillance. Counterfeiting real money is a federal crime as well as a felony in the state of California, and it carries a mandatory five years in prison if convicted. Though I was the one on probation and the mastermind behind the whole money-making scheme, the authorities had solid evidence that James was the one trying to cash the fake bill. They didn't really care that I was driving.

Before the cops showed up to my house, James and I already knew that the heat might be on. On the way home, we concocted a simple story so that, if we were to get caught, we would both be on the same page. Events turned out as we kind of suspected; pretty soon after the cops arrived, James and I were sitting in separate rooms with different detectives to tell the lie that we had spontaneously fabricated, which turned out not to be so much of a lie at all. We told the cops that, earlier that day, James had purchased food from a Panda Express at the local pavilions. He bought his lunch with a fifty-dollar bill, and part of the change that the grocery store gave him happened to be one of those twenty-dollar bills. So we both basically said that we were not aware that fake money was in either of our possessions at that time.

The only reason the lie appeared true was that fake money had been going in and out of that market now for several weeks, and the police had been investigating that store. Because both of our stories matched and seemed to be true, the police released us thirty minutes later with no tickets, no nothing, free to go. We'd just dodged a huge federal offense. I was actually surprised to hear that fake money was going around the hill from someone else besides us. Well, we were relieved to say the least.

Around the same time, I was doing a lot of credit card and check fraud also; only I was defrauding my own grandpa's checkbook and credit cards. I was ordering stuff on the Internet and selling the merchandise for cash when it would eventually arrive at my doorstep. I also used to call up any place that delivered food and took credit cards over the phone, place an order, give them a random address (usually the address I was standing in front of), and when they would show, within thirty minutes I would have about thirty bucks' worth of either sandwiches or pizza ready to grub. I was always sure to get two liters of Sprite with each order. Sprite was my favorite drink for a long time. If I didn't have any weed to smoke that day or any cash, usually one of my buddies would exchange a favor for a favor. I would give him food, and he would smoke me out.

The scam usually worked out pretty well, until I eventually got caught by my grandparents. I think that the bill one month just for ordering food was over four hundred dollars. My grandpa ended up having to get a new credit card because of me. I actually had the credit card number and expiration date memorized so that, whether or not the card was in my actual possession, I was still able to make phone and Internet orders with ease.

When that scam wore off, the time had come for something new. I really didn't respect myself at all. All my good friends, too, pretty much alienated me, and their abandonment kind of forced me to run with the only guys with whom I had something in common: the druggies, wannabe gangsters, outcasts, and soon-to-be failures.

Chow had this really attractive friend named Candy, who also went to Rancho with us. She was a year older than me and just beautiful, with long, blonde hair, beautiful skin, and a gorgeous smile. She was one of those pretty stoner chicks that all the guys definitely wanted to be around. Remember the losers I was telling you about? One of the Asian guys' names was Lunie Oddball; he was about four years older than I was. He would drive all of us in his crowd around to the rave parties and supply us all the drugs we needed.

One night at Chow's, Lunie came over with a few friends and a whole bunch of ecstasy, trying to sell it to us. No one really had any money right then. I was sitting there with Candy, and at the time Chow had her boyfriend, some big, dorky guy. We were all looking at each other, trying to figure out how to get enough money together so that we could all take some X and get high that night. I told them all, "Chill out; I'll be right back." I ran up the street to my house without thinking twice about what I was about to do, went into my grandpa's office where he kept his checks, took a check from his drawer, wrote my name and my grandpa's signature on it, and made it out for three hundred dollars.

I came back and told Mr. Oddball that the check was legit, that I'd had it for a while. Because it was late and the banks were closed, I could sign the check over to one of them, deposit the check straight into one of their accounts through the ATM machine, and withdraw three hundred dollars immediately. Lunie knew what was up; he wasn't stupid. But he also knew that the deal was on me and that, if anything came back insufficient from the bank, I knew what time it was. He made my responsibilities pretty clear to me. He convinced his girlfriend to put the check into her account. I knew that the fake check was going to mess up her account; I knew it. The check was fraudulent, a fake check, but I still told Lunie not to worry, that everything would be cool.

We did as I'd suggested, and I had three hundred bucks in my hands in a matter of minutes. I bought ecstasy for everyone there that night. Lunie was happy, because he got the cash and sold his drugs. And I also gave him and his friends each one pill of ecstasy after I'd bought it. I think that my motivating factor that night was that I was pretty stoked on Candy, and I thought that, if I'd hook her up with some E that night, we would all have a good night. She'd like me, and so I thought that maybe I'd have a chance with her.

The night was pretty fun. We had an interesting trip, to say the least, and Candy and I ended up in my pool house. When we were coming down off the ecstasy, we each took more than we needed. I remember towards the end of the night having hallucinations. I remember cuddling with Candy, but really wanting to do more because I was so physically attracted to her. The fact that she was such a sweetheart really made it hard to resist her. She was so attractive, and I couldn't believe I actually had her in my house cuddling and kissing me. But the night came to an end pretty quickly. Candy was always a really cool chick; we stayed friends throughout high school. She ended up getting pregnant later on that year by some bozo and moving out of Palos Verdes. I will always remember her.

That night, I took too much ecstasy, and the next morning it was really having its way with me. I got in a huge argument with my grandparents, and I ended up running away from home for a few days post-X dropping. My best friend was James Narino all through elementary, junior high, and all the way through high school. I was trying to lay low for a couple of days at James's. Basically, I was just trying to get back to a normal state of consciousness from all the hard drugs I had been inducing into my body. James's mom treated me like I was her son. I loved James's mom so much; she was always such a nice woman. In a way, she reminded me of Grandma Ginny, very loving and supportive no matter the circumstances. She was always so loving, caring, and under-standing, qualities I never experienced at home. I felt safe at her house. She didn't mind that I was hiding out there. She just wanted to see me doing better than I was doing, and she would always encourage me, nothing like being at my own house.

I knew that it was on; I had only a matter of days before Lunie would find out about the bounced check in his girl-friend's account. Well, I was right. James's mom was out of town that weekend I was staying with him, and her trip worked out perfectly. James and I had the house to ourselves. We chilled, smoked some pot, and watched movies. Slowly, I was coming back to reality. Then, James got the call through the grapevine from one of our friends saying that Oddball was looking for me. Somehow, Lunie got the heads-up that I was staying at James's house, called James, and tried to interrogate my whereabouts out of him. Like a good friend, James denied having any contact with me or any knowledge of my whereabouts. Somehow, Lunie knew I was staying there and threatened James that, if he didn't give me up, James himself was going to be having problems of his own. The last thing I wanted to happen was for my best friend to take the heat for my stupidity. I felt so guilty and ashamed; I didn't want my friend to have to face my burden, my prob-lems that I'd created on my own.

All of a sudden, Lunie and his boys showed up at James's house unannounced. I started freaking out. These guys weren't just some regular kids in our neighborhood. They went about things in a real gangster-like mentality, and that was that. As soon as they started pounding on the door, I ran into James's mom's bathroom, and I told James, "Please cover me, bro." James did all that he could. He stood by his word that he had no clue where I was and that I for sure was not there at his house.

I could hear what was going on from the other room. Lunie and the others tried to mess with James. I heard arguing coming from his room and could sense really bad vibes and that James was definitely uncomfortable. As I was sitting in James's mom's bathroom, rolled up like a little girl in a tight ball, I thought to myself: *I can't let my best friend take the heat for something I caused.* As soon as that thought came over me, at that very moment I came out of the bathroom, down the hall, and asked Lunie and his brother and the three other guys, "Leave James alone. He didn't do anything, and here I am to face my punishment." That confession seemed at the time like the standup thing to do.

Lunie had brought his little brother Blob, whom I'd never actually met before that night, but Blob definitely wasn't little. He was known for having knock-out power in his right fist and breaking kid's noses all the time. He actually knocked a good friend of mine out, Tyler Smith, and broke his nose a few years prior. Lunie also had this guy Tone Loc with him, who was from New York. Tone's dad was like a real mobster from the east coast or some stuff. And I saw this other kid, Ruthless, who originally was from the Mexican Mafia. All these guys were straight gangsta gang bangers, grimy kids who grew up in the streets. I used to hang out with Tone Loc and Ruthless and get high with them all the time, and they actually liked me. They were always pretty cool with me.

But as soon as I came out of the bathroom down the hall and said my piece, they came out of James's room. Lunie's brother Blob said, "Is this him; is this the kid?" The other guys with Lunie said, "Yeah." Blob got me by the collar of my shirt, walked with me down the hall about five paces, turned around, and just laid into me with a solid right, straight knocking me out cold. James later told me that I was out for a good minute or so. And my landing was ironic, because when I came to and regained consciousness, a huge mirror was right there in front of me at the end of James's hallway, just a reflection of my stupidity. Blob had shattered my nose with one punch.

I remember waking up in a puddle of blood with all of these crazy guys standing over me. I got up, and everyone was scuffling. I locked myself in James's bathroom. I remember just staring at my face in the mirror, thinking: *I can't believe these guys really just broke my nose like they did over three hundred measly bucks.* Believe it or not, my nose looked like a sideways V. Meanwhile, the gang was trying to break the door down to get me out of the bathroom. I was crying because my nose was so mangled. I actually had blood coming out of my ear; that's how hard this guy hit me.

I pleaded with them, "All right, all right; I'll get you your money." I opened the bathroom door, and I told Lunie and his posse, "Let's go. Take me to my grandma's, and I'll get you your money." The whole scenario was so surreal that it seemed like a movie. These four huge guys grabbed me and threw me in the backseat of their car. They put me in the middle of Tone and Ruthless in the backseat so that I wouldn't try to run.

We got up to the top of my grandma's street. Lunie made his expectations really clear to me. I should just go down and get the money, and then everything would be cool between us (except that I had a freaking broken nose now). If I couldn't get the money from my grandparents, then Lunie told me just to come back up to them to work something out and make some sort of arrangement. I was scared for my life. He also made the fact clear that, if I didn't come back up to them, I was going to make the situation a lot harder on myself, because they were not going to forget and they knew where I lived.

In my head, I said: *Forget that.* I had already made a conscious decision to stay home. Besides, why would I want to go back and be tormented by these thugs? But when my grandma opened the door to find me in tears with a bloody nose, a black eye, and a crooked face, she was incredibly mad and wasn't letting me go anywhere. I hadn't been home for several days, and now I showed up this way. There was no way she was paying these guys off. She must have really thought I was insane. She didn't care about my situation; she wasn't bailing me out again. I went into my room, where my dad was sleeping in my bed. I had a pounding headache. My dad was peeved at me like always when I was hurt or was in pain around grandma, but he got up and gave me some ice for my face to reduce the swelling and pain. I couldn't sleep; the pain was agonizing.

I really didn't really want to be home in the morning; so I got up before my family did, grabbed my skateboard, and headed to the other side of the hill to the house of one of my good friends, this girl at my school named Eileen Gutierrez, who was a good chick. She was a stoner friend of mine. We had one thing in common; we were potheads. Well, I guess we had the same friends, too. I got to her house pretty early in the morning. She was still asleep. I went around back to her room, knocked on her door, and woke her and her sister up. She was so concerned. My face was a wreck, and I looked sick and pale, she said. I told her the situation, and she graciously let me stay on her couch. Her parents were very nice people, too, and her mom didn't judge me. As Eileen had the same group of friends, Mrs. Gutierrez also knew Lunie, Tone, Ruthless, all those guys. She understood what had happened.

Within twenty-four hours, those clowns showed up at Eileen's looking for me. I was so bummed out, because I felt that I couldn't go anywhere without these guys finding me. They assured Eileen that they didn't want to hurt me anymore; they just wanted me to go with them so that we could come up with a solution as to how I was going to pay them back. Lunie, Tone, and Ruthless actually liked me. I think that the fact that Lunie's brother just grabbed me and knocked me out, breaking my nose, was not really part of the plan that night. Lunie actually mentioned that he didn't actually want what happened to my nose that night to go down like it did. Lunie admitted to me that Blob was out-of-control that night. He actually apologized and explained to me that all he really wanted was to make amends with the cash; so all I had to do was make his money back, period.

The guys basically ended up kidnapping me and holding me hostage until I got the money back that I owed them. They were actually being cool to me at this point; they smoked me out as we got in the car to go to Lunie's girl's house. I felt comfortable when Blob wasn't around, and because he didn't chill with his brother all that often, I started to feel just as if I were hanging out with some of my friends in the beginning. We would sit at Lunie's girlfriend's house, play video games all day, and smoke weed while trying to come up with a decent solution to pay him back.

I told them, "Check this out: I know how I can pay you and your girl back, Lunie." The plan occurred to me that, if I stole the color printer from Chow's house, Lunie and I could print fake money all day, come up with a few different ways to spend it, and get their money back. This solution was the only one I thought would work; so he agreed. I didn't care about anything at this point. I would have done anything, really, to break the chains that had me bound. Counterfeiting was my best idea.

So the next morning, we cruised up to Chow's house. I wasn't sure if someone was actually home or not at this point; I didn't really care, though. I hopped through one of the girls' back windows and into the house, and I really didn't show any signs of concern. I knew the house really well, as I'd been over there almost every day prior to becoming a numbskull. I kind of had an idea that no one was home. So here I was, this tiny, one-hundred-thirty-five-pound kid with a broken nose and a black eye, climbing unauthorized through a Rolling Hills residence window in broad daylight with intentions to steal a LaserJet printer.

The thing literally weighed about a hundred pounds. I approached the printer, pulled the cord from the wall, picked it up off its stand, and made a beeline through the hall to the window where I'd come in. I could barely pick this thing up because it was so heavy. By the time I got to the window with it, I was struggling. The car was right there with the trunk popped, and Lunie saw that I was exhausted and having trouble making my way the rest of the way up the hill from the window. He hopped out of his car and ran over to me, and we carried the printer up to the trunk of the car, threw it in, and went off unnoticed: shweeu.

Now when we got the printer to Lunie's girl's place where we were staying, Tone and Ruthless were there, chilling in the same spot where they were before we had left that morning. We plugged the machine in and started printing off fake twenties. Lunie knew about the copier and had seen the fake bills before, but Tone and Ruthless were in shock at the quality and how good the fake cash looked. I really felt like I only owed Lunie two hundred bucks, because I did give him some of his own drugs that night when the fraudulent transaction went down, and I bought all of my E from him anyway. And now I felt like actually I owed him nothing, because I already got a broken nose out of this whole situation. Wasn't a broken nose good enough?

Lunie thought at first that targeting drive-through windows, donut shops, and liquor stores would be a good idea. The first attempt to pass the fake bill was at a nearby Jack in the Box drive-through in San Pedro. We ordered a small drink and fries. The transaction worked. Not only did it get us cash, but we also got a free drink and fries. The plan was almost too easy, and so we went to another drive-through and experienced the same thing, no problem. We had hit about four or five drive-through restaurants successfully. Well, finally one of the drive-through clerks noticed that our bill was fake and brought that fact to our attention.

We played it off like we had no clue, like we were innocent, and we handed over regular cash to pay for the food.

We decided to try different targets. So we went to different donut shops. They ended up being our primary targets because the scam worked so easily. Ninety percent of donut shops seemed to be owned by older Asian families who seemed never even to look at the bill before putting it into the register. The scam was almost too easy; we must have come up with about a hundred bucks or more at donut shops alone that night. I thought that I'd pretty much squared up with Lunie and that my debt was comfortably accounted for now. They had accepted my efforts at making their money back for them; so we went pretty much back to old times, where we were just hanging out, getting high, and being clowns. Or were we? The money we made passed about ninety-eight percent of the time; so we decided to go home, make more money, and figure out a plan for bigger transactions. We were such greedy little kids.

Lunie came up with the idea to go to raves with the fake money, buy real ecstasy, and sell the real X for cash. He would make money a lot quicker that way; plus, we would also have free drugs if the plan worked properly. His idea was a good one. We began printing a whole bunch of fake twenty-dollar bills, located a rave in the middle of downtown Los Angeles, and went on our way. We thought that, if this plan really worked, we could really end up making some legitimate money and at the same time get high for free. Back then, if you did a lot of Ecstasy, you were considered an E-tard. So I guess you could say that we were all E-tards.

We got to the rave, where Tone, Ruthless, Lunie, and his brother Blob went inside and looked for somebody selling X. The plan didn't exactly work the way we'd intended. The kid selling the E somehow knew what was up, and tonight probably wasn't the first time that he had come across counterfeit cash. We left that night empty-handed but were still motivated to find a better working scheme with our fake money. But now the heat was back on me, because Tone, Ruthless, Lunie, and Blob each paid twenty bucks to get into the rave. They held the failure of the plan to go as we anticipated against me. There I was again, back at square one with Lunie, once again trying to figure out how I should make amends in this never-ending nightmare I'd gotten myself into.

So we headed home late at night to get some sleep and figure out what we were to do in the morning. Because Lunie was living at his girlfriend's apartment, I wasn't allowed to sleep inside with them. They were kind of holding me hostage to a certain point. At night, when the others would go inside to get ready for bed, Lunie would have me go to his car, which was this 1998 Ford Contour, and sleep in the back seat until morning. I slept there for a few days and hated it! Sleeping in the back of a car was very uncomfortable. I'd wake up every morning all sweaty and super hot. Lunie usually got me up in the mornings around 8 AM to take me into the apartment to have breakfast, smoke some weed, and play some video games. I felt trapped by the whole situa-tion. Meanwhile, my nose was still completely mangled, and I hadn't seen a doctor yet. If I were to leave in the middle of the night, an option which was completely possible, the gang would be coming to look for me; so I just stayed put in hopes that this nightmare would cease soon. I was basically scared for my own well-being, and I just wanted this whole situation to be over.

I didn't really have a choice, actually, about where was I to go. Nobody at home wanted me. Both sides of my grand-parents were extremely upset with me. I couldn't stay at Grandma Ginny's, because Papa Herman didn't want me there. My nose was broken, and my heart was broken. I was slipping deep down into a state of depression, and the only way I know how to fill that void in my heart was to keep inducing drugs into my system to mask my real and true feelings. I was just a lost soul in the world of darkness, slipping further and further away from life.

Blob's friend worked at a clothing store in Downey, and our next plan was to print some money, go over to the Downey shopping center, buy a whole bunch of nice clothes from his friend with the fake money, and return the clothes there or even to a different department store in the area for real cash later on that day. We thought that plan was going to be great, but Blob's friend chumped out. Again, the heat was back on me. The fake money plan wasn't working out as we'd all thought it would. We were back to square one, driving around and hitting up Jack-in-the-Box and other local drive-through windows.

Basically, coming up with a new plan was up to me to at this point. Meanwhile, I had violated my probation several times over now by not appearing for my drug test and not checking in regularly. Chow's dad called the cops on me about the missing printer. Somehow right away he knew that my running wild and their printer going missing simultaneously was no coincidence. Besides all that trouble with the authorities, I was on the run and being held against my own will all at the same time. No one even knew where I was or what I was doing. The police were after me. Really, all I wanted to do was smoke weed, take pills, and evade the law, and basically, I was doing exactly that to a T.

The last solution that I offered Lunie was just to do a home invasion on a home that I was familiar with to get anything worthwhile so that this debt of mine could finally be cleared. I figured that the easiest target would be my neighbor's house, the Wachs. Go figure: that house was my destination when in contemplation. I knew when they were in and when they were out. I was pretty sure that the guys in the guard shack at the gates to my grandma's neighborhood were probably on the lookout for me. I decided that Lunie and I would just park at the school library behind my grandma's and the Wachs' house and take the trail up there. The same trail where my mom dropped me off when I was about seven and the same parking lot that we used in that scenario ten years later was now coming into play in a much more serious situation. And this time, I was older, and I knew the consequences and had made the choice on my own. My conscience didn't stop me from entering the Wachs.

Once in, Lunie and I just started taking whatever we could find of any value to us. I knew deep down that I was going to be the one to blame for this heist, but I knew no other solutions for the situation I'd gotten myself into. This robbery was the only way at the time I could imagine to pay off my debt and get out of the hole I was in. The robbery was nothing personal; it was just what was easy at the time. We didn't really get anything of much value that day. We didn't find any cash, but Lunie found some earrings that we thought for sure were diamonds but ended up being cubic zirconium. When we found those along with a few other items, such as some vintage coins and some collector's items from Justin's room, we pretty much split.

Lunie actually wasn't very satisfied upon exiting our little heist, if you can call it that. All he really wanted was his cash right in his hand. Then I would have been free to go, I guess, and he would have been a happy man, I suppose. Well, I ran out of plans. I'd just dug myself deeper and deeper into a ditch that I knew I was not going to get out of. I was sick of sleeping in the back of his car every morning and waking up sweaty to the sun at 6 AM, and I knew that the probation and the police departments were on the lookout for me.

I went to fake sleep in Lunie's car, but I chose that night not to wake up in the car the following morning. I felt like I had given Oddball more than enough, that I had bent over backwards to make amends to the situation. The printer alone was worth a thousand dollars; I figured that if they'd just keep that and let me take the rap for it, that printer alone would've been enough, right? I headed towards Grandma Ginny's house that night to face what I'd been doing. Grandma Ginny would never judge me ever. She always just let me know if I were doing something wrong how disappointed in me she was, and that disappointment hurt me more than yelling at me could ever do.

Eventually, I made amends to the gangsters. I paid them back two hundred dollars in cash, and upon giving their cash back, I also got the printer back as part of the deal. I immediately took the printer that afternoon straight up to Chow's dad's house and rang his door bell. He wasn't there, but his friend answered the door. I dropped off the printer and asked the man who answered the door if he could please tell Mr. Sav-on that I was sorry for stealing his printer but that I'd gotten myself into a huge mix-up and that I would like for him to forgive me, please, if possible. Then I left the printer and went on about my way. I came to find out that Chow's parents were having problems with their marriage and got a divorce a few months later. Then the family moved out of Rolling Hills. I never really kept in touch with Chow after that whole situation went down. We just kind of drifted, and our lives took off in their destined directions.

Struggling Upwards,
and Sliding Back Down

I was letting my family down, the people who loved and cared about me the most. I never really thought that drugs were my main problem. I guess I was in denial. I was always quick to place the blame on others, a reaction that made justifying and coping with my own actions easier for me. Reluctantly, Grandma Ginny let me stay with her, as I was in violation of my probation and had decided to man up and face reality.

Upon showing my face after a week or so of disappearing acts, I turned myself in on my violations and went back to juvenile hall for a sixty-day stay. I really had hit bottom this time. I wanted change so badly; I just didn't have a direction. I didn't know how to go about really quitting drugs, changing my immature behavior, and walking on the straight and narrow line which would be beneficial. I just wanted to have the respect and trust back from everybody I had harmed. I was at a point where I wanted to make things right and work towards the next positive indicated step.

Being away for sixty days now, my body detoxified. Really, juvenile hall gave me a chance to sit down and write out some goals. I had a plan when I got released, something I'd been lacking since I started high school. My plan was to stop doing drugs first of all. I felt like the hard-core drugs that I was doing were the cause of my problems. That judgment didn't include weed, though, just the harder drugs.

Because I'd missed so much school, I was going to be very behind. And as I'd missed basically all my junior year wasting away, hiding, and being absent from my own life, I was determined to make up all the credits I was lacking, along with finishing some extra-credit classes to get me ahead during my senior year. I'd always been trying to play catch-up with credits ever since starting high school. When I started my senior year, I had somewhere around a hundred credits, maybe a little more. Each year, you're supposed to have about fifty-five credits to finish the year. Going into my senior year, I was at sophomore status, credit wise. I needed two hundred twenty-five credits to graduate high school, and I was a solid hundred twenty-five credits away from that goal. I had a lot of catching up to do, and that reality started to resonate in my mind and body.

I started my senior year with a determination from within that I had somehow tapped into. I guess that just being beaten down so hard and basically hitting a bottom made me decide that I was going to change the way I was living and make an effort to clean up my act on my own. Changing your actions is easy when your back's against the wall, when you've gone so far down the wrong path in life that the only way you can go is up. I was in that place and felt that way, kind of like the bow and arrow analogy, where sometimes going back is the hardest part. I'd gone back, and creating so much tension was so hard. I kept pulling, pulling, and resisting and going against what was right. When I just learned to let go of what I was holding onto inside deep down, I released that bow, and the arrows or the goals I'd set catapulted forward effortlessly, allowing me to walk in a mighty, upright way.

I think that life is arranged exactly how is intended to be. But when you go through such hard trials and overcome your demons, coming to the other side really builds character. God gives you strength and encouragement to go forward. Like the book of James says, "Count it all joy when you fall into various trials, knowing that the testing of your faith produces patience" (James 1:2). I didn't even know what faith was at that point in my life; I really didn't have any faith in any type of God or religious icon. I just had faith in myself that I knew I could do better than I was doing, and patience not to give up, to overcome, and to persevere. My senior year in high school, I didn't have any faith outside of myself, really.

I was raised in a non-Christian, non-religious home (or homes, if you will). From a very early age, I was always taught just to do what's right and work hard, and you'd be successful, like Grandpa Joe was. Basically our family trusted and believed in Joe and put our faith in him. He overcame adversity and conquered many trials and tribulations. Grandpa Joe passed away on February 5, 2006 at home in his bed from Alzheimer's or old age, same difference. I have been to funerals where friends had passed away and felt the sadness in the rooms. I really felt like my grandpa's funeral was more like a celebration of life because of the fact that Joe accomplished whatever he set his mind to do. He lived a very full and passionate life. He was an absolute success in every sense of the word: relationships, friends, career, family, and business. I love and miss Papa Joe so much, and I trust that he rests in peace.

Though Grandpa Joe was not religious, he was very much a Christian man from the way he showed love towards all. He was so slow to get angry over anything, and he was always helping those in need, like in the book of Proverbs: "The fruit of the righteous is a tree of life, and he who wins souls is wise" (Proverbs 11:30). Well, Grandpa Joe was married only once in his lifetime; so I guess you could say that he won Grandma Phyllis's heart and soul from the very start. He was the definition of wise in his actions. He didn't have to say a thing; you knew by the way he operated that Joe was a great, decent, solid man. Because my grandma loved Joe so much, that love she had for him made him shine.

My grandpa was healthier than your average teenager when he passed away from old age. The doctors always commented on how healthy he was, even in his old age. The Bible states in 1 Corinthians 6:9-10 that the unrighteous, talking about fornicators, adulterers, and drunkards, will not go to heaven. Well, Joe married my grandma in his early twenties and never smoked in his life, nor did I ever actually see him drunk. He would have a glass of wine here and there, but who doesn't? He never idolized anything, and he was biblical, even though he wasn't religious. Joe stood for love, patience, tenderness, dedication, and hard work. Once again, in the book of Proverbs, there's Grandpa Joe: "The soul of the sluggard craves and gets nothing, but the soul of the diligent is made fat" (Proverbs 13:4). Well not only was my grandpa's soul rich because of his diligence in his work ethic, but he became a very wealthy man as well.

So growing up, believing in Joe was easy. He always did things in the right way and honorably. Joe was straight by the book. He always paid his taxes on time, and he always showed great character when under any type of irregular circumstance. I always believed in this creed: have faith in Papa Joe and do as Papa Joe would do, and you'll be okay. I believed that Grandpa Joe was a Christian man without even understanding Scripture or Christianity in its purest form. He didn't even know Christ, but his actions to a T biblically crowned him a righteous, Christian man without his even realizing it. He was the closest thing I knew to Jesus Christ, just by his actions. Although he never even would think about opening a Bible for guidance or direction, he intuitively knew right from wrong and good from bad. Sometimes I think about whether or not Papa Joe got to heaven without even really knowing Christ. I know what the

Bible says about being saved in order to receive eternal life in Christ Jesus. I also know what every Christian brother of mine would tell me if I asked him from a biblical standpoint whether or not he believed that Papa Joe is in heaven. I'm okay; I'll find out one day.

For me, not being a Christian throughout high school left me to choose a belief either in my grandpa and the way he went about his choice making or in my own ability to buckle down and fly straight. Most of the time, I was a bird with a broken limb, spiraling downward. But I was so determined to graduate my senior year that I barely went out at all. I was still doing my drug tests for probation, but I still had those pills to clean out my system. I was home right after school doing my homework every night. I was staying up really late some nights just to finish extra work. Something inside of me clicked. I was sick and tired of being sick and tired, I suppose. At school, I was in class, completing assignments, taking tests, and participating regularly. I was getting student of the month awards in all my classes and completing all my assignments on time. I started to feel a sense of worth and really started to become quite positive on my outlook for my future. I was finishing credits so fast that I knew, if I kept up this type of behavior, graduation was in my grasp for sure.

At the time, Casey was in high school also. He was also attending Rancho with me. We were living together at Grandma Ginny's, and we had a really close relationship. I certainly was hurt when I found out that, the first time he got high, I smoked him out. I was just keeping the tradition going. But now, being the older brother and attending the same school as he did encouraged me to work hard and set the example. For the first time since elementary school, Casey and I were once again compadres at school.

Casey struggled with school about as badly as I did, if not worse. He had attention deficit disorder, which prevented him from excelling in his studies from young age. Though

I'm no doctor, I felt that, as he was diagnosed as ADD-ADHD before he was a teenager, we Mullenaux men all have a little bit of both of these disorders in all of us. The doctors put Casey on all sorts of different medications for his diagnosed situation. One of the drugs they were prescribing him was this drug called Dexedrine. Well, all Dexedrine was to me was a pure amphetamine: speed, but better and about fifty times stronger than anything you could ever get on the streets, for sure. When I found out that the doctors were giving my little brother drugs to remedy his deficiency, I was shocked. No wonder Casey was always depressed and irritable on a daily basis.

I started using Casey's Dexedrine to stay up late sometimes and finish my school work. One night I used a lot, way too much, and I was snorting it, too. The drug made me so focused on my work that I was staring at the paper very intensely for hours on end. My eyes then crossed, just like you would make them crossed on your own, but they felt stuck that way. Literally, I couldn't see straight for maybe an hour, no joke. The situation was actually scary. I remembered all those nights when I used to smoke weed and snort speed. But my drug use did not leave me cross-eyed like this, nor did it produce an even remotely close high. I had no control of my eyes, and they stayed crossed. My dilemma scared the life out of me. I was seriously scared from the beginning of when my eyes crossed to an hour later, when I started to come back to reality. As the Dexedrine wore off, my eyes slowly came back to normal, and so did I. What a relief!

Though I wasn't staying with Grandma Phyllis and Papa Joe anymore, they knew I was doing well in my studies, and even though I had lied to them, stolen from them, and betrayed them in the past time and time again, they were always very forgiving. There you go: Papa Joe with that forgiving heart of his. Papa Joe bought me a car my senior year. It was a 1991 Lexus ES 250 that was super clean, inside and out. He actually bought it from Mrs. Wachs' brother. It was in really good condition, and I was very thankful for it. I really couldn't believe that, after everything I had gone through with my grandparents, they were still willing to help me out, as were the Wachs, a generosity which tripped me out. I was so problematic that I'd cost my grandparents friendships in the neighborhood and a lot of time and money, not to mention stress and agony.

During the Los Angeles riots, Reginald Denny, a white man, drove a semi truck through the middle of the LA riots when they were fully raging, a decision which ended up being very bad timing for that poor man. He just happened to be in the wrong place at the wrong time. The riots were out of control when Reginald got caught up in the mix; a few black men dragged him out of his truck at a signal and started kicking and hitting him relentlessly. All of the sudden, a black man who had a brick in his hand came running at Reginald full speed while Reginald was helpless on the ground, beaten profusely. The man threw the brick right at Reginald's face. Miraculously, the brick didn't kill Reginald. I remember seeing the incident on TV when I was really young and just thinking to myself: *What is going on?*

Later on in my senior year, Grandma Phyllis went to a seminar on plastic surgery with Papa Joe. The doctor doing the seminar, whose name was Dr. Toffel, was a very well-known and highly respected plastic surgeon throughout the Los Angeles region. Well anyway, Dr. Toffel, the doctor who fixed Reginald's face, was the doctor giving the seminar, and my grandparents hired the same doctor to do reconstructive surgery on my nose. He was the softest spoken man I have ever met, and I liked him with a tremendous amount of respect. The procedure wasn't cheap, but Grandma Phyllis didn't mind paying. She wanted to get my nose fixed properly. She wanted to pay a good doctor to do the surgery, and she knew that Dr. Toffel was fit for the job. I could see why everyone liked him. Of all the times I've been to the hospital to see doctors, hands down Dr. Toffel was a nicest doctor of them all, just a real genuine guy. He did a complete rhinoplasty procedure on my nose, along with cleaning my deviated septum, which had given me problems for years. After my surgery, I could breathe better than I had ever breathed before, and the nose also looked perfectly normal once again. I was very impressed with the work of Dr. Toffel and his crew on repairing my nose back to normal.

I hadn't really noticed how self-conscious having my nose broken made me. My confidence came back, too. I missed a few days of school due to my surgery, but not too much. I kept hammering away at my studies, and I remember having the most credits completed in the whole school when Christmas break came around. I was doing very well without the help of anyone. I was getting respect back from my family and also feeling pretty good about myself. Things were looking up, and all from my making a choice to smarten up, start putting one foot in front of the other, and behave like a mature grown up. I chose that time to become a real man and to put aside the baby bottles.

During spring break of my senior year, I and a few friends went down to party and hang out at the house of this girlfriend of ours, Janis N. Most of my good friends were older than me and had graduated the year before I did: Keon, Nyman, C. Morgan, all those clowns. They attended colleges out of town. They came home for spring break, and seeing all of them whenever we got together was really good. That night, I was the designated driver for everyone because I was actually trying to be somewhat responsible at this point in my life. Remember, I'd brought myself to a crossroads around then and committed to myself to grow up and start making better choices. I remember having one beer that night; I was actually being very obedient in not getting wasted.

We were all having a great time drinking, playing pool, and throwing darts. The night ended pretty fast; so we began to round up the crew and cruise. When the time came to go, I loaded my car with everyone who needed rides home. Around this time, Grandma Phyllis had just bought my dad a beautiful, half-million-dollar, two-bedroom, two-bath condo in Rancho Palos Verdes. The place was gorgeous. After leaving Janis's place, the plan was to head over to my dad Scott's, party for a few more hours, and maybe have a few of the boys crash there as well. That was the plan.

Well, our trip was cut short that night when an LAPD cruiser pulled up behind me. The night was pretty late, but I was driving slowly and safely. My car was at capacity. I had current tags; I also believe that my insurance was legit that night, too. LAPD pulled me over after following me for about a mile through Pedro on Western passing 9th Street. The officers lighted me up around Weymouth. They probably ran my plates and saw that I was on probation. They immediately suspected me of drinking. They had me step out of the car and perform a field sobriety test. I seriously had only one beer in my system from hours before. I passed the field sobriety test with flying colors, and the officers were actually both in agreement to let me go with only a tinted windows ticket if, after they ran my name for warrants, everything was to come up clean.

The officers ran my name, and this skateboarding ticket that I had not paid in the past had gone to warrant and come back to haunt me. So the police were going to have to take me in, seeing that I was still a minor driving with alcohol on my breath, and book me on a DUI and a failure to appear on my skateboarding ticket warrant. That stop was just my luck. I felt inside my heart that I was actually straightening up and making better choices, maturing and growing in a sense, when all of a sudden here I was back to roots and dirt.

The arrest was a violation of my probation as well. I was so bummed out.

The cops that night were actually really cool, and they felt badly about my situation. But I guess they just felt that they were doing their job. Instead of impounding my car, though, which they were obligated to do that night as my circumstance permitted, they agreed to let everybody walk home at 2:30 AM in the middle of Pedro, leaving my car on the side of the street for someone to get in the morning. They told my friends to make sure that car did not leave that spot and assured them that, if it did, they were all going to get busted and face the consequences. Well, Keon and the few of the chicks that were with me that night pretended to walk away from the car, but as soon as the cops left the scene and were far enough out of sight, Keon drove my car back to my dad's and parked it for me.

That year was actually the year of my eighteenth birthday; so I was now tried legally as an adult. The authorities ended up booking me on DUI charges and sending me to the LA County men's jail facility for the first time in my life. Basically, they processed me in and released me within two days. I remember that, on my way to be released, the officer scanning my wristband looked at me, and looking back at my wristband, he said, "Mullen-X, how old are you?" I said, "Eighteen." He said, "What are you in for?" I told him DUI. He asked if I ever had been locked up before. I told him only in juvenile hall. He looked at me and said, "You'll be back; I guarantee."

Those words haunted me from then on. That men's jail was a nightmare. Because I was in violation of my probation once again for coming into contact with a peace officer as an adult, the state reinstated my probation on the same felony terms and conditions, only for some reason, now I didn't have any more drug testing. Stoked! No more drug testing was awesome. I was definitely happy about that change. All I had to do now was just check in with my probation officer once a month to prove my progress and pay my fine down on a monthly basis. When I got out of jail, spring break was coming to an end. School was about to be back in session, a time that meant no more messing around. Back to the books I was.

As soon as school started, I was on it. I really wanted to graduate with my class more than anything. I cracked the books open and was off to the races. I was getting high, but I was completing my work still. I was doing semesters of work in a couple of weeks or so. No one besides Casey and my grandma really saw me the last few months of my senior year. I was not going to end up a few classes behind on graduation day, for sure.

June came fast, and I was lacking two classes: history and math. I had made up over a hundred credits, but I was still falling short. The fact that I'd just accomplished a year and a half of work in only about seven or eight months didn't matter at the end, when I was one or two classes short. Now, if you're one class short, you can still graduate with the class; you just have to finish your last class that summer in summer school, which was an option the school gave us.

I knew I had all my classes done except history, and I had already made arrangements for summer school prior to graduation day. I completed one hundred thirty credits that year. You needed two hundred twenty-five credits to graduate, and I finished with two hundred thirty-five actual credits, even though I was lacking in history. Somehow, earlier in high school, I had completed two extra semesters of PE; so I actually finished with extra credits, only lacking one history class.

Graduation day came, and I needed to walk with my class in the ceremony, no matter what. I didn't do all that work for nothing. I knew I had finished my math class they mentioned I was lacking. The math teacher, Mr. Gold, got my little brother and me confused and forgot to make proper corrections on his paperwork indicating that Cody, not Casey, had finished his Algebra 1 class. That kind of mix-up was just my luck. But the mistake came to light, and the principal gave me a cap and gown. By the hairs on my chinny-chin-chin, I scraped by and was able to graduate high school. I was so happy that I'd finished. All this super hard work seemed to have paid off, and I felt a huge sense of accomplishment from inside of me come over my whole body.

Later that summer, I attended summer school, took the credits of my completed history course up to Rancho, and got my diploma, which was waiting for me in the office. That day was one of the best days of my life as a teenager for sure, because up until then, nothing but drama and chaos seemed to be occurring regularly. Experiencing something positive and healthy in my life for a change was a good feeling. It was about time, anyway, that I applied myself successfully, and I had succeeded at the task at hand. I'd challenged myself. Accomplishing a goal I'd set forth felt good. After that experience, I noticed that I am very goal oriented, and that self-knowledge gave me motivation inside to accomplish more and more goals as I grew older. If I acknowledged something I wanted to accomplish and set it as a goal, I usually completed it. Achievement started to become just that simple.

But that summer was a pretty reckless and out-of-control summer. I remember right out of high school my first months of being a graduate, cruising with Chris, Keon, and my boy Christian out to Costa Mesa where my buddy Nick was living at the time.

At Halloween, we left Nick's place and headed out to a party. Besides Chris and me not having a costume, Keon and Christian were a pumpkin and a vampire: stupid. We rolled up to this Halloween party in Long Beach where we didn't exactly know many of the people, just one of the girls and maybe a couple of the guys. We were so belligerent upon entering the house that evening that I can't believe that they let us in. We brought with us a plastic handle of Popov vodka, which we finished in like twenty minutes between the four of us upon cruising into the party.

Chris was trying to hit on some dude's girl while he was completely hammered, and he got a right hook that cut his eye open and left him dazed and bleeding all over the place. Keon came up to me while I was at the DJ table just trying to have the DJ put on some decent music, because whatever they were playing wasn't cutting it with me. I was standing there with this handle of Popov, which was empty by this time. Although I was drunk, I always had my friends' backs regardless of the situation. I treated my friends like I treat my family, and I expected them to have the same outlook as I do.

Here came Keon all aggressively towards me, telling me what had just happened to Chris. Without hesitation, I said, "Who?" I was hammered. Keon pointed out some dude that was for sure twice my size, but back then, everyone was bigger than I was. I immediately ran through the crowd of partiers with the bottle still in my hand but empty, came right up to the guy, and swung the bottle right at him. Being so intoxicated, I completely missed the guy. I was simultaneously falling but trying to grab onto his leg and take him to the ground to mount him or something. Actually, I didn't really have any type of plan upon hitting him; I just hoped that he would go down and that my boys were going to get my back, I guess.

After I completely missed this guy, all of a sudden, I started getting jumped from every angle by what at the time seemed to be about four or five different guys. The funny thing was that, as I stood up, I didn't have a scratch on me, and right away I started laughing and talking trash to these clowns for not doing anything to me.

The whole party was now spread around my friends and me as we grouped up and challenged these clowns to a straight up backyard brawl. The owner of the house then came out and ordered us to leave. We reluctantly left upon the owner's request, but upon arriving at Keon's car about to split from the scene, Chris was bleeding so badly that we thought: *Nah, we're not leaving like this.* I remember being in the car and Keon popping the truck, saying, "Grab your boards; we're going back in there."

We all jumped out, grabbed our boards, and ran back into this party like a bunch of monkeys. *Here we go!* I thought. We entered the back yard with energy, lots of energy! We were determined to let these clowns know what was really up and that, if we wanted to take their girls home with us, we would do just that.

I ran over to some kid, cocked my skateboard back, and swung it as hard as I could at him. My board flew out of my hands, and the grip from my board took off the top portion of skin from my thumbs. My target used his girlfriend as a shield; I guess he thought that I wasn't going to hit him while he was with his girl for some reason. Well, he didn't realize how drunk I was. I couldn't have cared less at this point who I hit; I just wanted to back up my buddy Chris at the time and not get thrown out of some silly Torrance party that was going on in Long Beach.

I scattered over to my board. Meanwhile, behind me Keon, Chris, and Christian were going to town on these kids. Keon was always known for the one-hitter quitter; even still to this day he packs a mean punch. Somehow I got in a head-lock face down on the grass before getting to my board. I remember yelling for Keon to help me out if he could hear me. I was in such a tight headlock that I couldn't get loose for the life of me. All of a sudden, I felt my assailant's arms go completely limp. Keon knocked this kid out cold while he had me face down; he heard my cry for help and came through, just as I was expecting him to do. I jumped up and ran over to my skateboard.

At this point, these kids backed off. They'd had enough. The whole party had scattered inside and was looking through the blinds at us throwing down in the back yard. We were done; we got revenge. The other guys didn't want any more; so we slowly started to cruise. Upon leaving, I saw in that backyard a plastic table full of drinks, chips, salsa, and paper plates, stuff like that. I flipped the whole table over and at the same time told those punks what was up! My friends and I straight handled a whole party of guys, just the four of us, and we went home laughing, except for Chris. He was crying and bleeding even more than before we got in the car to leave the first time. I guess he got popped pretty badly again; we had to take him home.

That summer again, I was partying with this chick from Palos Verdes that I didn't really know well; I just knew her through friends of friends. We'll just call her Hoots. I passed out at her house on a Friday evening and woke up next to her; we slowly rose and started our day like any other normal Saturday. This weekend, her folks were out of town, and she told me that, if I wanted to call up some of my friends, she wanted to have a party at her place. She wanted my friends to come. Having a party with all of my friends was a horrible idea on her part.

I did just as she asked, but as soon as that evening came, she was sorry she'd ever asked me to throw a party at her place. I was just starting to party when all of a sudden my buddy Wezel shows up with half the Harbor football team, a DJ, and like twenty other dudes all from Carson, Torrance, and other bordering cities. Hoots started tripping out. The party was cool; everyone was having a great time. But the fun started to get too overwhelming for her really fast, I think.

A few hours later, she approached me as I was drinking her wine straight out of the box I had found in her fridge upstairs. By this time, I had already drunk half of bottle of whisky and was super drunk. She approached me very rudely, blamed me like the party was my fault, and said that she needed everyone out. She ordered me to be in charge of kicking everyone out. I said, "Uh-uh, no way, Jose; you're the one that encouraged me to round up people and get a party started. How stupid would I look now telling everybody they have to go? No, I'm not doing it."

She got really mad, left the room for a minute, came back, and again started to plead with me to get everyone out! As I started to reply with the same answer, just as I started to open my mouth, out of nowhere Hoots broke out a can of mace or pepper spray and fired a direct shot clean and clear in both of my eyes at point-blank rage. I was on the verge of passing out at this point when she sprayed me. But as soon as that stuff was in my eyes (I kid you not), I went from drunk to sober almost instantly. The spray seriously woke me right up.

Because I could barely see at this point, Hoots tried to run from me. Squinting my eyes, I ran after her, grabbed her by her hair, and threw her into her pool in front of the whole party. At the same time, I started pushing anything in my way into the pool: planters, chairs, and people. That spray was the worst pain I have ever experienced, and I was no stranger to pain.

I took my shirt off, and at this time I was working out and getting in shape for the first time in my life. I guess you could say that I was pretty swelled up. I ran outside and couldn't for the life of me see anything clearly. All I could hear were voices and a lot of commotion. I exited the side gate and began throwing trash can after trash can over the gate into the party and into the pool. I was like a bull at a rodeo, basically as if something was causing me to act out in rage. I was relentless in revenge. Besides, she'd told me to have the party. I was so mad that I can't even describe my state of mind at this point.

My good buddy Wezel came up to me with his arm in a sling because he'd just had surgery on his shoulder a few weeks prior. I didn't know one person from the next; I couldn't see anything. I cracked him in the face out of rage, not knowing who he was. Right away, one of his good friends from the football team gave me a good, solid right, straight across my chin, which probably would have knocked me out had I not been on an adrenaline rage.

I guess that Hoots didn't know how to swim; so people were jumping in to save her. Everyone I knew wanted to calm me down. My friends went inside to get some milk and ice cream to put in my eyes to help reduce the pain temporarily. I couldn't believe that Hoots was the cause of all this pain and confusion. I didn't really get it. She was the one that wanted to have a party at her folks' home that weekend; I was just going along with her wishes. Trust me; I had really calmed down at this point in my partying and could have cared less whether or not my friends and I were partying that night or not. The next morning, I woke up with a little hangover, nothing too serious, and my eyes were perfectly normal. I had to thank God, because that spray was seriously one of the worst feelings in terms of physical pain that I have ever felt to this day.

I worked all year at the Hollywood Bowl. Management had changed; so a lot of the people that originally worked there were gone. The new manager came in and started changing everything around the way he thought it should be; someone should have told him the old rule: if it's not broke, don't fix it. He lost a lot of good workers with his controlling approach towards all of our servers. That year ended up being my and Hayley's last year at the Bowl.

When summer ended, the time had come for college. I attended Los Angeles Harbor College in Wilmington, California for my first semester. Although school is for some people, it just wasn't for me. I guess you could say that I'm more hands-on and visual, if you will. I basically just stopped going to class. I once again started to lose motivation, and I lost the forward momentum that I'd had at one point.

Casey and I were staying at my dad's new condo with him now, thanks to Grandma Phyllis. Things started getting pretty out of control once again very, very quickly. Casey and I were pretty much just having parties at our new place a few times a week. People were over continually. As Casey and I grew older, my dad never wanted to play the father figure; he would rather have just been our buddy. Scott wanted to hang out and be involved more or less in what we were doing opposed to what we should have been doing. Casey and I thought that arrangement was great. Scott would smoke weed and drink and party with us most the time. All of our friends thought our dad was coolest dad around because he let us do whatever we wanted to do. When we weren't around, our friends would just show up to hang out with Scott, smoke weed with him, chill, and basically treat him like our friends treated us. Scott pretty much became one of us, one of the boys.

My grandma paid Scott's mortgage every month as well as his utilities, and she bought the food in the fridge on a weekly basis. Scott's insurance, registration, and gas for his car, anything you could think of, were handed to him on a golden platter. Although I love my dad very much, I have been able to bear witness to very little progress in his life over the past twenty years. He still depends entirely on my grandma for everything, although she has little left to give. He still has no job and no goals; he just hangs out with his dog and his habits in the condo. Scott was in his fifties at this point, but my grandma claimed that Scott was a basket case. I realized as I grew up that Scott wasn't a basket case at all; my grandma was a control freak. Everything was either her way or the highway, seriously. And her support made doing nothing really easy for Casey and me, too.

Even though I can admit that I got Casey high off pot his first time ever, I figured that, if he was going to do weed, he might as well do it with his older brother in a controlled environment. I specifically told him that day that, if he ever got involved with any other controlled substances besides marijuana, he was going to have to hear from me. I made that line very clear to him early on. I went through that addiction, and nothing good came from it. I just didn't want to see him fail in the same manner his older brother had. Regardless of what I did or what I thought, Casey was going to do whatever he pleased. Casey ended up in juvenile hall, and the courts sent him to camp in Malibu for a six-month stay.

As Casey grew up, he wanted to do his own thing, and he started experimenting with different types of drugs and hanging out with the wrong crowd. Casey started hanging out with these kids from San Pedro, pretty much out-of-control, troubled kids with broken homes, to say the least. San Pedro kids and Palos Verdes kids, though we lived in bordering cities, never really got along for years and years. These San Pedro kids took a liking to Casey and me because we weren't like your normal Palos Verdes kids; they saw us as troubled kids, just like they were. I guess they felt that they could relate to us. We kind of formed an alliance with the San Pedro kids, who became our good buddies.

This kid Info always thought that he was so tight. He had tattoos everywhere, and he had this certain type of demeanor like he was better than you. Kids in Palos Verdes never carried themselves that way, and the type of image these kids portrayed was interesting. They really tried to portray some type of big shot, when most these kids had houses the size of my bedroom. They were a trip. Casey became good friends with one of Info's best friends, Danny B. God bless his soul, and may he rest in peace! And from then on, we pretty much partied every weekend. We started getting high every day.

Eventually things escalated, and we started getting into bigger and better drugs and robbing houses to pay for them.

Casey got arrested for residential burglary when he was under the age of eighteen. He went to camp for six months and got out. I felt that his attitude was worse after camp than it was when he got sentenced. He basically got out and went straight back to these no-good friends of his, and the vicious circle started right over. A few months or maybe a year or so later, he got arrested for grand theft property over four hundred dollars. That charge was a felony and a violation of his probation. He ended up in the LA County jail, the men's facility, just like I had at about the same age.

Casey was really always more of a knucklehead or numbskull than I was. I seemed to learn from my mistakes. When you put your hand over a hot surface and get burned, you find out really quickly that heat hurts you badly, and you don't want to get hurt anymore. I would get locked up and have remorse. I would get out with intentions of never going back again. But jail never fazed Casey in the same way that it would faze me. His type of mentality basically seemed to be that he just had some dirt on his shoulder, and he brushed it off.

But my little brother Casey and I are very similar in many ways. We both graduated from the same high school, and we both had most of the same friends growing up. He is somewhat athletic, and he has a very genuine heart and is absolutely one of the most caring kids I know. He struggles with the same things I do, such as having an addictive personality that succumbs to drugs, alcohol, lying, cheating, and stealing. Though I was able to find a solution to my character defects by getting sober and coming to God, Casey has not yet found that path. He is such a great kid at heart, but he doesn't have any tools to use to help him with his issues.

Right now, Casey is actually doing time up North for a little mishap he got himself into last October, but I am very confident that he will come out the other end of his wild days as I did. I'll be here to give him love, direction, and really lead by my actions in hopes that he will come to his senses and smarten up so that he can find sobriety, God, and some type of power greater than himself. His path to success is absolutely attainable, whether he feels that it is or not. I hope that, when he gets released this October 2009, he will have a plan and a direction that he is willing to seek on his own as well as the motivation to achieve anything he puts his mind towards. The kid is a good kid, just a lost soul with no direction from a young age. Now, being an adult, he is really feeling the wrath of a dysfunctional family.

Holy Rap Sheet, Batman;
It's Another Felony!

In the beginning of December 2002 when Casey was gone for six months, I started hanging out with his buddies, as they would be around a lot at my dad's getting high. We had formed a pretty good friendship throughout a few years of partying and running amok together.

I was always pretty good with credit cards, and I knew how to use ones that weren't mine for making fraudulent transactions. Buying stuff on the Internet or simply going to the mall and going on shopping sprees seemed to be my MO. I got Info involved one night around Christmas time.

We were broke, and being those stoners and knuckle-heads that we were, we tried to figure out how we could come up with some money for the holidays so that we could get high and have a good Christmas, because none of us worked legit jobs. Info would cruise over late at night, and we would go up into Palos Verdes from San Pedro and pull up next to houses which looked like either the family inside was sleeping or was not home at all. We would break into cars and steal purses, wallets, etc.

As it was around Christmas time, a few of the cars we robbed had Christmas presents. We stole one guy's wallet out of his car in the middle of the night, and the picture on his license just so happened to look just like Info. We scored. We had five credit cards, gas cards, and an American Express card. The guy was definitely wealthy; he must've been a doctor or some type of real estate agent or maybe an attorney. We literally took the ID and credit cards and headed straight to the mall. This Christmas, the malls were packed, and people were buying large quantities of merchandise. Our behavior seemed quite normal at that point, I suppose. The heist was almost too easy.

Once we hit the mall, we began buying anything and everything we wanted: clothes, video games, CDs, DVD players, jewelry, videogame consoles, huge boom boxes, and anything else you can imagine. We never got questioned on the credit cards or the ID because Info matched the guy on the ID. What we did just seemed like normal, last-minute shopping. That night (I kid you not), we filled my car with so much merchandise that we had to call my buddy Keon to come down and pick up Info because the trunk, backseat, and passenger seats of my car were full of the clothes and merchandise we had just purchased. We actually had bags of things, all brand names and brand new, piled to my driver's side, making driving safely hard for me. We actually had to throw stuff out of the trunk and leave it in the parking lot of the shopping center, stuff we didn't want that we had actually stolen days before from garages or cars.

That theft was the biggest rush; we probably spent ten thousand dollars in a matter of maybe two hours, maybe even less. As I was driving home, I remember checking my rearview mirror every two seconds for cops. I was tripping out the whole ride home by myself with a car full of stolen products. If a cop were to pull me over, I would have been so done. I was on probation at this point; so I was definitely nervous. But eventually I ended up getting home safely.

We got to my dad's condo, unloaded the car, and separated all the goods between us. We looked like we'd just come home from winning a shopping spree or a game show. I could just hear in the background: "Cody Mullenaux, you're the next contestant on *The Price Is Right*; come on down." Then you would just see me come running down the aisle all stoked. But I didn't have to guess any numbers or wait in any crazy lines; no, I just walked in, got exactly what I wanted, and walked out. That was it.

This was the type of action I was choosing at the cost of innocent people. No wonder my baby brother was locked up for similar behavior. I told you how I was either a good or bad influence; well, go figure. I tell you this story because I think that understanding the type of behavior that drugs cause you to do is very important for people. Drugs make you become selfish, self-seeking, and dishonest, and most of all, addiction makes you slowly lose your sanity or regards for yourself or anyone around you. The world is all about you, you, you. If you're going to benefit at the cost of some-body else, that choice is a no-brainer for a drug addict-alco-holic. If you're a drug addict, all you're interested in is what you want, when you want it or need it, and how you're going to get it. That's it. You never think about anyone else, plain and simple. Making this point is important to me.

Our success that night with a credit card scam was a boost to our confidence in fraudulent transactions. Like I said, the scam was too easy. We continued to terrorize Palos Verdes as Christmas was drawing even closer. Here we were about a week or so later, and Info and I were back. We didn't get caught; no one even knew the type of stuff we were doing. We kept our activities pretty low-key.

One night when Info was driving, we stopped outside this house behind the gates in the middle of the night. He hopped out and saw a purse in the passenger's seat of this SUV. The doors were unlocked, and he grabbed the purse. Off we went to fill up our gas tank and get some bud (weed). Only fifty bucks in cash was in the purse along with the gas card. We proceeded to the nearest gas station, filled the tank with gas, and bought as much junk food as we could from the gas station mini-market as well: another successful mission completed.

But Info for some reason left the purse from the SUV in my car accidentally, and somehow I never noticed it. Later that week, I picked him up to smoke some weed, just chill, maybe try to pick up some chicks or just get a few forties (bottles of liquor), and lay low at my dad's, our usual program. So I remember noticing the purse that day as I picked him up. Right then and there, we tossed it. Upon getting rid of the purse, Info dropped a business card down the seat of my car, a mistake which ultimately led to my getting arrested on December 18, 2002 and charged with grand theft personal property over four hundred dollars, just like Casey.

I was with my friend, Joking, which was seriously his name: Joe King. We just called him Joking. We headed out to Santa Monica because my buddy Christian was selling weed at the time. I called Christian and told him that I needed an ounce. An ounce typically runs about three hundred dollars. As I'd grown up with Christian and we were tight buddies, the weed ended up costing somewhere around two hundred fifty dollars for us. Christian was my boy; so he told us no problem.

He was on his way to work that day, and so we ended up meeting him near the Fox Hills Mall right off the 405 and the 90 freeway for the exchange. For me, the location was cool, because it was a little closer than Santa Monica, where Christian was staying at the time and where we usually rigged from him. I didn't even have a license at the time. Because of my DUI, the state had revoked my license for a year, but I still drove everywhere. Who was going to stop me? I was back in the whatever mode, which meant that, no matter what anyone wanted me to do, I did whatever I wanted to do just to go against the grain. Law, family, teachers, whatever: nothing mattered!

We went there, got the weed, and proceeded to head back home. On the way home, we hit a little bit of traffic. Joe was in a hurry to get home that night, and he kept rushing me from the moment we left to go get the weed. Joe wouldn't shut up about having to be home at 5 PM, because he had plans with his folks, and he insisted that I hurry and get him home. We finally got back to the neighborhood a little before five. I was speeding to get Joe home, but before I dropped him off, the plan was to smoke somewhere. Besides, I didn't take him all the way out and hook him up with a good deal on some good chronic not to get broken off even a little bit; that share was part of the whole plan.

I was approaching a main intersection after exiting the freeway near Joe's house, and I was definitely speeding. I was approximately fifty yards out when the light turned yellow, but I gunned the engine to get through the yellow light instead of slamming on the brakes. I was already committed not to stop because of how fast I was going. The light was definitely solid red as I flew through the traffic signal, maintaining a speed of more than seventy miles an hour. Joe's house was only about a mile and a half away at this point.

As fate would have it, I didn't see him, but I guess that, as I flew through the intersection, a police officer was on the opposite intersection. He watched me speed through the red light. I didn't even see him behind me at all for at least a minute after running the red light, a fact which would've meant that I was a mile from the signal at this point because of my speed. The officer thought that I was evading and that I'd actually seen him, a false assumption. He lit me up right before Joe's street, actually somewhat near my house.

The cop was very angry at how fast and erratic I was driving. I didn't really even care or think about anything at that time but being able to smoke some weed and get that head change I so sought on a daily basis from an early, early age. Everything else was minimal to me when I had my mind set on something. Usually at this point in my life, my mind was always set on things that would harm or affect my life in a negative way. When he came to my window, the cop got more even upset to find out that I didn't have a license, insurance, or current registration on the car I was driving, which happened to be my dad's. The fact that I was on felony probation at the time he ran my license didn't add to his good humor, either.

Once he found out about my probation, he was obligated to search the entire vehicle as part of the terms of my probation. Unbelievably, he didn't find the ounce of weed in Joking's crotch, but what he did find was a business card from one of the residents whose house we had burglarized a week prior. Info must've accidently left some evidence under the passenger seat of my dad's car when we tossed the purse just days prior: bozo.

I didn't care that all the crap I was doing needed to come to a halt at some time or another, and I wasn't going to be the one to tap out and say, "Hey, I've got a problem; I need help." No, I was going to need something of this caliber to get my attention and really smarten me up. I always seemed to be getting busted at the expense of other people. Don't get me wrong. I'm always involved in what I do wrong and always have a hand in it, but I have an unusual inability to cruise under the radar, with friends or not. Someone would go through my backpack when that knife was in it or leave a business card in my car for me to get popped, but I always set myself up.

The name on the business card matched the lady's name whose purse we had stolen. At that point, the woman had already filed a report at the Lomita Sheriff's Department that her purse was missing and that her car had been burglarized. The rookie deputy that day must've looked like a real hero when he found one little business card and questioned me about it. Either I couldn't come up with a quick enough lie or whatever lie I gave him wasn't really matching up or making sense; so he put two and two together. Here I was, going to jail again.

I wasn't a very good criminal, and I knew I was guilty. I felt convicted that night to be honest inside the interrogation rooms, and that tactic never gave me a good court case, because I never utilized my fifth amendment. Everything I did, I admitted, and I always took the blame for my actions when I got caught. I never placed blame elsewhere, because I didn't need to get off. I needed the help.

The police booked me on felony receiving stolen property, driving on a suspended license, and violating my probation once again. I was headed back to the county jail. This arrest occurred around Christmas 2002, a week before my twentieth birthday. The police took Joe with me, because he had a warrant for an unpaid ticket, and that ticket really came back to haunt him. When we got to the police station, as a normal procedure the officers searched us once again before throwing us into any cell. This time, unfortunately, they found Joking's weed in his crotch. They ticketed him and gave him a misdemeanor for possession of marijuana, and later on that night he was released to his mom.

For me, things weren't looking too good; once again, I had come back to the big house, just like the sheriff had predicted. The judge gave me ninety days of county jail time, restitution to be paid in full to the victim, and three more years of reinstated probation from the day of my release forward. I got arrested on December 18, when my twentieth birthday was five days away. I spent my birthday, Christmas, New Year's Day, and even Super Bowl Sunday in jail.

I used to be really addicted to smoking cigarettes before I got arrested this last time. I would smoke a pack a day at the least. The day before I got arrested, I'd probably smoked a whole pack before 7 PM. When I got to jail, I wanted a cigarette so badly, but I couldn't have one. This time, I was actually doing some considerably decent jail time. Five days went by, and I was coughing up phlegm and black stuff. I made a commitment to myself on my twentieth birthday that, from that day forward, I would indulge in no more drugs, no more cigarettes, and no more adolescent mishaps.

Now was the time to grow up, mature, be responsible, and stop leading the life my parents chose. I was over that life. I was only twenty years old, and all I knew how to do was smoke weed, steal cars, lie, use women, and create havoc amongst family and friends. I looked as if I was going to be just like my mom and dad. I was so depressed this time around that I was determined to change when I got out. Inside the county, I did a lot of writing and reading for those ninety days. I made a conscious decision that, if I didn't want to come back to jail, I would have to change all of my actions, every single one of them. If I used to put on my shoes in the morning on my right side first, from that day forward I was going start putting my left shoe on first, and that was that.

During that few months I did in jail, I met a very knowledgeable, elderly man from the Middle East. I remember waking up one morning to somebody arguing in the day room over a newspaper. In the county, some guys always think that they can run things. In this case, I was for some reason boarding in the medical unit, where the blacks were in charge, even though all races, blacks, whites, Hispanics, and Asians, were all together in the same module. Usually the paper came at about 4:30 AM, and each module got one paper. The blacks usually had access to it first. Then, throughout the afternoon and evening, the paper would get passed around the module, and eventually you'd be able to get up to date on the recent news.

But this one morning, new fish had arrived. Fish were the guys who were just in, the new guys; so they didn't really know the rules of the module. You didn't want to break the rules and create conflict amongst your comfort zone, which we all shared. This little Middle Eastern man didn't even care. I was sleeping when I heard the commotion coming from the day room. I was a little edgy and nervous about altercations. I just stayed in my bed. From what I could hear, somebody had taken the newspaper first that morning, and the offender just happened to be one of the new fish. Although I know that not all black people are the same, the black men in my module were extremely loud, rude, animated, and somewhat obnoxious. The newspaper was missing, and one of the leaders of the black guys was raging. The Middle Eastern man was up before anyone because the fish arrived at the module around 3 AM. Not knowing the rules, he'd taken the newspaper into his own cell and started reading it, not knowing that doing so could be detrimental to his safety.

Someone pointed out that the new fish had the paper and was reading it in his room, and the black man approached him as the Middle Eastern man stepped out of his room with the paper in his hand. Keep in mind that this new man was in his older sixties, probably a hundred fifteen pounds, and maybe five feet five at the most. The black man was well over six feet, a good two hundred fifty pounds at least, and had a very aggressive look about him. All I remember was loud arguing back and forth. You would think that the little man would have submitted and handed the paper over immediately, right? Well, he didn't; he didn't even flinch. He held his ground, and he didn't give the paper up. He actually was louder than the black man, and he wasn't going to back down.

Now as I was in my bed, I just remember hearing the commotion. And when I got up to hear the news of the new fish standing up to the black dude, which was the talk of the module in the morning, I was curious about this guy. When I saw him, I was very surprised to find out that this little man had so much courage and such a big heart. His bravery was very surprising to me, and I was very intrigued as to how that guy, being so small, acted so big in such a frightening time.

For the next month and a half, this man whom I'll call Hercules became my spiritual mentor and mental guidance instructor. He had so much wisdom and poise about him. He said that he was locked up for spouse abuse, but from his story, I came to believe that he was innocent. He said that this was the second time his wife had called the police on him and that she was actually the aggressor, although he was doing the time. After the whole O.J. thing, women had the upper hand on domestic altercations. Whether or not the male was innocent, the women always had the police's sympathy.

Hercules taught me a lot about myself. He taught me a lot about God, Jesus the Son, the Holy Spirit, meditation, the power of being quiet, and the ability to use your mind in ways we think are impossible as human beings. He explained to me that, after tapping into this source of power we have as humans mentally, nothing was out of our grasp. He taught me the benefits of prayer. He showed me that faith outside of myself would be crucial to my success, as someone with an addictive personality.

He told me a story about himself. Things seemed to be pretty rough for him at one point, being married, having kids, and struggling with a drinking problem. He had always been a spiritual man. Due to his drinking problem, he was losing his spirituality and losing his relationship with God. He explained to me that his drinking problems stemmed from the problems he was having at home with his wife, who was cheating on him regularly. He had hired someone to investigate, and he had actual evidence.

I barely knew this guy, but I felt very connected to him. Even though he was much older than I was, I felt like we had a lot in common. I shared every day with him. I started reading the Bible and praying at night. He broke the Scriptures down to me in a very plain and simple way. He made the Bible very easy for me to understand, and whether I understood it or not one hundred percent, I was still willing to try to learn and understand something outside of myself that was completely new to me. I would pray and meditate daily and nightly, just like he taught me. After less than a week or so, I began to feel empowered spiritually. Keep in mind that, before I even met Hercules, I hated God, if there was a God, and I didn't believe in any type of spiritual realm. This study with Hercules was actually my introduction to the spiritual world, along with an understanding of faith and the power of our minds.

Hercules said that he was a Christian man, although he was very convinced about meditation from a Middle Eastern perspective. He had a crazy way of meditation, yet he praised Jesus Christ as his Lord and Savior. He taught me how to close my eyes, get very quiet, and relax my whole being. Once I was in that state of mind and had a black consciousness, where everything around me was quiet, he encouraged me to go into the next step of meditation.

I'd make my limbs as heavy as boulders and would visualize my arms and legs sinking into a muddy surface. I would then visualize some type of cleansing liquid or light detoxifying my entire body. I liked to visualize orange juice or a citrusy type of fluid flowing throughout my whole body and taking away all the toxins that were in me. After a few weeks of doing this exercise, I could actually feel like my body was being cleansed internally. I would then imagine some type of release valves at the end of either my feet or my hands. With my mind, I would bring the fluids up and down my whole being two or three times, and once the cleansing fluid was towards the lower portion of my body, I would open the valves and release everything out of my body and into the atmosphere. Right at that point, I would fall into such a relaxed state of mind.

Then I would visualize something beautiful, something that made me feel at peace, something that made me happy or just comfortable. I would usually choose a beautiful flower, and I would visualize it right in front of my face. I could actually smell it, see the water dripping off the petals, and feel it tangibly. Sometimes I would also visualize a hummingbird flying at an extremely fast rate, right in front of my face; I could see all the beautiful colors on it and feel the air being pushed past my face by its wing as I was observing it. I would do that exercise for about two to three minutes.

Then I would just put myself on a beach somewhere where I could hear the waves crashing and feel the sand in my toes and the breeze in my hair. I would feel myself breathing very steadily. Meditation would relax me so much that I would almost fall asleep. I would also do that exercise for two to three minutes.

The next step of my meditation would consist of visualizing my life twenty years from my present state. I would always think of myself in a hammock in my backyard surrounding a pool, a backyard I had never seen. I just made up in my head a backyard of my own house some time in my future. I'd swing with a glass of lemonade in my hand, my dog to my right, and my wife sunbathing across the pool on the deck. I would just sit in that state of mind for a few minutes and really feel like I was better, that I actually owned that place. Those thoughts were very real.

The very last portion of the meditation would conclude with absolutely nothing, clearing my mind of everything and visualizing empty space, blackness, quietness, and solitude. I would then wake up out of my meditation literally feeling like I'd slept a solid eight hours, and I'd have immense energy and a positive outlook on my life. I felt like Hercules was sent from God to come into my life just to put me on a path where I could at some point be used by God in a positive way. I felt very healthy throughout the duration of my imprisonment. I take that sentence as a positive thing instead of seeing the negatives in it.

Along with my meditation, I was doing push-ups on a regular basis, increasing my strength and stamina, and I was mentally conditioning myself for my release. Everything I was doing while away was healthy. I made the commitment to myself that I wasn't going to smoke cigarettes anymore once I got out, either. I also made the commitment that I wasn't going to get high anymore, that drugs were the root of all of my downfall and my poor choices. I didn't acknowledge that alcohol was an issue with me; I did, however, tape above my bed in my cell the twelve steps of Alcoholics Anonymous. I was introduced to AA first in Utah at that super fun school in the middle of nowhere. Gosh, I missed that school. Anyway, AA was part of boarding school as a requirement of part of our program. I was about fourteen or fifteen then; so I kind of had an understanding about the twelve-step program.

But along with my reading, prayer, meditation, and push-ups at night, I would also try to memorize one of the twelve steps, repeating it over and over in my head before I would go to sleep at night. God was really working on me at this point in my life. When I look back and think about the type of people and the type of guidance I was so freely given, I can only conclude that the positive influence was a godsend. Looking back, meeting Hercules was somewhat of a miracle. Hercules also encouraged me to write down five things that I was to complete every day upon awakening, whether the goal was fixing a cup of coffee, doing fifty push-ups, having lunch with my grandma, or just doing my prayer and meditation at night. He encouraged me to write down a list in order to keep me focused throughout the day, and I was to write that list every night before going to sleep or even doing my prayers.

I'm proud to say that, since I was locked up on that day of December 18, 2002, I have not smoked one single cigarette: not a one. I managed to quit something completely to which I was so addicted. Once I'd had a year without a cigarette, I knew that I could do anything I set my mind to do through faith, discernment, obedience, and follow-through. I also managed to stay drug-free for over a year on my own, thinking that drug addiction was my main issue. I didn't have any more run-ins with the law for all of the year of 2003.

I was released sometime in mid-February of 2003; I only ended up serving about forty-five days of a ninety-day sentence. I didn't smoke cigarettes, but I did continue to drink alcohol. I was lifting weights now, becoming healthier mentally and physically, and feeling great about myself. I was actually working a few different jobs at family-owned businesses run by the families of friends of mine, seeing that finding actual work with my background was hard for me. I was doing pretty well.

When I got out, Hercules had also encouraged me to pick up a few books he had read that helped him in his faith and also helped him in his quest of a sober lifestyle, and I also encourage any of you reading this book to get these books: *Psycho Cybernetics* by Maxwell Maltz M.D., F.I.C.S. (the first edition because several of them are out there)[2], and *The Power of the Sub-Conscious Mind* by Joseph Murphy[3]. I had a paper Hercules had given me when I left the county jail that gave instructions on my meditation steps and reminded me to write down five things at night to be completed the following day. Hercules assured me that, if I was to lead this type of lifestyle he had written out for me, by 2007 I would be a very successful young man. As I'd never had any type of real guidance or any type of spiritual mentors growing up, Hercules in my life at that point was very influential.

Even though I continued to drink through all of 2003, not once did I have any real altercations with the police. I'd seemed to be having problems with the law on a monthly basis before making a conscious decision to become drug-free. I did, however, start to become quite the drunk. Upon my release, I started by not wanting to do any type of mind-altering substances or smoke cigarettes at all. But a week following my release, I was drinking forties with my boys and partying weekly, although I was managing to stay drug-free and pill-free on my own accordance, an abstinence which was very remarkable if you knew the type of spell drugs had on me.

December 23, 2003 marked over a year since my arrest. I had not smoked pot now on my own will for over one year. To me, that record was an amazing feat of its own. I also had not smoked a single cigarette! Wow! I felt really good actually setting goals just attainable enough to feel some type of really tangible success in my life that I had achieved willingly and on my own. I had lasted that one year that I promised myself without getting high. So now what? My goal was accomplished; what was my next goal to be? Maybe I didn't think that far ahead in order to give myself some type of safety net.

December 23 was my twenty-first birthday, and some friends and I were out at a bar in Redondo Beach. I think that about six of my really close friends at the time came, and this little twerp Slow-ik came with one of my good buddies (just kidding; we love you, Slow-ik). Whatever, the party ended up being cool. My cousin Hayley was bartending at the bar where we went that night. On my twenty-first birthday, I was being served in the exact manner you would expect, especially having your cousin as your own personal bartender.

Drinks were flowing, and energy was high. A very memorable night looked to be in store for me. I remember one of my buddies thinking that he was being funny getting me what turned out to be a traditional twenty-first birthday shot. I'll never forget the shot my cousin poured for me that night upon my friend's request, but she didn't have the decency to give me a fair warning. My friend called the shot a Mexican Thanksgiving: one part Tabasco sauce and one part Wild Turkey, hence the name Mexican Thanksgiving. I was taking shot after shot. By this point, I was already pretty hammered.

I slammed the shot back and literally felt like my eyes were bleeding. They started tearing up, and while everyone was laughing at my expense, I took the pain like a solider and laughed it off with them. Hayley looked at me kind of quietly, said, "Happy birthday; I love you," and gave me a hug.

My friends and I went home from the bar to my dad's condo, where we continued to drink and party. My good friend all through high school, Keon, was with us that night, and being the stoner that he was, he came prepared. I have to admit that night that, being all drunk and in the moment, a hit of some weed to finish the night seemed so innocent. Keon passed me the bud, knowing that I had been drug-free for over a year now, and assured me that I was cool, that one hit of some chronic on my birthday wasn't going to change anything. Or was it? I remember reluctantly hitting the pipe. I didn't even really feel any significant head change from the bud at that moment, but maybe I was so drunk at the time that I couldn't really notice it. Maybe I had been clean so long that one hit of some weed didn't really have any type of effect on me. Either way, the night ended somewhere around there with the weed back at my dad's condo.

I remember waking up the next morning with a very heavy and crippling feeling of guilt. I had gone one whole year without smoking bud. Upon awakening, the fact that I decided to go against what I strongly believed to be my downfall really scared me. Maybe if I hadn't been drunk, I would have made a better choice; maybe if I had set a longer goal, like five years instead of one, I would not have gotten high that night. All these different crazy thoughts began to plague me. I was so disappointed in myself. I felt like I had let myself down, and that failure was releasing something so toxic and negative into my whole body that I just wanted to lock myself in a closet somewhere, never to appear again. My lapse was that horrifying for me. The fact that I had actually smoked the weed that night wasn't so much what had such a great effect on me mentally; the fact that I knew the outcome of my addiction upon taking that hit was what was so disturbing to me.

My intuition was right. Only a week or so later, I was back on the scene with the wrong hombres, getting high, taking pills, and piling right back into the mix of chaos and confusion once again. For me, a downward spiral usually happened really quickly. My mind was so strong in letting me know my emotional state that, when negative emotions surfaced, I shut down and became very withdrawn, completely blocking anything that could be of any benefit to me. I was kind of like a turtle; when they feel threatened or bothered, they retreat into their safety zone. Well, for me that safety zone was drug inducing myself until I either died or got locked up just long enough to tap into a positive source of direction. I could only seem to tap into that realm of life when I was at some type of bottom or forced with my back against the wall. When my back was against the wall, I tended to make better decision, better choices, which tended toward a better outcome in my life positively.

Well, needless to say, a few months following my twenty-first birthday, I had caught a few new cases. I started selling prescribed medication, such as Xanax, Oxy-Contin, Vicodin, colodipins, any type of pills you could imagine that you weren't supposed to have unless you had a doctor prescribe them to treat some type of mental illness or disorder. I had access to them all.

The very end of 2003, I actually had gotten a job at Sharper Image in Palos Verdes. I was a salesman for the store and was doing decently well. A woman came in one afternoon who looked horrible, with sores on her face and a really skinny frame. She looked like she hadn't slept for a few days. She started talking to me normally about one of our best-selling products ranging from two hundred fifty to five hundred dollars. There we were, face to face with each other, while I was trying to make a sale, only to find out that she was also trying to make a sale: my purifiers for her prescription medications. Somehow the conversation took a turn and got way off course. She all of a sudden out of the blue just asked me if I was interested in taking pills. Did that question come from the devil or fate? Why couldn't she have asked one of the other salesmen in the store that day; why me? I asked her what kind of pills she was talking about. She said that her friend, a real good friend of hers who had AIDS, had an unlimited access to any amount of any type of pills I could imagine. She wanted the purifiers, and I wanted the pills. So we made arrangements and exchanged numbers. I actually got some pills at one point from this lady after meeting her, and I was very impressed with the type of medications she had. We became friends, I guess you could say.

My life got bad fast again. I stole a purifier from work retailing for about five hundred dollars and traded it to her for five hundred dollars in pills. Now five hundred dollars in pills is enough to get anyone addicted to them, especially the ones she had in her arsenal. That amount was almost two hundred pills or something like that. I started selling them, because for the price she was giving me on these pills individually, I could sell and double my money easily. I got hooked.

I lost consciousness of my spiritual journey, and I lost sight of maintaining the significant goals and standards I'd once come to know and believe. Nothing else mattered to me, nothing! Probation? What was probation? I didn't care. I didn't care about anything once again but seeking that high, that high I knew that was so toxic and detrimental to my health. I knew the path it would take me down. I knew the type of turmoil I would start to experience once again, but after I hit the weed on my birthday that evening, I knew subconsciously that I would soon be right back in this exact position with little or no effort whatsoever. Wow, I was right.

Late one weekend night in Palos Verdes, a few parties were up on the hill. I was the guy you found if you wanted to get some pills and have an awesome night. The supply I had was about to go dry that night, and I called up my hook so that I could stock up for the weekend and not have to stress on people calling when I was having a shortage. I was actually making cash getting high, and I always had some new little random chick around me to keep me company.

From my house to my connection's house in Redondo Beach was a short drive, but I never actually got to see her house with my own eyes, because we would usually meet in a parking lot near the Redondo-Torrance beach area bordering Palos Verdes. At the time, I was with this underage girl who was quite the pill head, and in the months leading up to this particular moment, I couldn't remember how or where I met this chick. I couldn't tell you what month it was or what my own name was half the time, actually. I was in bad shape. Everything was kind of a blur for those few months. I had my mind on pills, pills, pills: wake up pills, go to sleep pills, and go to the bathroom pills. I was literally a zombie. I figured that if I got four hundred dollars' worth of pills from my hook that night, I could easily turn that four hundred into eight hundred in the blink of an eye and also have some pills to myself.

I got the stuff I desperately needed that night at the spot and was heading back to Palos Verdes to the parties to get high and get the people what they wanted. At this point, I had a 1991 Honda CRX two-door; my grandpa had just bought it for me a few months before because I seemed to be doing so well for all of 2003. But now it was 2004, and my whole perception of life had once again changed, not in a positive way but in a demonic, controlling, possessive way.

My car was low, loud, and obnoxious. It was a red flag for any cop, to say the least, especially at 1:30 AM driving through Palos Verdes with a pocketful of pills and an underage girl in my car. How did I get so smart? Can you say numbskull? Thank you. But guess what? The parties were in Palos Verdes; so that's where I needed to go. I had tinted windows on my car, too, which were also illegal, and come to think of it, I don't think that anything I was doing at the time was actually legal.

Sure enough, upon entering Palos Verdes, the police began to follow me. I was so startled. I was still on felony probation for my last little run-in, as well as being completely under the influence of prescription drugs, which anyone who tried to hold a conversation with me would be able to detect almost immediately. I didn't have a license or insurance on my car, and the registration actually had a hold on it because I failed to provide the DMV with proper insurance coverage. The girl sitting next to me was seventeen. A thousand things were going through my mind.

The police lighted me up. I panicked. I scurried and tried to give the girl with me the pills to hide in her crotch, but she was not very cooperative. So I put a handful of them in my mouth. I swallowed maybe a hundred dollars' worth of all sorts of different pills. I still had a little plastic container with quite a few pills in it which I tried to conceal in my crotch at the time as well.

I was approached by the officer, and by this point the whole force knew me by name, which is never a good thing. The officer that night had sympathy for me; he was being somewhat chill. He pulled me out of the car after asking me several times if I had anything on me. I kept assuring him that I was clean. He asked if he could search the car, and I agreed. "No, go right ahead, officer. Nothing here to hide, officer." I really didn't have any other choice. What if I said no? Then I'd look suspicious, and they'd search it anyway.

The police didn't actually find anything in the car, because the rest of the stash was in my crotch. When the officer's partner, who had me on the curb, stood me up and asked me to spread my legs so that he could search me, here came the pills in the little plastic container, clinking and clanking all the way down my leg until they stopped at the bottom and rested on the cuff of my pants. The officers took the girl home and booked me on possession of a controlled substance, once again in violation of my probation, and another felony charge for the record. That charge would be my fourth felony.

On the police ride back to the station, I began to feel really woozy; all those pills I'd taken started to kick in. The officers were asking me all sorts of questions, but this time they actually (I think) felt bad for me and were asking me regular questions, trying to figure out why I was such a numbskull. Upon arriving at the substation, the officer opened the door and guided me out graciously. I could barely stand on my own. I couldn't feel my legs, and I started feeling very nauseated. With handcuffs on, I started to throw up all over myself in a standing position. Basically, I was dry heaving because I didn't really have much to eat that whole day. The officer kindly guided me over to a trash can, where he allowed me to vomit for several minutes.

All I remember from that moment on was waking up and the police releasing me on Easter morning. I couldn't believe it. They were letting me go? I wasn't dead? They wrote the incident up as a misdemeanor? Didn't they know that part of the terms of my probation was to stay away free and clear from all substances, including alcohol, and to avoid contact with the police? When and if I were to violate my probation, the violation would take me back to the county jail with a new charge. Clearly, I was in violation of my probation. Also, having a prescription medication without a prescription was a felony on its own. Somehow, the felony drug charge only appeared as a misdemeanor, and the police released me, citing me with a court date. I could barely walk that next morning. I was so discombobulated. I was aching all over.

A Couple of Come-to-Jesus Moments

Though my prayers and faith were at a standstill, how I was doing so well for all of 2003 never eluded me. Prayer the same year as success was not a coincidence. Remembering the little bit of insight I was so blessed to experience when I got locked up with Hercules for that forty-five days bugged me for months and months. Getting back into the serene routine of prayer and meditation after I started back on drugs was very hard on me emotionally for awhile, because I was so disappointed in my own actions that I really was at that point my own worst enemy. My conscience kept telling me what a drug addict I was and how much of a loser I was and would always be. I acted on those thoughts, allowing them to drag me down further and further into becoming the isolated inhabitant of a life where anything to my benefit was not an option: not sobriety, job hunting, or going back to college to get a degree. I had dreams, goals, and even aspirations, but they were all cut short because my drug usage led me to a depressed mind state in which I didn't have any love or respect for myself.

Even though I knew that I had court dates coming up in a few months and that my drug use was a direct reason for why I had new cases, I continued to drink, get high, and party on a regular basis. Every year, my mom's side of the family planned a vacation to a little island right off the coast of Long Beach called Catalina, and attendance every June was almost mandatory because, besides the fact that it's nice to be able to see everyone in our large family once a year, Great-Grandma Mann always celebrated her birthday out there, too.

At this point in my life, I could honestly say that I was definitely coming to a very crucial spot. Either I smartened up now, or I was for sure off to prison for a three-year bid at the least. Before I set foot on the boat ride over to Catalina that June, I made a decision to call my attorney, Bruce McGregor, to see if he had any type of clarity for me. Although I was vacationing, I could only think of the sentence I would be facing because of my violations upon returning to the mainland after my vacation came to an end. Bruce broke the situation down to me pretty clearly and simply. Basically, I had gotten myself into a really ugly scenario with the courts because of priors and probation violations, and even though Bruce had some pull over at the Torrance courthouse, he was skeptical about my sentencing. He just encouraged me not to go on the vacation but to check into some sort of rehab or sober-living type of program with management, sober people, accountability, and a program to get my mind in a clear and conscious state and also to influence the court that I was showing a willingness to change my lifestyle. Really, the reason I was in all this mess was my drug use, and Bruce was planning to use that dependence as my alibi for all of the mischief and run-ins I was having over such a small period of time.

I thanked Bruce for his advice, but I still booked the next boat over to Catalina that following evening. My buddies Drew D. and Dan M. cruised with me that next night, seeing that I had a place to stay where the family wouldn't be for a day after we arrived. We figured we'd have the place to ourselves for that night, party it up super hard, and wake up the next morning to the family. Basically what happened was according to plan, but in a much more embarrassing way than I foresaw.

Drew and Dan and I met some guy on the boat ride over that worked on the parasailing boat in Catalina, and we found out that this guy was a little fiend for opiates. We made a new friend on the boat ride over, and the timing was perfect, because he had all sorts of pills with him. *Perfect,* we thought. Before we even got to Catalina, the night was very young, and all three of us were pretty much intoxicated to the point where standing in an upright position was humanly impossible.

None of my family actually knew that I'd planned to come over a night earlier than everyone else and throw a party with the islanders and my buddies from high school in the rented house we specifically have designated for us every year on the third week of June, but this year I really outsmarted everyone. I always felt so clever when I would get away with sneaky, outrageous escapades at the cost of others.

Well, that night was pretty blurry. I remember having a very in-depth, emotional conversation with the parasailing guy that night in the restroom of our rented house. We were almost in tears, and then tears turned to angry emotions and almost into fists flying for no apparent reason. Hard liquor and strong, strong, medications were fodder for some hard, hard, emotional conversations that you would normally never have. Everything was so blurry that night that I just remember waking up on the living room couch.

All my weed was gone, and Dan and Drew lay to either side of me. Grandma Ginny and Great Grandma Mann were awkwardly standing over me, wondering how in the heck I got into the house. The family was just arriving as we were arising from one of the last intoxicated nights in my life. My friends and I arose and began our day very sluggishly. That morning, I clearly remember swimming, eating a sensible lunch, and heading over to Hamilton Cove for some weight lifting and a dip in the Jacuzzi.

The night came fast, and for us it couldn't have come fast enough. The freaks come out at night, as I once heard; I think that song was written about me. Dan and Drew left that evening on the 7:30 PM boat ride back to Long Beach; so I had to make do with what I had, which at that time wasn't much. As I had just turned twenty-one in December, I was able to hang out with the adults this year and do the whole bar and club scene with them. In the years before, usually my cousin Tyler and I would look for someone to buy us alcohol, and then we would proceed to the nearest secluded, quiet place near the water, drink, get high, and maybe try and pick up on some island girls. Eventually, we would stagger back home and crash at a relatively late time of the evening.

This year was different; I got hammered with the older cousins, aunts, and uncles. I remember just completely embarrassing myself time and time again in front of my aunts, uncles, and other people I respected. The morning hangover was one of the worst of my entire drinking career. My family, when I eventually woke up that morning, was looking at me in disgust. Their body language said it all. I didn't even have to ask. I knew I was being obnoxious and acting just like any alcoholic would act with that much alcohol in his liver over a one-night period: like a jerk! To say the least, my family was very disappointed in me; the energy I was getting from my family from the beginning of that day to mid-afternoon was very uncomfortable.

I had just hit my very, very worst bottom as a drunk in the eyes of my own people, who had loved and cared for me my whole life. Their disapproval just about killed me inside. I knew that I was a better person than the one I was portraying. I had no control over my body or my tongue when that liquid courage would enter my stomach.

I didn't take long to come to the conclusion that maybe Bruce was right, and whether or not the choice was going to look good in the judge's eyes, I truly needed to seek some type of drug rehab and counseling. Believe it or not, the choice came to me from my heart, deep down inside. And even though I didn't want to quit partying and acting out in all sorts of crazy, absurd ways, I had really left myself with only one option, and that was sobriety! Yep, sobriety was the last resort on my list, but I had excluded all my other options with a large red mark through them. Family, friends, and people I thought were my friends turned on me, and my family shunned me. I felt so alienated by my loved ones and my peers that I was determined to make a comeback in the most positive way I knew.

I caught the next boat back into town with my cousin Tyler, called an inpatient rehab in Orange County, and got a bed opened for the following day. I got back to Tyler's house that night and smoked the very last bit of weed I would ever smoke again. I got so high that night that my eyes looked as if they were bleeding. A crazy feeling of willingness and clarity came over me that night, telling me that everything was going to be okay, and inside my heart I knew that voice in my head to be the truest thing I had ever heard. I sincerely believed it.

I arrived at Chapman Medical Facility the following morning, June 25, 2004, at 8 AM, just as the staff had asked me to do. I had officially started on the hardest and craziest path of my life that I would ever know. Rehab was basically for me a seven-day detox because, in my heart, I knew that I had just left a part of my life back in Catalina that I never, ever wanted to experience ever again. I knew with a little willingness, patience, and open-mindedness, I would be able to do anything I put my mind towards. I started back on the spiritual journey from which I had previously detoured and began practicing all the tools and guidance I had received for free from Hercules in the county jail.

I had something that no one else at that rehab had, and that unique ingredient was faith. I believed from day one that I was going to be better, and I visualized for the next seven days what sobriety actually looked and felt like. While the other patients in the morning and afternoon groups were holding back stuff and not really knowing for sure if they in fact were ready for sobriety, I just opened up, put everything out there, and just kept telling myself that I was already sober. Sobriety came like first nature to me. It made real sense from the start; I believed I was where I was supposed to be. Prayer, writing, and push-ups were an absolute must every day, no questions asked. I was conditioning my brain to get ready for the real world, because I couldn't wait to take it on. I was on fire, I guess you could say. People in sobriety talk about being sober like being on a pink cloud. Whatever I was experiencing was so pure and so gratifying that I just wanted more and more of it.

A week passed, and I made arrangements with a sober living recovery home in Huntington Beach, California to come and live there for at least ninety days while all my court issues were being amended. The rehab didn't exactly feel that the timing was good for me to be checking out of there and embarking on a new path of my recovery so quick. The staff felt like maybe another week would be perfect, and then I could choose whether or not I was to start a new chapter in my life or not. The staff kept emphasizing program, AA, spirituality, and sober peers. I wanted all those things for myself more than they wanted them for me. I had already subconsciously checked myself out of that rehab a day before my actual release and visually prepared my mind for sober living.

New Life was the sober living home I picked. It was in a great location, ten minutes from the Huntington Beach pier and only five minutes from the Huntington Beach skate park. New Life was a Christian-based recovery home, a quality which was strange for me at first, but I learned pretty quickly to adapt to the format and just appreciate where I was and what I had. HOW hall was about three blocks from my recovery house. HOW was the club in Huntington where all the people in that area in AA attended their regular meetings.

I remember my roommate at my recovery house; his name was Jamison. He was about four or five years older than I was, and he was kicking heroin. He was actually a very key part to my sobriety from the beginning. He attended HOW hall every morning at 6 AM, and he had a commitment there as the coffee guy. Basically, every morning before 6 AM, he would be at the meeting, making coffee for everyone so that, when they arrived, coffee was brewed fresh and everyone was happy. To get a commitment like that is kind of honorary, because you have to be appointed that position; the people in the morning meeting acknowledged Jamison for some reason or another and felt he would be a good candidate for that spot.

I thought: *How crazy of these people to show up in the middle of summer at 6 AM to talk about their drug addictions and alcoholic tendencies!* Of course, those thoughts crossed my mind quite regularly, but after I started taking action in my own recovery, opening my mind and taking advice from the guys that were there every single morning at 6 AM sharp, I started feeling a part of the meetings. At the same time, I really started to understand what was going on between those walls every morning at 6 AM.

I started to become noticed. The leaders of the meetings started to call on me quite regularly, and I started making quite a few new friends. I was the youngest kid in that room. At twenty-one, I was religiously attending an AA meeting every morning at 6 AM, even on the weekends, and those people in those rooms really started to like me, kind of take me under their wings, and teach me about sobriety, recovery, and a life that I never knew existed. For the first time in my life, I felt like I really belonged somewhere. I felt right at home every morning when I would show up at HOW. I knew that good old Robert would always be there in his corner seat. I knew that Camey and Robin would for sure always be there as well. I had a great group of people around me, providing me with accountability.

One morning, I woke up expecting to see Jamison getting ready for the meeting like always, but this morning was not like the rest. Jamison had not come home the night before, and word had it that he went out with his ex and started shooting H again. For me, his lapse was a real shocker. Here was this guy who was so serious about his sobriety every morning. His so consistently suiting up and showing up at the 6 AM meeting was very influential and inspiring to me at an early stage in my sobriety. And his lapse was my first experience in sobriety feeling let down.

No one heard from Jamison from that day forward. But I didn't let Jamison get to me. I didn't have a car, any money, or even a job. The only object of my focus was my sobriety, and I wasn't going to let something like one guy's failure derail me that easily: no way. I started waking up even earlier than I would normally, praying, reading, and making that meeting at 5:35 AM every morning, Jamison or not. I would walk to HOW hall every morning with my big book of AA in one hand and make sure that I would start each and every day with program. I ended up getting appointed as the coffee guy. I felt so privileged to have a commitment at such a prestigious meeting, and that perspective is just how I looked at it.

HOW stood for Honesty, Open-mindedness, and Willingness. Those words for me really became the mantra for my recovery. I got a sponsor and started working the steps of the program as a requirement for long-term sobriety. AA requires twelve simple steps, and from my experience, if you don't fully commit to those steps, balking on a few of them or not really opening up fully and getting completely honest from the very beginning of your new sobriety, you could very easily compromise your own well-being. Holding back would be a complete waste of time.

A lot of people go in and out of the rooms of AA and NA, getting sober and then getting loaded, getting sober and then getting loaded again. Simply, no one is promised sobriety. Sobriety comes the harder you work at it. The steps are the program, and if you don't really truthfully work the steps to the best of your ability, you are going to be one of those who just sit around saying that whole AA thing is a hoax. You'll never, ever experience real, tangible sobriety. I know what I'm saying for a fact, because I actually experienced sobriety in its purest form. I achieved that level of sobriety at one point from shutting up, listening, and working the steps exactly as they were outlined.

Sobriety came for me, and great things started coming to my life. My faith in God was growing at such a profound rate, and the effect it was having on me was indescribable. My faith started as Hercules planting the seed, and taking direction in the rooms of AA really made those seeds bloom and blossom. At first, the program is hard if you don't really believe in God or have any type of real faith in any religious icon. So you just start to pray to your sheets at night or your door knob in the morning. That practice grows into conversations with yourself at night on your knees before bed. Even at that point, still kind of doubting but at the same time feeling like something GREAT out there really is orchestrating this so-called life, you start to pray that, if He really is out there, He reveal Himself in some profound manner that really grabs your attention so that you can really start to believe without any doubting, right? Well, I got to that point in my sobriety-faith about one month after attending meetings regularly.

My grandma was paying my five hundred dollars in rent every month, but that provision wasn't giving me any money to have in my pocket just in case maybe I wanted to see a movie with the boys or maybe cruise over to El Pollo Loco for some dinner once in a while. Part of living in the sober living home was the responsibility to be job hunting on a weekly basis. I ended up getting a really chill job in Signal Hill right next to Long Beach with the dad of my buddy Dan M.

I had to put my morning meetings on hold for the mean time, seeing that I just got a great opportunity to make some solid cash. My roommate at the time was working very close to my new job, and God just seemed to be looking out for me. My roommate started dropping me off every morning around 7 AM, and then he would head off to his job. The arrangement was working out perfectly. Although the job was laborious, I was making ten bucks an hour under the table, a salary which was way more than any of the other guys at the house were making, and the conditions of my work were pretty straight-forward. I liked my job; I liked it a lot.

Well, all of a sudden one early morning at 2 AM, my roommate and ride to work at the time came home all high on speed. He got caught and ejected from the sober living home immediately. I had work that morning at 7 AM in Signal Hill, which was probably a good twenty-five miles from Huntington, where I was staying. I was perplexed. *Why? What in the world?* I thought. I had just started this job three days prior, and I loved it. Here it was now 2:30 AM the morning before work, and I didn't have a ride. Without seizing, I remembered that the bus schedule was always in the kitchen for anyone's convenience. Not knowing anything about buses or how they ran or which one I was to take in the morning or what time I actually had to catch the bus to get to work at a decent time, all these crazy thoughts started flowing through my head but not deterring me from getting to work that morning on my own. I found a bus that went to PCH (Pacific Coast Highway) at 6 AM; so I figured that, once I got there, I would be able to figure out the rest of the way how I was going to make it to work on time. I didn't realize it at the time, but when I look back at that day, I was running on pure faith alone. Faith told me that I was going to get to work, and faith gave me the confidence to persevere.

I ended up getting lost coming off the OCTA (Orange County Transit Assistance) and into LBT (Long Beach Transit), which runs only to certain perimeters of the county, because I really had no clue what I was doing. I got off a second bus that morning and sat at a LBT bus stop, not knowing when or if a bus was coming or even if whatever bus came was going to be taking me in the direction that I needed to go.

I remember being on 2nd and PCH in Long Beach in front of the In-N-Out Burger, just hoping that a bus was coming soon. I had a list of goals written on a piece of paper in my room back at the house, and one of the goals I had written and was very avid about achieving was buying myself a motorcycle as soon as I saved enough money. Just as I was thinking about the motorcycle I was going to buy one day, a street bike rode by in the opposite direction. As I was following it with my eyes, simultaneously a cherry red 1962 El Camino stopped at my bus stop.

Okay: this coincidence was the most random experience I would have early on in my sobriety. Some guy in his late forties stopped to ask me if I needed a ride. At first, I thought the request was very strange, but the beauty of the car stood me up and walked me to the passenger window to talk to the guy. He seemed like he was just in good spirits and was trying to do a good deed perhaps that morning, and I was on the receiving end of a nice gesture at a very crucial time of need. I told him, "Well yes, actually I do."

He told me to hop in; I jumped in as fast as I could. It was about 6:45 AM by this time, and I was stressing that I was going to be late to work for sure. The guy had a joint of weed lit as I entered. He asked if I wanted a hit, and without breaking my anonymity, I respectfully declined. He was going to the Veterans' Hospital, which was only a few blocks from where he picked me up. This part is where the story gets weird for me. He had a doctor's appointment for his recovery from a motorcycle accident in which he was involved a year before. In the accident, he had lost his whole left leg from the femur down on his left side. I looked down, and sure enough, he had a prosthetic leg. No wonder he was smoking weed so early the morning; I would be, too, if I only had one leg.

To me, the craziest part about the whole thing was not so much the guy stopping to give me a ride to work that morning and go out of his way in doing a stranger a favor. No, the strange part was the fact that, as I was thinking about a motorcycle that I wanted and was going to buy one day, I was watching one go by at the same exact point. And at the same exact time, this guy randomly pulls up to give me a ride on his way to a check up for a motorcycle accident he'd had one year prior. The motorcycle coincidences just blew me off my seat! They were really quite intense. What would you make of that morning?

The guy was so cool, a very calm and collected type of guy. He shared with me that he had lost his family in a car accident just months after his motorcycle accident. He told me that, basically, the reason he picked me up was that he was trying to ensure a spot in heaven for himself when he died, because he wanted to make sure that he got to see his wife again at some point when he passed away. Then he told me that he had cancer and that the doctors gave him just six months before he was completely consumed with the disease. He was on his way to heaven as we spoke. Was he an angel? I came to believe so later on.

He got me to my destination and then offered me money (and I am not joking when I say this); he offered me his own money. I didn't even know what to say. I didn't even know this man. He picked me up when I was stranded, gave me a ride to work in the earliest part of the morning, and then, as he was dropping me off, tried to give me money out of his own pocket. The whole situation was so crazy that I respectfully declined his money and walked into work ten minutes early that morning.

I shared the experience with my friends and my boss that morning at work, and they thought that something must have been wrong with a guy like that. You would normally think so, right? Then, as the days passed, I started thinking that the guy must have been an angel from heaven. My conclusions made me realize that, no matter what I did now, God was going to be there watching from that point on; so I had better really kick myself into gear. God sent angels over me to guide and protect me in the purest form. In regular, human life, angels are here, real, and so is God. I really, actually started to think and believe in that way for the first time in my life. The craziest part about that whole experience itself and just tapping into minimal faith is that you automatically think: coincidence, not divine being, for sure. You're questioning still. Is God really there? Is God really real? The experience is telling you that this appointment you just endured was through God for sure, not coincidence, but you're still skeptical because you just tapped into something crazy you have never experienced. So you try to be as quiet as you can about your experience before getting too mouthy, because you're afraid of embarrassing yourself.

My next step in doubting was also on my way to work. Even though I had a strong, new belief now that some type of crazy energy was out there for sure, I really wanted to be sure that this presence was real, and I really wanted to experience it firsthand, if possible. The bus schedule was still a mystery for me the next morning for work, but I managed to get on three different buses and get to work on my own for the first time since I had started my job in Signal Hill.

219

The bus became my normal means of transportation for the early stages of my sobriety. I would take my big book of AA with me some mornings to read. Sometimes I'd take the Bible, and other times I'd take this book called *Psycho Cybernetics*, which was a self-help book that was very inspiring for me early on. Having a little reading material with you in the mornings on the way to work and in the evenings on the way home just helped. Reading was therapeutic for me, to say the least.

Every morning for the first three weeks of catching the bus, upon exiting the first bus, the second bus to catch so that I could get to work on time was the LBT. The third bus always seemed to have me waiting thirty to forty minutes to come and get me the rest of the way to work. It was always cold so early in the morning, and having to wait that long for a bus that the schedule said would intersect accordingly but never did was just annoying. My faith and my patience were being compromised for those weeks taking the transits. I got to a point where I was showing up thirty minutes late to work every morning, because the bus format showed different times for each bus I was catching.

What was happening was depending on the lights where we would stop. Coming out of Orange County into Long Beach, the signals would affect the times the buses were running by just minutes, but I didn't even realize that effect at all, ever. That missed timing wasn't even something that crossed my mind; I just thought that the schedule was wrong forever. I was getting to a point where I wasn't being patient anymore; I was just getting quite agitated, actually.

I started telling God, "What's up with this, God? How come that bus is never there when it is supposed to be?" One night before work, just like every night, I hit my knees and said my prayers. This night, I was really questioning where I was in my sobriety and in my faith, and I cried out to God, "If there is a God at all, then change my heart, God, and make me a for sure real believer in You. Prove to me You're real, and I'll never, ever question that You're out there again." That prayer seemed very demanding of me and very doubting, but at that point in my life, I felt that I needed something I could see and grab onto in order to change my heart and make me a real firm believer in something I didn't actually believe. I prayed that, after getting off that second bus that next morning, I wouldn't have to sit and wait in the cold for an extra thirty to forty minutes for the silly LBT to get to work. I prayed, "If You, God, are almighty and all powerful, then You, God, could spare me this morning and see to it that that bus is there waiting for me and that I don't have to wait at all. If You, God, reveal Yourself to me in this way, I will never, ever again doubt You." I needed evidence, and I felt like, if that prayer was to be answered, the answer would be enough tangible proof for my faith.

Here I came the next morning, cruising to work on the bus just like every other day. I got to the second bus, and everything seemed to be going smoothly, the regular way. We were about two lights from the stop that I had prayed about the night before. We cruised around the corner down PCH, and I could from my seat actually see my next stop. Guess what: NO BUS!

I thought: *Cool, I knew it in my mind. God is not real, because if He was, He would have just had the bus waiting there for me like I asked, right?* That little favor wasn't much to ask for a kid on a mission of faith, was it? I exited the bus with my book and skateboard in hand. I looked across the street at the gas station on the corner, which was an Arco gas station. I was bummed out, disappointed, and inside cursing that there ever was a God. If there really was a God, then if He couldn't make a bus appear through one prayer, what did I want with Him, anyway?

Just as all this negativity was overwhelming me, I noticed that the top of the Arco station gas price sign was stocked with pigeons. Just as I noticed all the pigeons, the sun started appearing directly over the sign, and in the direction I was standing, from the street behind came the LBT bus. As I noticed the bus arriving, the sun was rising and all the birds simultaneously flew away over the bus with the sun shining just perfectly on the horizon. Chills went down my spine. A sense of warmth came over me, and I felt that God had actually, really proven Himself to me that He was actually real and that He was actually capable of answering prayers.

That bus arriving was my experience, which was all I asked for and really needed for my faith to start to become more and more real! And the bus wasn't just there on time, either; no, God had me wait first, then doubt. And then, all of a sudden with the birds, the sun, and everything, He used everything beautiful that morning to let me know how real He actually was. If he was capable of that arrangement, then what else could He do? I was now on a crazy mission of faith and God. The bus picked me up no more than sixty seconds after the second bus had dropped me off. Never, ever had that happened in the weeks prior.

I got to work on time that morning, and I was in complete awe for the remainder of the day. I tapped into the divine being who was orchestrating this world where we're living. I believed I had actually experienced God in His purest form, and I started living for God from that moment on. I can understand how people live their whole lives worried, afraid, mad, and depressed, without an understanding of whether or not something out there really does love and provide for us upon faith and asking for Him to show some crazy sign of being real. God isn't real if you have never experienced God. There is no God for you if you can't feel His presence or His love because you have never before felt Him or His presence. Unbelief is understandable without experience. I had to hit a bottom and surrender my life to something I didn't even believe was real in order to come to the conclusion through my own experiences that there is no other actual answer. The word coincidence for me from that point on was not even in my vocabulary. Everything for me served a meaning and a purpose. My life became something beautiful, something I wanted to be a part of, something I really wanted to experience to the fullest.

Late September 2004, my spiritual journey had taken off down a path I never knew existed. I was excited about the newfound love I had for sobriety, health, and my overall well-being. The choice to put myself in rehab also proved to be very beneficial in the outcome I had for my probation cases. I ended up having to do a little bit of time in the county jail, but nothing major, for all the stuff I had piled up once again over those few silly months of numbskulling.

The courts gave me one hundred eighty days in the Los Angeles county jail, a three-thousand-dollar fine for my driving on a suspended license as well as for tickets that I had also gotten, and three more years of reinstated felony probation following my release from the county. Only this time, I had a joint suspended case, a ruling which meant that any more run-ins and I'd be off to prison, no questions asked.

For all of the mess I was in, Mr. McGregor sure did save me from years of agony and having to have a prison term on my record. I ended up only doing fifty-four days in the county because the jails were so overpopulated and the state needed space for new inmates. Fifty-four days on an actual one-hundred-eighty-day sentence? I was so blessed. The state was weeding us out. I got lucky to say the least, or maybe I was experiencing just another blessing from God due to the faithfulness and positivity I had before taking my sentence.

I went in with an extremely positive state of mind. When the courts gave me my sentence, they also gave me twenty-four hours to turn myself in. I resolved every day in jail to pray and seek God, read, stay focused, and not get distracted by all the negativity going on around me. God, program, God, program would take up my time, and that was it. Another part of my deal, I guess you could call it, that the judge cut me was a drug diversion program called prop thirty-six that I got along with everything else. Prop thirty-six was a twelve-month program during which I was to attend four meeting a week in Torrance and submit to drug testing on a weekly basis.

When I had gotten released from jail, I was something like six months sober; so program was part of my daily regimen anyhow. Aside from the four diversion meetings I was attending, I was also doing six AA meetings a week on my own. I was hitting a solid ten meetings a week all together and really fixing my eyes and my heart on the purest and most tangible sobriety possible. At this point, I had not really been seeking any church or anything like that. I don't even know if you could say I was a Christian or if really I had any religious preference; I just was a spiritual solider, I guess.

Back in Huntington at HOW, this chick named Kathleen knew that I was from the South Bay because of my shares. When I would speak, I would speak a lot of my hometown. She was familiar with this guy named Pete B. who attended a Monday night meeting almost every Monday in Hermosa. He had some good sobriety; so she encouraged me to find a specific meeting she told me about and find Pete when I got back to my hometown area. So I did. He ended up becoming my sponsor, and for the first time someone really actually took me all the way through steps one through twelve, one by one.

June 24, 2005 came around quickly. I had one year sober, and I was enjoying life. Grandpa Joe had acknowledged my sobriety by buying me a 2001 Dodge pickup. It was so clean and nice, and I was very thankful to him for that gesture. I was being blessed in so many different ways. My goal to buy a motorcycle came to pass about a month after I got my truck. I had saved up forty-five hundred dollars and bought myself a 2002 GSXR 750 street bike, just like the bike I had envisioned. Everything was coming together.

I started to become very comfortable, resting on my laurels, if you will. I had sobriety, a new truck, a street bike, and a decent job going on. Nothing was going to stand in the way of my goals and my vision to have a successful and prosperous life; at least, I didn't think that anything was. I started cutting my AA meetings back but still attending my prop thirty-six program classes four times a week, just like the courts had asked. I was just about done with all that nonsense. I was strong, healthy, goal-driven, and determined to be somebody. I was getting too comfortable with the way my life had just turned around so quickly.

Summertime was always fun: cruising down to Hermosa, skating on the strand, peeping some chicks, getting some sun, and relaxing. As Great-Grandma Mann had a beach house right on the strand, friends and family and I were down there regularly, summertime or not. I rolled up on my street bike this summer and met some of my cousins and relatives down there at our place.

One of my cousins was with one of her friends that I thought was super cute. I was so attracted to her in such a crazy way that I got butterflies in my stomach when I was introduced to her. A week went by, and our family had a little camping weekend planned just outside Malibu on a little camping site called Leo Carrillo. That site is one of our family's regular spots to go camping yearly, seeing that it was right on the coast and the surf was usually good there. My cousin's friend, Ursula, came with her again, and this time I was sure to get to know her a little better. I got her number so that we could hang out some time. She only stayed that evening and left later that night with my cousin. I was so stoked!

I gave her a day or two, and then we got together for some lunch and a little date. I had an extremely rare physical connection to this girl, for some reason. We shared a couple of stories and talked about our families a little bit. We had a lot of things in common. She said that she was a Christian woman and that she attended a little church in Gardena, and she encouraged me to check it out with her. Going to her church sounded like a good idea because I didn't go to church. I was very interested in attending one, but I never found anyone to encourage me to go somewhere specific. I took the invitation as a perfect opportunity. I ended up liking the church but liking her even more.

I started drifting further and further away from my meetings to spend time in the new infatuation I was having with this girl. We really seemed to like each other. We started getting really physical, and we eventually started dating. I knew nothing about dating all through high school; my only relationships had been with weed, pills, alcohol, and court dates. Come to find out, when I met this girl, she was just getting out of a very toxic and unhealthy relationship that had lasted for a while, but I knew nothing about break-ups and the back and forth, back and forth that goes on with a couple after just ending a pretty serious relationship. I was educated on those terms pretty quickly.

The unreal amount of love I had for this girl grew rapidly. I wanted to impress her and make her feel special; I put all my other goals and the good stuff I had going on in my life on hold. Besides, I was doing well now, anyway. I lost sight of what was real, what was good, and what had gotten me to the place where I was before meeting Ursula. My motivation, goals, and striving attitude were being compromised by long, drawn-out nights feeling like this girl was messing with my heart.

I crashed the truck my grandfather bought me into a parked car one morning, trying to find out where Ursula was. She hadn't come home, and she wasn't at her house. So I was all caught up emotionally and couldn't sleep that night from only thinking negative thoughts. I ended up having to call in sick to work the next morning. I was struggling to say the least.

She was cheating on me, I came to find out, but before I knew for sure, I was getting played like a fiddle. I was doing everything I possibly could to keep this chick in my life. I would take her flowers to work on Valentines Day to surprise her. I traded the truck my grandfather had bought me months before for a 2003 Jaguar X-type, having my boss at the time co-sign on the contract. I was doing everything I knew to make something work out that was never, ever supposed to be and to make this girl like me and respect me.

But everything I did just seemed to make matters worse. Why didn't she like me? What was wrong with me? I started to focus on all the negative aspects of life once again, and I was blinded by the trickery really of the devil. "Whose ways are crooked, and who are devious in their paths; to deliver you from the immoral woman, from the seductress who flatters with her words, who forsakes the companion of her youth, and forgets the covenant of her God. For her house leads down to the dead; none who go to her return, nor do they regain the paths of life" (Proverbs 2:15-19).

Even after all the fights and late nights, Ursula and I ran off to Vegas and got married one night after moving up into my grandma's pool house. We had probably been dating on and off at this point for one year, tops. Our relationship had been on and off, though. I wanted to be with her so badly for some reason, but she had her eyes elsewhere. And my eyes for God had been plucked out with an ice pick, it seemed.

Our marriage lasted only thirty days after we got into a huge fight one night on our way to look for apartments to rent. Emotions were high, and negative energy was in the truck that Mac just co-signed for me once again. (I had my Jaguar for about eight months, and at this point I had traded that car in for a 2005 Dodge quad cab 1500.) Ursula and I headed out towards Manhattan Beach to look at some places. Along the way, arguments began to flare. Our relationship was very unstable. My serenity was being compromised, and my patience at every minute was being tested. She was yelling at me about something or another, to go down this street or go down that street to look for some places for rent. I was supposed to have been meeting a guy in Manhattan, and we were already late. So I was getting frustrated, and my patience was really being tested.

I admit it: I blew up. I said, "You know what? That's it." I turned the truck around and headed straight back towards home. I made an illegal u-turn in the middle of a busy street with no signal, no nothing. I then started to accelerate to speeds probably up to sixty or sixty-five miles an hour on a regular street with a speed limit of forty.

Ursula began to hit me with the rent guides, and then she reached over and put my gearshift in park as I was driving. Immediately, I grabbed the knob and threw it right back down into drive. My truck seemed fine, but her interference just created so much anger inside me that I started to drive faster and faster and get hotter and hotter. I pulled the truck over abruptly, stopped at a gas station, and told Ursula to get out and find a ride home, because after she pulled that little stunt, I couldn't tell what she would pull next. I didn't trust her.

Here we were, a young newlywed couple just trying to find a place to live, thinking we were in love but finding out it was only lust. I compromised with her at the gas station. She got back in the truck, and I took as deep of a breath as I could. Once we proceeded back down the street towards home, I was in a somewhat calmer mode. I was driving much slower now and had calmed down very much. She was yapping in my ear, but I was trying my best to ignore her.

I was so mad and at the same time just hurt. I decided that I was going to pretend to call this girl I used to date just to make Ursula mad, because she had seriously broken my heart five times before this night. Here I was married to her, and she was still treating me with no respect. I had had my limit; that night, I really started to think of the type of respect

I was displaying towards myself by staying with a girl with such a temper and such bad intentions.

We were going up Crenshaw Boulevard in Torrance over by Hoff's Hut, and we were at a stoplight. With my right hand, I dialed the other girl's number, and I put the cell phone in my left hand. Simultaneously, I accelerated from the signal as the light turned green. As I was driving with my right hand, Ursula reached over, grabbed the gearshift, and jammed it into park, but this time, she turned the key off, too. My steering wheel locked at a slight angle to the right, and as the power was now off, the brakes were inoperable. As I stepped on them, they went all the way to the floor. A Chevy Silverado approached to my right, and just as I saw it, though I could do nothing about it, the truck slammed into us on Ursula's side, pushing us sideways for a moment, up a curb just missing a fire hydrant, directly into a four-foot retaining wall, and bringing us to an abrupt stop.

I couldn't even explain the emotions I was feeling right then: rage, such anger! I jumped out and ran to the victim's truck to see if everyone was okay. The driver was a woman by herself; she was fine. My airbags didn't deploy because the engine was not on. My truck was mangled. Luckily, everyone was fine, no injuries. The police came and took a report, and even though I had just been put through one of the worst experiences of my life by my own wife, I went home with her that night and assured her that, whatever we were going through, we were going to come out the other end.

To make a long story short, Ursula decided that she wanted to keep on being a numbskull, doing whatever she wanted, seeing her ex, partying at the bars, and leaving me home alone night after night. I was forced to file for a summary dissolution of marriage just months after we eloped. The dissolution was really my only option, based on her choices. I really wanted to be with her and seek God together with her, as she showed me where church was. But marriage is not a one-way deal; it's actually a covenant between a man, a woman, and God.

My short marriage was a huge step forward for me in my faith. I felt forced to elope so fast because I knew that I was living in sin, and I knew what the Word said about living in sin and premarital sex. I wasn't educated enough on a spiritual level to make such an irrational decision. I really thought I loved this girl. We tried going back and forth afterwards and working it out, but our relationship was never the same. I loved her deeply and cared about her more than I think I cared about myself sometimes, but we had a huge trust issue.

Upon the divorce and filing all the paperwork and going through that whole process, my heart became heavy with hate, anger, resentment, and remorse towards Ursula. As a matter of fact, from that day forward, my heart became darkened, and a once openhearted, loving kid who was making forward progress digressed and became withdrawn and bitter towards women. I had trust issues of my own now, with walls as high as the Grand Canyon. I felt like I had been manipulated so badly, and I felt used and dirty.

God and I stopped having conversations at night, and I started for the first time since I had gotten sober started going out to bars and clubs and hanging out with the old homies I used to kick it with and get high with. I remained sober, drinking energy drinks on those occasions, but I tried to let loose and let what I had just gone through fade into my past experiences, moving forward the best way I knew how. And that forward motion wasn't through prayer yet; my faith was still at an infant level. I started going back to old characteristics that I used to display when I was out there using; only this time, I was sober.

Some friends and I cruised out to Long Beach one night to go see this group called Metal School play at a club called Sachi. The band was a really flamboyant 80s cover band. If you saw them live, you would laugh hysterically; they are super funny. I was having a good, chill night; everything was cool. Towards the end of the night, I was dancing in the mid-front of the crowd in a tank top, when all of a sudden some random chick tapped me on the shoulder.

Over the years, I had been getting quite a bit of tattoos all over my body. From coming to God, I had a cross dead center on my back, with praying hands saying, "Only God Can Judge Me!" From my right shoulder all the way down my back is a picture of a guardian angel watching over these two little kids crossing over a bridge. On the left side of my back is a picture of Jesus holding His hand up in an awkward position with a dove descending upon Him. I got the body art because my faith had became so real to me that, when I had my shirt off, I wanted everyone to know that I was representing Jesus Christ as my Lord and Savior but still seeking to find true serenity and true peace.

This girl approached me because she noticed Jesus on my back, and my being a Christian at a bar was intriguing to her. I didn't really pay much attention to her, honestly; I just kept on dancing and enjoying my evening, trying to avoid all chicks and really trying to focus on making the evening a guy's night out. I reluctantly turned as she started lifting my shirt up on her own, trying to see my tattoo.

I glanced at her briefly, not even long enough to get a really good look at her face or anything. Actually, I kind of just kept on keeping on. I was letting loose that night, and I wasn't going to let some random broad ruin my night. She wasn't in my plans. After the concert was through, B. and all the boys with me that night met around the exit at the front of the club.

That girl who was checking out my back actually appeared to be waiting for me at the exit. She signaled me over to her and her friends, and she was cute! I didn't really get a good look inside because I wasn't even interested, to be honest, but she was very attractive. She told me she was a born-again believer and asked if I was willing to meet her some time to get coffee and maybe get into the Word a little.

I was kind of caught off guard, but we exchanged numbers. Six months later, we got engaged. She dug the fact that I was younger, attractive, and goal-driven. She had made a very good life for herself, starting her own real-estate company when our economy was booming. She owned her own house in Long Beach and seemed to have her life together. We clicked. We had chemistry; we had the physical connection and the spiritual connection as well. This relationship almost seemed too good to be true. She was actually a few years older than I was, which I didn't mind, because I had a thing for older women. She was a special type of woman. Noticed how I said "woman." I proposed to her in February 2007, and life seemed to be looking very positive for me at this point.

The truth was that I was acting like someone I really wasn't. I loved my fiancée, but I had all sorts of skeletons in my closet. The actual fact of the matter was that I was doing all sorts of shady things behind her back. I wasn't even working much at the time we met, but somehow I managed to get her a seven-thousand-dollar princess cut diamond ring, just like she wanted. I was living in Torrance now with my buddies Wezel and B. I was renting a room from B.'s mom for five hundred dollars a month, which was a great deal for the place. I had just bought a new 2006 Kawasaki Ninja zx-636 street bike, because I'd sold my GSXR a year before and had been itching to ride a bike ever since I got rid of my old one. You must, at some point in your life, ride a street bike; if you have never experienced it, it will blow you away. That bike plus insurance cost me about three hundred dollars a month. My finance card and my credit cards all ran around three hundred dollars a month each. I had an income of six hundred dollars a month if I was lucky, because my job was very slow. I was working part time as a casual down at the docks in Long Beach and Los Angeles, working to become a longshoreman just like I had always wanted to do from a young age. After I got my fiancée her ring, I had another three-hundred-dollar a month payment; plus, the new truck I was driving was five hundred seventy-five dollars a month. Life slowly started getting out of control. I was looking at somewhere around two thousand dollars a month just in bills, and this amount didn't include gas or food or anything else like that. On the outside, I looked like I had it going on, but in reality, I was about to fall flat on my face if I didn't figure out a solution. I had all the nice things: a new truck, a brand new street bike, a fiancée with a rock. All of the juggling bills and not working much but trying to stay faithful and godly was just not working out. I had so many demons haunting me daily, plaguing me with failure and defeat! At the same time, we were planning our wedding. Grandma Ginny was kind enough to intervene and help out financially. She helped out in anyway she could, and her gifts helped me out a little bit.

Bills still piled up quick. I ended up having to sell my truck for probably half of what it was worth, because after the collision it was never the same. I was now fifteen thousand dollars in debt to my boss who co-signed on the truck, because I sold the truck for fourteen thousand, kept four thousand, and gave my boss Mac ten thousand, but the truck was worth twenty-five thousand. I had all these nice things, but I still couldn't figure things out.

I made a really poor choice without thinking about the consequences or the outcome, and I did it without anyone knowing. A thought came to my head one afternoon. As I had insurance on the street bike that I couldn't afford anyway, why didn't I make a false insurance claim and report my bike stolen, but keep the bike, sell the parts, and make some extra cash on the side apart from the settlement from the insurance? I would not tell anyone. I would just see what happened.

The scheme worked. Insurance paid what they called my "fun-ancing" card, all five thousand dollars of it, and the insurance company cut me a check for about three thousand dollars. I was somewhat relieved, but at the same time I was scared. I had the bike in my possession, still just sitting in my garage at home. Nobody knew the type of silly choices I was making.

Every day, seeing the bike there would haunt me. So another bright idea came to mind, and I acted upon it. I cruised out to LA by myself one afternoon, because I remembered going down to Alvarado Street and getting fake IDs in high school. On top of doing insurance fraud, I had made a decision to sell my bike fraudulently under an alias. I bought a fake ID, fake title, and fake DMV registration. I was very intricate and deceiving with this whole situation, but I felt like I really had no other choice. I posted the bike on the Craigslist website and immediately began getting inquires. I ended up driving the bike to Santa Monica one evening and making a solid four thousand four hundred dollars in cash from some random kid who was victim to my fraudulent scheme. I threw in my five-hundred-dollar helmet just as a good faith gesture. Lies upon lies upon lies: when was all the deceiving going to come to a stop?

The next few months were very uncomfortable for me. My fiancée and I were fighting and not seeing eye to eye at all. We began to grow distant from each other because of my own selfish actions. I was being haunted even more now by self-seeking motives, and my once happy, spiritual existence had come to an abrupt halt, even though I was still portraying the faith of a Christian man from the outside. I thought I really had everyone fooled, but I was actually only fooling Cody.

That July 4, 2007, I made the conscious decision to pull the plug with my fiancée. From my perspective, I was toxic to her, and I didn't want to involve her in the mess I was about to be in really soon. She was devastated. I had no other excuse except that I wasn't ready to commit to someone fully, and I wasn't even mature enough to let her in on my dirty little secrets.

Almost immediately following our break-up, the devil was tugging and tugging on my heart with so much strength and brute force that the type of choices I was about to start making didn't seem possible to avoid. I had become such a lost soul in a matter of months. My self-esteem was at an ultimate low, and my confidence was lessening daily.

This little voice inside my head kept telling me just to go back to my ex-wife, Ursula, and try to make everything work out. I went with my stupid head once again, and instead of letting God guide my heart or lead my heart and my thoughts, I once again put myself right back in a toxic situation for no other reason but selfishness and insecurity. Ursula and I did well for about two weeks, maybe. Two weeks seemed to be the longest time she could go before everything would just start to fall apart. Being with her actually felt good for those few days, but the honest to God truth was that I knew I wasn't supposed to be mending things with her. I had so many other life-changing situations about to occur, but I selfishly chose to add her into the mix once again.

She was still in party mode when we tried to go for round two, but some people just weren't made for each other. Either we weren't destined, or I was just tired of being home at night by myself when my girl was out dancing and drinking. I was still sober and had no other options but to stay sober unless I wanted to go to prison for three years. That sentence was always over my head. Whatever the case, I was confused, and I needed a rope to get me out of the hole I had just dug for myself.

I moved out of the Torrance house a few months later and moved in with my ex-fiancée in Long Beach, not to work things out but just to try to get my head out of that cloudy, foggy state of mind. My ex-fiancée was such an amazing woman. After all the pain I had put her through, she was still willing to help me out when I was in a state of helplessness. She allowed me to stay in the back room at her house for several weeks for free. She gave me the opportunity to go to church with her and start seeking God on a much higher scale than I had been previously. She didn't judge or criticize me, just influenced me and helped me when she was able.

I was very thankful, and my walk with God started to become very diligent once again. I was programming, writing, doing my visualization, and seeking God, just like I had when I first got sober. I was feeling very good about myself once again. I began to go against my flesh and started obeying those good thoughts once again, encouraging me back down the path to peace and serenity.

With the money I had from selling my bike to that kid, I spent two thousand dollars on a little car, trying to humble myself and pay some bills, also. People say, "What goes around comes around," a lot; you hear that expression almost on a daily basis. The car I bought had a junk title; so I couldn't get it registered, a barrier which meant that I really couldn't or shouldn't even drive it. It was worthless. I had to go to the DMV and get the runaround to find out that the car was unable to be registered to the streets of California. I was trying to find a job, because I was only working maybe a day a week at this point. Although I had crazy bills piling up once again, I had made a choice this time just to let go and let God orchestrate and guide my path faithfully.

I was living in Long Beach, but I sponsored some kid from Redondo Beach in the AA program. He needed to talk, but I didn't have legal transportation. I had no money, maybe two bucks to my name, and I just seemed to be right back at square one with myself in the midst of my own stupidity and sobriety. I was trying my best to stay sane, and by regaining my spirituality and my faith, I stopped struggling and worrying so much. I started feeling a relief, like everything was going to be good, that God was faithful and was going to get me out of this mess I had got myself in once again. I remember that morning walking down the stairs of my ex-fiancée's place and exiting the front door with the intention to hop in my little illegal car, cruise over to Redondo, try to influence this kid who was struggling with a crazy cocaine addiction, and try to spark a sense of peace within him that he had hope and that sobriety was a definite possibility if he really was willing to go to certain lengths.

Well, upon exiting that Saturday afternoon from my place, I looked at my car. Then, with two bucks' worth of quarters in my hand inside my pocket, I looked across the street at the bus stop. Right then and there, something clicked: car, Cody's way; bus, God's way. What was I going to choose? I put the key back down deep in my pocket along with the change I was holding and cruised over to the bus stop. I waited there for a while before I looked up at the bus stop and called the LBT number to see what time the bus came. Well, on Saturday that particular bus didn't run that day down that street; so I asked the operator if she could direct me to a nearby bus that was active. She gave me some crazy, far-out directions that seemed like getting from where I was to where I needed to go would take me a half a day. I was sitting at the bus stop, and straight across the street from me just sitting in my ex-fiancée's driveway was my little car, saying to me, "Don't worry; just come, get in, and cruise over to Redondo. It's no big deal." I was holding the key in one hand and the quarters in the other hand.

I glanced once more, and then I put my head down and started cruising up Woodruff Boulevard in Long Beach towards the nearest bus running that afternoon. I was pretty distraught but running on faith at the time, pure faith; I was allowing God to guide my steps. Well, what do you know? About fifteen minutes later, walking down the street, I came

237

to a point where I was now lost and very confused; I saw no bus stops and no bus benches.

Out of nowhere, a LBT bus coordinator in a Ford Explorer pulled up to the intersection where I was standing. I didn't even notice his job at the time; I just approached him and asked him if he knew where the nearest bus was I could catch to get to Redondo from where I was standing. He told me to hop in; so I did. This guy was an angel.

We started talking, and I told him my situation. About five minutes down the road, I came to find out this man was a man of God. He was listening to the inspirational radio, and he had his Bible to the right of him. This energy from him that I have never, ever felt from anyone else was extremely peaceful and comforting. We started talking about God, and he started asking me questions. "So you're a Christian," he asked, and I said yes. He said, "Well, if you're a Christian, then what kind of fruit did Eve pick from that tree in the Garden of Eden?" Of course, I replied, "An apple." He said, "Open that Bible to Genesis; where does it say anywhere in there anything about an apple?" The answer was nowhere. He began to school me in what I believed to be a direct message from God, telling me that I'd better learn my stuff if I was going to be on this so-called Christian path. He then asked me, "How do you know for sure you're going to heaven if you die today?" "Well," I told him, "That's easy. I'm a born-again Christian, and I accepted Jesus Christ as my Lord and Savior. That guarantees me a spot in heaven, right?" He said, "Well, have you ever been baptized as a Christian?" I said, "No, not yet."

He continued to have me read Scripture, and I found that I really knew nothing about certain things I thought I knew. He showed me in the book of John that, if you are not baptized in the name of the Holy Spirit, you are not going to enter the kingdom of God. This conversation was too odd. This man had me mad, but in a good way. I wanted to know more now about the Bible than ever, and I wanted to be educated to the fullest. He gave me a free ride all the way down to downtown Long Beach, sat with me for a few minutes, and encouraged me in a way no one until that point in my life had encouraged me in my faith. He told me to seek and pray and get baptized, dropped me off right when the bus showed up, and gave me a free token and his number and a God bless. Then I was off. TRIPPY!

That encounter was what I needed, though. I got to Redondo and met with the kid I was sponsoring. He was struggling in a really bad way when we met. He had been sober about a week and was really feeling like getting high. I told him about my little run-in with the bus guy and encouraged him to come with me in the morning. We would get baptized as Christians and start a new path of life together. He totally agreed, and we made arrangements for the following morning. I called up the bus guy, and I met him at his church the following morning with my friend El, my ex-fiancée, and the kid I was sponsoring. The kid and I got baptized in front of the whole congregation that morning after church, and I felt a real sense of worth now.

I was this man on a mission to get right again, just as I was before in the early stages of my sobriety. I was feeling great again. I was amazed at how just taking a simple step away from what Cody wanted to do (get in his car and cruise down to Redondo illegally), turned into my getting baptized a day later at some random church in the most ghetto part of Long Beach with this guy I didn't even know. Everything worked out perfectly, though, and right then I realized that I needed to start making more choices against my own will to see what kind of path God really had planned for me. I realized that, if I kept making Cody choices, I almost always for sure was going to get myself in a rut. I needed God to steer my rudders if I was going to be successful in this world.

The next few days following my baptism, I began to feel extremely down and depressed out of nowhere. I was up in my room, reading the Word of God and trying to get out of that funky feeling, when all of a sudden I decided to check my email, because I had been job hunting online. I opened my email, and there was an email from Ursula. All of a sudden, those feelings in my heart, good feelings like for sure it was love I was feeling, came over me, and without hesitation I emailed her back with my new cell phone number and told her to contact me ASAP.

I was home alone at the time, feeling guilty about using my ex-fiancée's computer to contact my ex-wife and knowing that this one was a Cody choice, not a guided choice. That kind of decision meant that more trouble was in my near future, but I couldn't resist. Months had passed since I had talked to Ursula, and I wasn't even really thinking about her. But when I read her email, I couldn't wait to see her again. My feeling about her was pure and complete insanity at its best: continuing to do something over and over again that you know is bad for you, thinking that you're going to get a different result.

Once you put your thumb on the cigarette lighter when you were five and burned your thumb really badly, you learned really quickly never to do that again, right? Wrong! You learn when you get burned that it hurts; so you don't do it again. But I couldn't learn; I guess that I liked getting burned by Ursula.

I didn't ask God for guidance or direction; I chose not to pray about this choice. Ursula called me back quickly. I told her that I was staying in Long Beach. She said she was in Orange County, and she agreed to come pick me up. That's exactly what happened. I had butterflies in my stomach, and I couldn't wait to see her. Seeing her again felt like seeing someone you love for the first time after years of being apart.

All the negative craziness that went on between us went right out the window when I saw her again.

She picked me up, and I just couldn't keep my hands off her. The devil knew exactly what my weakness was and used it to his advantage: Devil 1, Cody 0. I was definitely not strong enough in my faith or my Christian walk to resist Ursula, no matter what the circumstances were. We talked and seemed like we made up. She seemed to have mutual feelings towards me, but that fact was that neither of us trusted the other. I didn't trust her because she was really shady, and she didn't trust me because she knew that every time I would feel betrayed or disrespected I would just get up and leave her.

I don't know why, but I remember that day so clearly. Why did something I knew was wrong feel so good? I just felt like something was different, that this time we were going to be cool, that everything was going to be okay. Without giving my ex-fiancée a really good reason as to why I was leaving or even where I was going, I pretty much just picked up all my stuff that evening, left her house, and moved in with Ursula and her roommate in Huntington Beach. I knew that this move probably wasn't the best idea, but I couldn't deny that fact that I truly deep down inside was in crazy love with Ursula and was willing more than ever this time to make our relationship work because I couldn't see myself without her. We had a good long talk, and we seemed to be on the same page with each other.

I kid you not; four days later we got in an argument because she wanted to go out to some club with her girl-friend in Newport Beach when all I wanted to do was chill and watch a movie with her. I submitted to her reluctantly and chilled at home that night all alone, watching TV by myself because I didn't feel like arguing with her anymore. She didn't come home that night. Her phone was off, and I was so worried again about her. The disappearance reminded me of the first time we were together before we got married; when I couldn't sleep, I'd gotten up, cruised the town like a madman, and crashed my truck by sideswiping it against a parked car. I was just so flustered.

At 5:30 AM, I had literally probably only gotten one hour of sleep that night. I knew that HOW hall was just down the street and that I could hit that 6 AM meeting if I so chose. That meeting was my only option at that time to release the pain in my heart that was clogging my throat. I wanted to break down with tears, but I was just numb. I felt so betrayed once again, so used, so lied to. I was humiliated and so disgusted with my actions.

I showed up at the meeting, and even though I hadn't been for a year or so to that meeting, the same people were there. They welcomed me with open arms and let me lead the meeting that morning. That kind of welcome was what was good about AA; if you had an issue going on with you, no matter what it was, you could always show up to a meeting and release that negative energy off your heart and just get it off your chest. Releasing that energy that morning helped me a lot.

It was Sunday morning, and I had church that night at my newfound church where I was baptized. I had Ursula's car because her friend had picked her up the night before. I was thinking about her all day in all sorts of different scenarios. She was together with some random guy at a club, or she met her ex-boyfriend from Manhattan Beach and stayed with him last night. Maybe she just got too wasted and passed out at her friend's house. All these crazy thoughts were running through my head. Her phone was off, and I had no way to contact her to know if she was okay or not. I started thinking that maybe she was in jail or something. So many crazy thoughts came over me that day that thinking about anything else was impossible.

Church was a blur, and I knew that God was disappointed in my actions once again. I left church, hopped in Ursula's car, and headed back towards Huntington. Just as I was leaving the parking lot, little Miss nowhere-to-be-found-or-heard-from called me with some crazy, far-out excuse and lie. I went to pick her up from her friend's house in Long Beach, where she said she passed out.

Whether she was telling the truth or not was hard for me to know, because it was a whole day later. But I didn't believe a word that came out of that woman's mouth. She ended up confessing to me that she was doing all sorts of cocaine. She had actually smoked crack that night for her first time ever, and she didn't want to come home to me because she thought I would have known she was on a good high.

Well, she was so surprised, but I didn't yell at her. I didn't even get mad at her. I actually just told her how much what she had done hurt me. I forgave her and told her not to worry, that we would just put the night behind us. I was trying to have that good type of heart, and I actually in my heart forgave her and felt okay. I felt like I was being Doormat Louie or something, though. Louie Diamonds! The next week, Ursula and I saw eye to eye. Our physical relationship and quality time together felt good.

My twenty-fifth birthday was right around the corner. Ursula and her roommate threw me a surprise party, which I thought was very thoughtful of them, and I was very thankful. All my friends came over, and we went out to eat in Huntington on the strip. My actual birthday was the following day; so I thought I'd take Ursula out and just spend some good time with her, just try to make things between us more comfortable. Her roommate's friend had the same exact birthday as mine, and they had plans to go to Sachi, where I had met my ex-fiancée lifting up my shirt and looking at my tats. Being sober and with Ursula again, I really didn't feel like going out. Besides, I'd gotten tattooed for six hours that day for my birthday, and I just wanted to lay low, stay in, and relax.

Ursula agreed that, even though she had planned on going out partying that night with all her girls, she would compromise, stay in with me, and keep me company. That decision got to her friends, who were not too cool with that whole idea; so they gave her a hard time about staying in. She ended up leaving me by myself once again on my birthday. That abandonment was the limit for me. Once everyone was gone from the house that night, I packed all my stuff and cruised back up to Rolling Hills with my grandma. I had decided I was going to stay with her again. I moved without notifying her or anyone else. Trying to stay with Ursula when I was getting left time and time again on my own was jeopardizing my well-being. With her, I endured heartache after heartache. I had taken enough, and I decided that I was completely through with a girl who couldn't comprehend what type of love I had for her. I left and never looked back.

Something Gets through
My Numb Skull

On December 24, 2007, I was eating Christmas dinner at my Aunt Suzanne's house, a regular family occurrence every Christmas Eve. All day, I was receiving messages and phone calls from Ursula wondering why I just picked up all my stuff like that and left. How could I be so inconsiderate? Why was I such a jerk? I was over her. Once again, I had to change my cell phone number and leave the past behind me, this time for good. I made a commitment to start attending my AA meetings regularly like I was doing in the past, make church my first priority, and direct the love that I felt towards Ursula back towards God once again. I got a commitment at my Monday men's stag meeting in Hermosa Beach at 8:30 PM every week, and I also picked up a volunteer ushering job at my church on Sundays after second service. The new year was right around the corner, and I wanted to do everything I possibly could do to make sure that I was on a good, strong path to bettering myself. Accountability was at the forefront of that decision.

The beginning of the year, I was sitting at my house up on the hill in a really depressed state of mind, doubting God and doubting my faith for no apparent reason. I was just down. I cruised into the garage to get some fresh air, and I looked up at the ivy plant in complete doubt of my faith and the path I was on. Even though I was seeking God, I was really on the fence about whether or not I was really going to walk in a Christian lifestyle for the rest of my life. Was Christianity just something I was doing to get myself out of the mess I had got myself into?

With a real sense of doubting and disbelief, I looked over at the hose reel in our driveway, which was made by this company called Ames. It was a trip. Next to "Ames", the hose reel said "Hose King", and in front of the part that said "Hose" was a picture of a wound-up hose that mimicked the shape of the letter C. *Chose King,* I said to myself. Then I looked again at Ames. Well, I was enough of a Christian that I knew some of the Scriptures, and I knew that a book called James was in the New Testament. I felt like God was telling me James Chose King. Wow! The message clicked. I felt like God was telling me, "Go open the book of James; do it now."

Right then and there, I ran inside at an abnormal rate and opened the book of James. Right away, right on the first page was my answer. Within the first couple of sentences, James was talking about faith. I'll give you the Scripture that really lit a fire under me on that day! "If any of you lacks wisdom, let him ask God, who gives to all liberally and without reproach, and it will be given to him. But let him ASK in FAITH, without doubting, for he who doubts is like a wave of the sea, driven and tossed by the wind. For let not that man suppose that he will receive anything from the Lord; he is a double-minded man, unstable in all his ways" (James 1:5-8, emphasis mine).

I read that passage, and right then and there I began to pray to God to give me faith. I felt like I was lacking in faith. And faith isn't something that we as people are born having; no, faith is a gift that God gives us upon asking. After I prayed, I felt way better, a lot more at peace inside.

All of a sudden, I had this energy to get up and start being productive by cleaning my house. The change was amazing; just like that, my whole outlook brightened. That negative energy I was experiencing was gone. Reading that chapter and understanding why I was feeling the way I was helped me a lot. I was faithless and doubting.

For me, having support and people around me who influence me in a positive way helped me to create stillness within myself, and through that support, I was able to be quiet and help to influence people around me who were going through trials and tribulations. But I couldn't do anything unless I was first taking the right precautions, achieving higher standards of living for myself through God and through Him only. Sometimes I seemed to conform to what was going on around me and struggle with being pressured by peers. When I was going to meetings regularly and attending church regularly, those temptations and influences were easy to dismiss, and I could keep on moving forward with positive momentum and positive energy.

I set some really good goals entering into 2008. Girls were not on that list at all. God was first; I made a three-hundred-sixty-five-day deal with God, which I promised I would complete throughout 2008. I also made a commitment to myself to learn God's Word and spend more time with God intimately on my own every single night. Every night, starting with New Year's Day, I was reading a chapter of Proverbs each night and memorizing a sentence from each that stood out to me particularly. Also, at night before bed for twenty minutes a night, I was writing all my prayers on paper and a checklist of things to be completed upon awakening. Along with the whole memorization of a verse from Proverbs, I was right back on track. I was being very diligent and consistent with all this stuff for two weeks straight starting the new year, and I felt amazing! I felt like now God could start using me to further His kingdom or whatever His will was to be done.

As an example, I have chosen January 15, 2008. I am going to read you my prayers for that night and what verse from Proverbs I had chosen to memorize right from my journal.

January 15, 2008
1. Wake early; eat a good breakfast
2. Gym, pray for Pastor Mays
3. Church 7 PM
4. Read, work, and meditate
5. Prayer and journal

And here is the prayer I wrote that night.

Lord God, Father, thank You for Your bloodshed. I love You, God, and ask that You take all of me, Lord. Humble me, Lord, in a way indescribable, and make me whole in You. Thank You for my sobriety, Lord God. Keep me sober one more day, Father. May You keep Pastor Mays safe, and may Your Holy Spirit communicate through him to reach those to whom he will be ministering. May he be that vessel, Lord God. I pray that You keep my family and friends safe, Lord: Jennifer, Ursula, Eliot, Jonny Boy, Mike E., B, Chris, Casey, Keon, Dad, Grandma and Grandpa Herman, Pete B., brother Duke, Mark D., and Heidi. Lord, I ask for tolerance and patience upon each and every one of their souls tonight. Lord, forgive me for my past sins and failures. Remove all the evildoers and dwellers from my life. Show me true serenity and peace of mind. In Jesus' name I pray; AMEN.

"In mercy and truth atonement is provided for iniquity; and by the fear of the Lord one departs from evil" (Proverbs 16:6).

You have just seen my exact five things to do in the morning, my exact prayer, and the exact verse of Proverbs I read that night and meditated on before going to sleep. January 16, 2008, at 9 AM, a loud and abrasive pounding at the front door of my grandma's house woke me up abruptly and uncomfortably. At the door was a task force which had taken on my insurance case and had been looking for me for a few months. They had finally tracked me down.

Now at this point, the last two weeks of my life was the strongest my faith in God had ever been in my life! I actually at one point heard God telling me, "Change your name from Cody to Thomas, because Cody is the old you, but you are Thomas in Me now." That message was weird, because although my first name is actually Thomas, for some reason I had always gone by my middle name, Cody, ever since I was born. I started to tell friends and people at church to start calling me Thomas from now on. I liked Cody too much, though, and would always answer to it anyway. I started off the new year on a very positive note and was staying humble and consistent to the goals I had set out to accomplish. Just praying every night and studying God's Word and meditating on it nightly gave me such a profound strength deep down inside me that I felt great.

When the cops pounded down the door, they came through with guns drawn and everything. My poor grandma was so startled. She had no idea what was going on. About fifteen undercover police officers in normal street clothes must have come. They got me. I sound crazy to say so, but I was thanking God from the moment those officers walked in the door to getting to the Hermosa Beach substation, where I gave the police a full, detailed, and thorough confession of exactly what I did: how I got the fake documents and how I sold the bike, to whom, where, what time, and everything. I knew that what I did was wrong, and I knew that I was going to have to make amends for my past poor choices. I went into the situation with my head held high, understanding the circumstances of my arrest and its extent, and I was preparing myself for what I thought was going to be the longest time in jail I was to serve in my life. I was actually thinking more like prison time.

I had been doing well for the past few years, not coming in any contact with police. A year prior to this arrest, I got off probation and was a free man for the first time since I was fifteen years old. Insurance fraud alone is a five-year federal offence; so I thought that I was going to be gone at least two and a half years at the least.

I was in the holding cell by myself. I got a Bible from the officer on duty and just put the situation I was in now directly into God's hands. I started reading from the very beginning of the Bible, right from Genesis.

With one of my two phone calls, I called my AA sponsor to let him know that he was going to have to cover that Monday night commitment I had filled because I was going to be gone awhile. I could really count on my sponsor and confide in him better than anyone else in my life; so he was already informed about the fact that I did insurance fraud months before the police got me.

Then, for my second call, I called one of my buddies from church to let him know that I wasn't going to be able to fulfill my Sunday morning ushering commitment. I let him know the circumstances of my situation and asked him just to keep me in prayer.

I made a choice after hanging up the phone that, whether or not doing so was going to be to my benefit, I would represent myself legally in this whole case. I was charged with filing a fake police report (a misdemeanor), grand theft of the victim to whom I sold the bike (a felony), and insurance fraud (another felony). I was looking at some pretty solid time; plus, I had serious priors.

A night went by, and I ended up having to stay at the substation for the whole weekend. As I got busted on a Friday and no court was in session until Monday morning, I had a lot of time to think of what I was going to tell the judge. I continued to read my Bible, pray, and do pushups for the whole weekend in my cell by myself. Sunday morning, the on-duty officer woke me to say that my attorney was there. I didn't call or ask anyone for an attorney. I wanted to stand up and take what I had done like a man and get it over with and behind me. I was willing to take what I had done on my own accordance, but when grandma saw me those past few weeks writing, praying, and going to church, she felt obligated to lend a helping hand. Grandma Phyllis, bless her heart, hired my attorney, Bruce, to take my case, which ended up costing almost twenty thousand dollars in cash.

Luckily, Bruce happened to know the DA; I guess they went to high school together. So they were able to come up with an extremely lenient sentence for the type of crime I had done. The court dropped the fake police report charge and dropped the insurance fraud (believe it or not), only charging me with grand theft of the kid to whom I sold the bike. The court gave me six months in the county jail and also put me back on felony probation. What! That sentence was impossible, seriously! Part of that deal, though, was that the victim had to be paid in full that day in the amount which the courts indicated: forty-six hundred dollars. Before my verdict, I was in prayer with God that whatever the case might be, whatever the verdict was to be was in His hands. No matter what, I was going to serve my time honestly. And now I had only six months for what I did! The sentence had to been a mistake; I couldn't believe that I was really hearing the verdict.

My grandma forked over another forty-six hundred dollars on top of the attorney fees, court fees, and filing fees. At the time, my grandma was pretty much struggling financially; so I was very thankful for her help in getting me get a lesser term then I would have gotten for sure if I'd tried to represent myself like a numbskull with priors. The judge probably would have laughed at me and thrown the book at me. None of the charges would have been dropped, and I would still have been sitting in a jail cell right now finishing my sentence. This book would never have been written.

I was back in the county jail, which seemed all too familiar this time. The first time is the worst, the scariest. After a couple of times, you're like, whatever, but this time I knew the routine. I knew what to expect, and I knew I only had a few months to go. The state shipped me to one of the county correctional facilities called Wayside, all the way out by Magic Mountain. I was in a low security yard because of my crime not being violent or anything. The state tries to put you with similar cases, segregating the multiple offenders and high-risk guys.

I was in a one-hundred-twenty-man unit, or module as they called it. The blacks were in another part of the facility by themselves, while the whites or "woods," Mexicans or "south siders," and the "pisas" all shared one module together, because in the county, the south siders and the woods kind of got along, in a sense. Well, for each group of guys, one guy was the leader for the individual groups of guys. And for each module, one main guy ran the whole show, I guess you could say. The system was a good one, actually, so that no one got out of order, a potentiality which could happen very easily. Also, the less conflict we had as a group, the less heat we would get from the fuzz.

The system was pretty straightforward. You just handled your own stuff, stayed out of each other's way, respected one another, and kept as neat and clean as possible. You didn't want to be known as a "dirt bagger," because then you could end up getting beaten. The wood representative in our module was real cool, and I came to find out that he was from San Pedro, right in my area. We clicked quickly. He was in his forties, and right away for some reason he took a liking to me. In the beginning, his friendship made things really easy on me. We started talking one afternoon, and I found out that this guy knew some of the same people I knew. As we kept on talking, we discovered that he actually knew one of my uncles really well.

Each representative had a vice representative, kind of like a chain of command, if you will. Usually, to become a representative, you had to be doing some decent amount of time. In the county, doing six months or more was considered a lot. Well, anyway, when our wood representative got released, because we got along so well, he gave me what people called the keys to the house, the power. He appointed me the responsibility of being in charge of thirty to forty other white dudes.

I had to make sure that none of my guys were mouthing off, leaving stuff out, or creating any type of problems amongst any of the other races around us. The proper way of dealing with troublemakers was a break off. If one of my woods stepped out of line or brought attention to himself for any particular reason or another, then to make sure things were being run smoothly and to keep things in order, seeing that the Mexicans outnumbered us whites by at least five to one, probably more, I was obligated to break my men off.

I would take the offender to the back, still inside the module, move some beds, and have two to three of my men underneath me in my chain of command lay hands on or basically beat that particular guy everywhere on his body except for his face for thirty seconds or more. Break offs were my prerogative as the representative. The south siders respected me when I would break off my woods, because I was showing respect to the whole house and teaching the new guys coming in that, if they "dirt bagged," they knew what time it was.

That discipline really made things run smoothly. The south side representative was my bunk mate, and we got along really well. Our module ran very smoothly, a lot smoother than the ones next to us, which were always getting raided by the cops because of fights and no solid leadership. Our place never got tossed up, because we were running a tight and solid program. Everybody got along, pretty much.

The type of power I just had handed to me all of a sudden was crazy. I could go against the grain. I made my own schedule, and I was able to do pretty much what I wanted when I wanted. It was a trip. However, being locked up with a bunch of knuckleheads started to rub off on me. I couldn't have that intimate relationship with God like I was having at home every night, because I was constantly surrounded by a hundred and twenty guys twenty-four seven. I started conforming to those around me, rudely judging them, and using my power to my benefit, not God's benefit. I was in a tough situation.

Time went by pretty fast in that position of rank and power, I have to say. I applied for house arrest because I qualified for it, and I was feeling like home would be better for me to get closer to God, because I felt like my faith was being compromised around all those numbskulls. This kid Travis whom all the south siders didn't like from day one was one of my woods, and we just kind of clicked from the beginning when we first met. He was from Huntington and skated. We kind of looked alike, and we just got along. He had a big mouth, and because some of the south siders wanted to get him back for talking trash a couple of times, when he was new, even though we were cool, I had to break him off like three times in one week. He was creating a little unnecessary tension amongst the module.

Well, as soon as I got the okay to go on house arrest, it was now my turn to appoint someone the new wood representative. I had already kind of let Travis know what was up and that, when I left, he was going to be the new representative. That night, leaving the module, I left Travis the keys. I had all my woods coming up to me tripping, saying that if I left Travis the keys to the house, there was going to be war amongst the south siders and the woods for sure. But I was on my way home; do you think I cared about what happened after I got home? I absolutely did not. I did my best to maintain sanity in that place while I was there; now that I was going home, I had a different state of mind.

I did about half my time in the county and the other half on house arrest. Really, after everything was said and done, altogether I did ninety days on a six-month sentence. The jail time was more a lesson for me than anything else.

I got home, and my grandma was so sweet and so supportive. She kept telling me that insurance fraud was a white-collar crime, that corporations did it all the time. "Don't worry; it's no big deal," she said. Once I got home, I began reading and praying, just as I had before I got locked up. Being locked up once again put me in reverse on my walk, but I would regain forward momentum and keep seeking God at home as if I had never been locked up at all. Coming home, seeking God just seemed harder now. Even though home was all quiet and peaceful, for some reason, connecting with Him like I had in the beginning of the year was harder; nonetheless, I was seeking Him daily. I woke up one morning in my bed at home in the back room of my grandma's house, and I felt like God was pulling at my heart and encouraging me for some reason to start writing a book on my life. So I acknowledged in my heart what God was indicating. I got a pad and a pen, and I just began to write everything in my life that I could remember that was significant or meaningful in one way or another. So that's how I started.

After I got off house arrest, I was pretty much back to my normal self, except now, as I was back on probation, getting a regular job was out of the question. No one wanted to hire a felon of my caliber. I was struggling with my finances still, but I was working a little bit with my old boss, the one who bought me my truck that I had sold and now owed a debt. Even though I still owed him money for that truck, he allowed me to work for him, and at the same time he was paying me, not even concerned about the money that I owed to him. I can honestly say that Mac is a one-of-a-kind guy who is kind of like a surrogate father to me. I respect and look up to him a lot. He hooked me up, and I was working, making a little cash back on the construction scene. Doing work felt good. I was outside, making cash, getting up early, and just making forward progress again.

My prayer life was once again solid, and although I didn't go to any more AA meetings, church was another regular part of my life. I was feeling great. Through all this craziness and madness, I was able to hold on to my sobriety, which has been one of my great accomplishments. I am quite sure, though, that if you were to get into contact with my sponsor, Pete B., he would most definitely tell you and me the positive benefits of attending AA meetings regularly. Quite honestly, I would have to agree with him. I just seemed to have found a spiritual high, if you will, which allowed me to crave drugs and alcohol no more.

When I first attended AA meetings, God Himself was never clear; only the word God came up quite often. I made my own choice to seek a God of my own understanding in order to get a better understanding of the God in the rooms of Alcoholics Anonymous. I know very clearly now that the God in the rooms of AA and the steps outlined for that program are in complete alignment with what I believe and what I do and don't want to do as an addict. Drugs and alcohol are the least of my worries today, and I am very thankful to be able to say so honestly. I am completely surrendered to God right now and walking faithfully. I know that God has some type of really crazy plan in store for me, yes indeed.

I was cast for a TV show called Bully Beatdown, which was a new show premiering on MTV in March 2009. The producers liked me a lot and ended up choosing me out of several hundred participants to be on the show. Basically the show was me hopping into a cage with a professional MMA (Mixed Martial Arts) fighter and going two rounds. The first round was just straight grappling, with no punches, no knees, no kicks or anything like that. I started off the show with ten thousand dollars in my pocket, basically. But every time I tapped out in that first round, every time the pro fighter got me in a choke hold or put my arm in an awkwardly twisted position which forced me to tap out or give up, every time within that three-minute round he would make me tap out, one thousand of my dollars would go to kids I had at one time or another in my past punked or bullied. They were going to be standing there watching me get beat down in the hopes that they would win a little cash for themselves. The second round was to be Muay Thai for two minutes. Just say that I tapped out five times in the first round. Well, two beat ups (the bullied kids) would split that cash fifty-fifty. I would still go into the second round with five thousand dollars in my pocket. This round was different. Every thirty seconds I stayed on my feet without getting knocked down, I would accumulate one thousand dollars back from the beat ups from the first round's loss. I was totally game and super hyped on the show.

When I found out I made the cut, I started training really hard, lifting weights, and running the sand dunes with my boy Danny A. I was prepping myself to walk out of that ring possibly with ten thousand dollars in my pocket, and that win was my focus. It didn't seem too far-fetched. The producers cast me about thirty days from the day of the fight. As part of the procedure of the show, I had to get a mandatory complete physical: eyes, EKG, blood samples, and even an MRI of my skull. Leaving the hospital, I felt like the appointment went well that afternoon.

Later the following day, Friday, I got a call from the secretary of the doctor's office where I'd had my physical. She told me that I needed to come back first thing Monday morning to go over my MRI. Now I was pretty concerned, because by the sounds of the lady on the other end of the phone, coming back didn't seem like normal protocol. Actually, I asked her whether something was wrong with my MRI and whether coming back to have a follow-up on the MRI was normal procedure for all patients. She would not release any information to me that day over the phone. For the whole weekend, I was somewhat concerned, but at the same time feeling extremely healthy. I figured that everything was cool and that this second appointment was just part of the procedure. Well, it wasn't.

Monday morning, I showed up at the doctor's office with Grandma Ginny and Papa Herman. The doctor came into the holding room where he'd had us quietly waiting for several minutes. Right away, he came in and said, "Well, there is really no easy way to do this." I was very curious as to what in the world he meant. He began to put my MRI up on the screen, and right away I could see from a mile away that something was irregular in my brain.

The doctor said that I had a tumor, and a pretty good-sized one at that. My first response was, "Well, I can still fight, right?" Although I was trying hard to hold back tears, when something of that caliber is brought to your attention in your own body, I'm sorry, but it is very shocking and unexpected, to say the least. I had a million questions going through my mind right then. *Could I fight? Was it cancerous? How long had it been there? What was my next indicated step into taking care of this in a timely and proper manner?*

So you mean you're going to have to cut my head open, go into my brain, and remove this son of a gun?

I was scared and in shock at first. I just wanted to lock myself in a closet somewhere and not even deal with this situation at all. I was in complete shock. I didn't have insurance, and I wasn't actually really working at the time. So the following morning, my dad and I went down to the ER at Harbor UCLA hospital in Torrance. We ended up waiting over thirty hours. Well, I did; my dad left after about five hours. I waited there patiently for a proper evaluation of exactly what was in my head and why I had not been experiencing any symptoms thus far.

I finally got to a room and sat down with a neurologist to review my MRI. The doctor that looked at my film was pretty impressed that I was in such good shape movement wise and verbally, because the tumor literally was the size of a baseball, with a nodule, which was the actual tumor itself, the size of about a quarter or so. The doctor I saw encouraged me to come back ASAP to get the tumor out, because the longer I waited, the worse my condition could get. The doctor didn't know just from looking at the film whether the tumor was malignant or benign.

Well, four days after finding out that I had a huge tumor on my brain, I was admitted into Harbor UCLA hospital, getting prepared for brain surgery. The night before my surgery, I stopped by the house of the parents of a good friend of mine, seeing that his folks were very intuitive with the Holy Spirit and very faithful Christians. I explained my situation to my friend's mom and asked her to pray over me for a safe, successful surgery. She told me that several days before, she was at a healing seminar of some type or another and had actually had a cotton swab of some sort that had been anointed and blessed by this faith healer himself. She blessed me with it, laid hands on my head, and prayed for me faithfully.

I left there that night, headed home, hopped in the shower, and prepared myself for one of the hardest and craziest experiences I would ever have. In the shower, I was singing in good spirits when all of a sudden, out of nowhere, my tongue started taking off by itself. Like I have heard at churches before, a tongue of a different language was coming out of my mouth. I was speaking in a different tongue, and I had uncontrollable chills all up and down my entire body for what seemed to be at least forty-five to sixty seconds. I knew that the book of Peter said something somewhere about speaking in tongues. I never had faith in that experience, but I really, actually experienced it. It felt really good, like you were getting a good back-scratching or something; that image was the only way I could explain it. I was somewhat embarrassed of the whole situation and hoped that no one randomly heard me accidently.

I had my surgery, a five-hour operation, on February 9, 2009. The crazy thing was that I had been through surgeries before more than once; so surgery wasn't anything new to me. I actually knew what to expect. Besides, the doctors sedate you, and when you wake up, everything is better. I had a lot of faith and people's prayer for me coming into my surgery, gifts which made going through something like that ten times easier than when you do not have even the least amount of faith. Entering the surgery room, I was beginning to get strapped down, and surgery was just minutes away from being in progress. I remember being strapped down and the doctor coming in. I told him, "Hey, Doc: do me a favor. When you get in there, upgrade me to Spanish and also Windows XP 5.0." The nurses and doctors laughed as the anesthesiologist then began to put the night-night mask on my face. I said, "All right, see you guys in a few hours," and that was that.

All I remember after that was waking up in the surgery room in what I thought was the middle of brain surgery in a complete panic. As I came to, I asked the doctor if I was having a seizure. I was in quite a panic post-operation as well. Then the reason for my panic came to me all at once. I was panicking because I'd had a clear and vivid dream of God while I was under the anesthetics. That dream was seriously the most real thing I can honestly say I have experienced in my life as I continued on this spiritual journey.

I remember seeing an illuminated light, like basically a bright, white background. Although I know how cliché this dream sounds, there I was in front of the pearly-white gates, not like a metal type of gate or anything fancy like that, but I could just tell that some type of gate was restricting me from going forward if I wanted to go. But something was wrong. Standing in front of these huge arches was what looked to be God Himself, but I couldn't be sure. All I could make out was a Man standing in front of me with His arms crossed, and a shadow from His cloak hid His face. I was at the bottom of what appeared to be three or four steps leading up to this cloaked Man. In my visual experience, behind me was completely pitch-dark blackness. I couldn't go forward, because God was standing there in what seemed to be a disappointed body language. If I took one more step back, I was for sure going to fall into a deep, dark hole that I believed to be bottomless. I took the image as meaning that God wasn't going to let me into heaven. I started panicking. I began to thrust my body back and forth in my dream as if I were in a straightjacket and couldn't move. Simultaneously, I woke up in the surgery room, thinking that I was having a seizure, to the doctor telling me, "Good job, Cody; we are all done. You did great. It's all done: no more tumor." Wow!

The dream was so real, so vivid that, coming out of my surgery in my dream, I was panicking deeply. I literally thought I was seizuring upon waking. The dream stayed on my mind as the nurses moved me from the operating room to the holding room before I was to be moved to ICU for the night.

In the holding room, however, I was in a completely different state of mind. I'd just had brain surgery, but my right eye felt like either sand or a piece of hair was in it. Now having had anything interrupt, scratch, or even touch my eye post-operation was impossible, because before surgery, my eyes were taped closed and screws were in my forehead and the left side of my skull to stabilize my head during my surgery just in case I was for some reason to happen to convulse or seizure. Well, I didn't; none of those things actually happened. And before my surgery, my eyes were fine.

Afterwards, though, my right eye was watering so badly that I couldn't open it because the pain in it was worse than the pain I was experiencing from where the doctor had just gone inside my brain to remove my tumor. At the same time, the entire left side of my body was completely numb. I am not kidding; this is how I woke up from a five-hour brain operation. I had no feeling from my fingers all the way down to my toes.

Then the doctors from my surgery approached me all at once with about a thousand questions. I told them that something was in my eye that was bothering me so badly that all I wanted to do was get whatever was in my eye out. I would worry about the other things later. One of the neurosurgeons took a look in my eye with a light only to find that nothing was in it, and he assured me that I would be fine. He walked away. I looked at the nurse with one awkward eye and said, "Nurse, I'm not crazy. I know what it feels like to get something in my eye, and it feels exactly like this. Please, believe me." She said she believed me but couldn't see anything; so they didn't know what to do. I seriously thought that the doctors triggered something because they were just in my brain, and I was now for the rest of my life going to have trouble seeing properly out of my right eye.

Five minutes later, an ophthalmologist came down, shone some type of blue light in my eye, and found that somehow

I'd gotten a scratch right on my retina. Wherever the scratch was, my eye just killed. The nurse put in some numbing drops, and instantly I could open my eye again pain-free. But the drops only lasted a few minutes or so. Then I explained the type of numbness throughout my whole left side, and the surgeon assured me that the numbness was normal. As the doctors just went into my brain, I was probably going to experience a little numbness, but only for a few days at the worst. So now I was relieved that the pain in my head wasn't too bad. I could deal with it. The numbness was fine; it was only temporary.

The only thing on my mind now was my dream, and I couldn't stop thinking about it. It was making me so sad, like I didn't deserve to go to heaven or like maybe it wasn't my time yet. All these thoughts came to mind, but I couldn't figure out what the dream was about. All I knew was that I just came face to face with my Creator. That's what I believed and what I felt to be true. A message was behind all this madness.

The first people to greet me in ICU after my surgery were my best friend Wezel and my friend Brittany. As soon as they came to my bedside, I started crying like I had never cried before. In tears, I told them my exact dream, what I saw and what I thought it meant to me. Britt was so touched by what I had just experienced that, when she and Wezel left, she went to the house of Wezel's friend, who was a pastor of a local church, and right then and there she accepted Jesus Christ into her heart as her Lord and Savior. I then told my dad, who doesn't believe in anything, and he even said while I was in tears still, that the dream just meant that it's not your time to go, Cody, not your time. For my dad to have that kind of insight was shocking to me, like the dream touched him in a crazy way, too, maybe. Then my boy Klingon came through shortly afterwards, and once again I told him the same story, because it was all I could think about post-operation. So with one eye open, one eye closed, my whole left side completely numb, and four titanium plates and a whole bunch of screws in my cranium, I was sobbing about this crazy dream I had just witnessed.

Upon accepting Jesus, Britt confessed to Wezel that she had been struggling with taking prescription medication for the past two years, but from that day, she has not taken another pill, as far as I know. Klingon, who didn't believe in Jesus Christ but thought that the stories in the Bible were cool, came to church with me for the first time a few weeks later post-operation, and he surrendered and admitted that he, too, also had a problem with prescription medications. He is also now walking on a different path. My buddy Wezel told me that, before I told him my story about how I met God at heaven's door, he had a similar dream the night before my surgery, and I was in it with him. That dream repetition boosted his faith to another planet, and he is now more on fire for God than anyone I have ever seen.

What was God really doing in my dream? What was God's real plan for me in this so-called crazy life of mine? What did this message really mean and actually have to do with my life? Or was it not so much supposed to affect my life as others? Since my surgery and all of these crazy spiritual encounters, as I guess you could call them, I've felt like I was a robot for God and that I was going wherever He wants me to go.

"His will be done every day in my life" is my new motto upon wakening. I am just sitting back and interested to see what kind of plan God has set out for me, because He has a plan for each and every one of us whether we believe it or not. 1 Corinthians 1:27 says, "But God has chosen the foolish things of the world to put to shame the wise, and God has chosen the weak things of the world to put to shame the things which are mighty." The more we resist, the further and further away from God's final destination our own self-wills are going to take us, and I know where my self-will takes me. Do you know where yours takes you?

As soon as I found out about my tumor, I called MTV to let the casting coordinator, Kristi, know that I was not going to be able to do the show because of the surgery, and I explained the situation to her very thoroughly. Honestly, the next day of the weekend before my surgery, I received a card from her wishing me luck and just letting me know that everybody at Bully Beatdown was pulling for me and that I would be in their prayers. I felt so blessed and so gifted to have such great friends around me during this whole procedure.

All the prayer and faith healed me so quickly that the doctors couldn't believe what a speedy recovery I was making. First they said that I was to have about a five-to-seven-day recovery in the hospital. Well, they ended up coming back the following day while I was eating some cheese enchiladas that my brother Chris brought me when I was supposed to be on a liquid diet. I was actually keeping down solid foods, and the doctors couldn't believe it. They took my IVs out a few days early as I was keeping down food, and I was up and around, feeling good actually. I didn't even feel like I'd had any type of surgery at all. To tell you the truth, I wanted to walk out of that hospital right then and there.

The hospital released me the following day, and I was sent home under the supervision of my family, who were to be my new nurses now for the next few weeks. Unfortunately, that night at home I had one of the worst headaches in the world; go figure, right? I'd just had brain surgery. I couldn't sleep, and when morning came around, I was feeling sick. I started feeling panicky all of a sudden and went into a seizure right in front of my poor friend Britt, who happened to be there at the time. She said that she literally thought I was dying. I just thought I was mad about something that triggered my reaction; I just didn't know what. I don't even remember convulsing, really.

Next thing I knew, the firemen were at my bedside at my house putting IVs back in me and giving me valium to stabilize the levels of shock in my body. I went back to the hospital from which I had just been released the night before, only to have two more seizures before arriving. Then I had a focused seizure. I can literally remember going into convulsions, thinking I was having a heart attack, but being unable to verbalize how I was feeling at that moment. I woke up a day later in a hospital room in a hospital gown with an IV in me again. I went through a pretty intense four to five days, to say the least. A lot of stuff was going on with me, and I just wanted to go home, relax, and read some good literature at this point. I was exhausted. The hospital monitored me for several days, did some tests on my brain, and put me on some stronger seizure medications.

I went home within the next couple of days, and ever since I've been recovering terrifically: no more seizures, no more headaches. I feel healthy and more positive about life then ever. My best friend Wezel went through the trouble of getting custom made rings for the both of us, to encourage us on our walk with God. The ironic thing was that the ring was made out of titanium, the same stuff that was now in my head, and he was completely unaware of that fact. Also, inside the ring was a Scripture he personally had engraved from Matthew 7:21-27:

Not everyone who says to Me, "Lord, Lord," shall enter the kingdom of heaven, but he who does the will of my Father in heaven. Many will say to Me in that day, "Lord, Lord, have we not prophesied in Your name, cast out demons in Your name, and done many wonders in Your name?" And then I will declare to them, "I never knew you; depart from Me, you who practice lawlessness!" Therefore whoever hears these sayings of Mine, and does them, I will liken him to a wise man who built his house on rock: and the rain descended, the floods came, and the winds blew and beat on that house; and it did not fall, for it was founded on the rock. But everyone who hears these sayings of Mine, and does not do them, will be like a foolish man who built his house on sand: and the rain descended, the floods came, and the wind blew and beat on that house; and it fell. And great was its fall.

The crazy part about Wezel bringing me that ring was that, exactly three years to the day on that day at that time, I was in a ring store in San Pedro putting a ring on my hand after I was married the night before to Ursula, three years earlier exactly. Because our wedding wasn't a planned event, we didn't have a proper ring exchange; so that following morning I got my ring, after we came home from Vegas. Wezel put this ring on my hand three years later exactly from my wedding day. It was just so obvious that God did that on purpose to grab my attention and really open my eyes through this whole experience.

The Scripture in that ring was about building your relationship on a solid foundation, and Wezel had no clue that that was the day on which I got married years before. When I actually told him, Wezel said, "That is crazy, because I was supposed to have the ring the day before, but for some reason it took an extra day to get the ring. I was supposed to have it on February 18; so it just worked out that way on God's time, not my time." I like it when God does stuff like that. What I used to call coincidences just remind me how much He cares and how much of His presence I am able to acknowledge in my life. Knowing Him has been a wonderful experience.

Also, I put the pieces together about the real cause of my eye feeing like a stick was in it post-operation. The reason is quite clear now. After sharing my experience with a cousin of mine who is also a brother in Christ, we found a Scripture that points out exactly this: "So if your right eye causes you to sin, tear it out and throw it away. It is better for you to lose one of your body parts than to have your whole body thrown into hell" (Matthew 5:26).

What makes perfect sense is that, while I was literally standing before God, I felt it possible that I was about to face my judgment. At this point and time in my life, I said I was a Christian man. I went to church on Sundays. I attended Bible studies on Wednesday nights. But did I really, truly, and honestly have an intimate relationship with Jesus when entering my surgery? My answer to my own question, I can truthfully say, is absolutely not, even though I was seeking and acknowledging Him every day. Was I walking perfectly with Him, and did my actions point out that I was in fact a righteous follower of Christ? No, they didn't: not a hundred percent.

Now being a saved Christian because I have accepted Him into my heart and thinking that I am walking a righteous path in my own eyes, doesn't necessarily mean that in God's eyes I am being obedient and honoring His Word; now does it? Actually, my actions up to that point would definitely declare otherwise: having unmarried sex, having a foul mouth (which I work to change every day), judging people, not being able to tame my tongue in certain situations, and lashing out when really I am supposed to be practicing patience. My actions showed very clearly how disobedient I was to God's Word and how my self-will ran riot, basically. I wouldn't have been surprised if God cast me down into that bottomless pit where I was teetering. I was unworthy, as my actions declared quite clearly.

God came to me in this way, I feel, because I doubt a lot in my faith. I go up and down with it. My first name really is actually Thomas, like "doubting Thomas." I feel like seeking God on a level of better understanding is an everyday adventure, and with this state of mind, every day is literally an adventure, never dull. Whether or not at the end of the day I had a good day, I am always thankful and grateful for a day I come through alive now. I am focused and seeking God faithfully every single day. We all fall short of the glory of God, but that is an understatement. Nobody is perfect, but we can learn from each experience, which can either strengthen us or cripple us. The effect is really our own choice.

I can honestly say, though, that this whole experience brought me a lot closer to my older brother, Chris, a bond for which I am very grateful, because I love him. I love my family and want nothing more than to have great relationships with the people around me, lifting each other up regularly in a positive way, no matter what. I am very blessed and thankful to be sober today, also, and June 25, 2009 marked five years of being completely drug- and alcohol-free. Thank the Lord! I can honestly say that I love God today, and I feel so lucky and grateful to know God on the level of faithfulness that I do. I am no numbskull any more; that's for sure.

As for the show Bully Beatdown, well, I didn't get to do the show, no, but God really does work in mysterious ways. That girl I mentioned, Kristi the casting coordinator, the one that sent me the card, well she and I are together now. Kristi and I are very much in love with each other, and the type of chemistry we have is just crazy. MTV's Bully Beatdown offered me a job as a recruiter on the show after they heard that I had made a one-hundred-and-ten-percent recovery, and I am making a weekly salary, which is completely crazy and new to me. But I am enjoying it. One door closes, and another one opens!

If I'd never found out about this show, Bully Beatdown, I would have been home jobless with a huge tumor in my head, quite possibly beginning to experience symptoms of headaches and all sorts of painful things health wise within the next few years. I wouldn't have a beautiful girlfriend, either. I really want to thank Matt Vener, MTV, and the show

Bully Beatdown for basically saving my life, in a way. Who would have known?

I can't really explain how, but my life seems to have done a complete one-eighty. I am not living at home anymore with my grandma. I moved in with my girlfriend, and we are renting a room in Redondo Beach, California, one block away from the strand and the water! My life is crazy and beautiful at the same time today. I also would like to recognize that, after going through all these trials and tribulations, I really feel like God is tugging at my heart to go into some type of ministry work with youth. I plan to attend a Bible college next year in Temecula to start my college degree and also to get more educated on the Word of God and the Holy Spirit. I am in deep thought with my girlfriend about moving back East to Charleston, South Carolina to go to school, work, and just start a great life of my own pursuing my dreams and goals. I really feel like anything is possible at this point in my life. I am on a mission to live a life of meaning, and I don't mind looking like a nerd in doing so. If you really knew me and how I was back in the day, you would only conclude from this type of attitude and behavior I portray today that something out there is very capable of changing a man's thoughts, heart, mind, body, and spirit to better His plans for all of us. But no matter where I live or what I do, as long as God is working in my life, I'll be safe and on a good path. None of us is perfect; in fact, we are far from it. We can try hard every day to better ourselves and encourage those around us by our actions and moving forward in a positive state of mind.

My story just goes to show that, no matter how hard times get or how down on yourself you may be at times, you will always find a light at the end of the tunnel. The choices I made along the way were not always right, but somehow I managed to stay clean and sober through every trial that tested me. I managed to keep my eyes on God as I went through extreme circumstances at times, and although I fell short regularly, I never forgot my early experiences in sobriety through willingness, suffering, and follow-through again after suffering, lessons that allowed me to connect with a God of my understanding and allowed me to be on this spiritual journey today.

Although I will always have a numb skull because of my operation, I don't have to keep suffering in my walk as a Christian man. I understand that God wants to use me. If I continue to be a numbskull spiritually by repeatedly making wrong choices like the ones that affected me negatively earlier in my life, then I as a man of God will never align my will directly with God's will, a lack which will eventually affect my testimony as a man of faith and compromise my authenticity in leading by example.

If I could encourage people reading this book in one thing that would benefit them that I have learned from all my ups and downs, that one thing would be consistency: consistency in prayer, accountability, church, and Bible studies. Consistency in these disciplines will really set a great foundation from the beginning of your sobriety and your spiritual journey so that you will be able to acquire the type of spiritual serenity God wants us all to enjoy.

Good luck on your missions, all of you, and I pray that my story will help those out there struggling with addiction to drugs and alcohol. I encourage you to give faith in God a try. Hey, if you're struggling with such serious and destructive issues anyway, what more do you have to lose? You have probably already lost family, friends, and relationships, and you may even have pending court dates. Am I right? So give God a shot; you really have so much to gain from something you don't understand now. Just try faith, and see where your life goes over the next few months.

If you suit up and show up, setting a solid foundation from the beginning, then the rest of the way is up to you. Remember consistency, accountability, prayer, and focus on the positive (not the things with which you don't agree) and you will (I promise when I say this) be sober, successful, and most of all, respected by those people who once despised you.

If you enjoyed my story *Numbskull* but didn't quite feel an ending to my story, then please understand that, because I am only twenty-six years old, this story really has no ending yet, only a beginning of many beautiful blessings and great happiness to come. Volume 2 is coming in June of 2024!

God bless you all.

Afterword

I am Cody's maternal grandmother. The first time I saw Cody was Christmas Eve day. He was born the night before on December 23, 1982. He was lying facedown in his little hospital bed, and I could see that his nose looked red where he had rubbed it on the sheet. I wondered right then and there as I looked at him: *What lies ahead for you, little one?* I felt apprehensive, as I was well aware of the fact that both his parents were drug addicts. His mother, Pam, the third of my five daughters, has had a drug problem since she was about fourteen. I was hoping and praying that, because she and the boy's father, Scott, had brought children into the world, they would become responsible and stop using, but that didn't happen. Cody's parents were blessed, I mean just blessed, with three beautiful, bright boys, but instead of becoming responsible parents, they led their children into their world of drugs, alcohol, chaos, and hell.

Eventually, my husband and I as grandparents, along with Scott's parents, could see the need to intervene. The four of us collectively took the boys, as both parents were in and out of jail. The boys were headed for foster homes if we didn't do something soon. I told Pam and Scott that we would raise the boys until they could get themselves clean and sober. They never did.

Although the boys were raised in upper middle class neighborhoods by two loving extended families, including aunts and uncles, all three boys had a great void left in their lives by the absence of their parents. All three boys have dealt with their sense of desertion and pain in their own ways.

It seems to me that most of our society thinks that living in a lovely home in a good neighborhood makes life easy. How false that notion is! Living in the protection of a stable, loving family did not keep Cody away from the evils of drug pushers that lurk in all neighborhoods and that led him to spiral down into an unbelievable existence.

Cody and I have literally been best friends since the first time I held him, when he gazed into my eyes with all of his innocence. I promised him then that I would always be there for him, and I have tried to live up to that promise. I have been there through the peaks and valleys of his young life. He has come through the darkness and into the light. He is experiencing the joy of a new inner spirit and looking forward to a more spiritually-led life. I was with him when he was diagnosed with a brain tumor, and we cried together.

I know that God has a special plan for Cody's life. I hope to be around long enough to see his dreams come true.

Virginia Moreno, Cody's Grandma Ginny

Scripture

I chose the following passages of Scripture because they have each been meaningful to me in my growing walk with the Lord. In some of them, I saw descriptions of me as I was before I knew God and descriptions of others who haven't found Him yet. In others, I found direction along the way or comfort in difficulty. I have arranged these passages in the order they appear in the Bible, and I hope that they are as meaningful to you as they are to me.

Now if a person sins after he hears a public adjuration to testify when he is a witness, whether he has seen or otherwise known, if he does not tell it, then he will bear his guilt.

Leviticus 5:1

Then I was senseless and ignorant; I was like a beast before You.

Psalms 73:22

For the lips of an adulteress drip honey, and smoother than oil is her speech; but in the end she is bitter as wormwood, sharp as a two-edged sword. Her feet go down to death, her steps take hold of Sheol. She does not ponder the path of life; her ways are unstable, she does not know it. Now then, my sons, listen to me, and do not depart from the words of my mouth. Keep your way far from her, and do not go near the door of her house, or you will give your vigor to others, and your years to the cruel one; and strangers will be filled with your strength, and your hard-earned goods will go to the house of an alien; and you groan at your final end, when your flesh and your body are consumed; and you say, "How I have hated instruction! And my heart spurned reproof!"

Proverbs 5:1-12

The fear of the LORD is the beginning of wisdom, and the knowledge of the Holy One is understanding.

Proverbs 9:10 NASB

Foolishness is bound up in the heart of a child; the rod of correction will drive it far from him.

Proverbs 22:15

Take away the wicked from before the king, and his throne will be established in righteousness

Proverbs 25:5

He who robs his father or his mother and says, "It is not a transgression," is the companion of a man who destroys.

Proverbs 28:24

Surely I am more stupid than any man, and I do not have the understanding of a man. Neither have I learned wisdom, nor do I have the knowledge of the Holy One.

Proverbs 30:2-3

Love is always patient; love is always kind; love is never envious or arrogant with pride. Nor is she conceited, and she is never rude; she never thinks just of herself or ever gets annoyed. She never is resentful; is never glad with sin; she's always glad to side with truth, and pleased that truth shall win. She bears up under everything, believes the best in all, there is no limit to her hope, and she will never fall.

1 Corinthians 13:4-7 ISV

Sorrowful, yet always rejoicing.

2 Corinthians 6:10

Consider it pure joy, my brothers, when you are involved in various trials, because you know that the testing of your faith produces endurance.

James 1:2-3

Is anyone among you sick? He should call for the elders of the church, and they should pray for him and anoint him with oil in the name of the Lord. And the prayer offered in faith will save the person who is sick. The Lord will raise him up, and if he has committed any sins, he will be forgiven. Therefore, make it your habit to confess your sins to one another and to pray for one another, so that you may be healed. The prayer of a righteous person is powerful and effective.

James 5:14-16

My brothers, if one of you wanders away from the truth and somebody brings him back, you may be sure that whoever brings a sinner back from his wrong path will save his soul from death and cover a multitude of sins.

James 5:19-20

So that the proof of your faith, being more precious than gold which is perishable, even though tested by fire, may be found to result in praise and glory and honor at the revelation of Jesus Christ.

1 Peter 1:7 NASB

Endnotes

1. Lettie B. Cowman, Charles E. Cowman, and James Reimann, *Streams in the Desert* (Grand Rapids: Zondervan, 1997), page 121.

2. Maxwell Maltz, *Psycho-Cybernetics: A New Way to Get More Living Out of Life* (New York: Prentice-Hall, Inc., 1960).

3. Joseph Murphy, *The Power of Your Subconscious Mind: Complete and Unabridged* (Radford, VA: Wilder Publications, LLC, 2007).

LaVergne, TN USA
08 September 2009
157112LV00002B/2/P